POLITICAL RHETORIC AND THE MEDIA

THE YEAR IN C-SPAN ARCHIVES RESEARCH

The C-SPAN Archives houses the online C-SPAN Video Library, which has recorded all of C-SPAN's television content since 1987. Extensive indexing, captioning, and other enhanced online features provide an unparalleled chronological and internally cross-referenced record for deeper study. The Year in C-SPAN Archives Research series presents the finest interdisciplinary research utilizing tools of the C-SPAN Video Library. Developed in partnership with the Center for C-SPAN Scholarship & Engagement (CCSE) in the Brian Lamb School of Communication and with support from the C-SPAN Education Foundation, this series is guided by the ideal that all experimental outcomes, including those from our American experiment, can be best improved by directed study driving richer engagement and better understanding.

SERIES EDITOR

Robert X. Browning

Faculty Director, Center for C-SPAN Scholarship & Engagement, Purdue University, and Executive Director of the C-SPAN Archives

OTHER TITLES IN THIS SERIES

The C-SPAN Archives: An Interdisciplinary Resource for Discovery, Learning, and Engagement

Exploring the C-SPAN Archives: Advancing the Research Agenda

Advances in Research Using the C-SPAN Archives

The Year in C-SPAN Archives Research: Volume 4

President Trump's First Term: The Year in C-SPAN Archives Research, Volume 5

The Evolution of Political Rhetoric: The Year in C-SPAN Archives Research, Volume 6

Democracy and the Media: The Year in C-SPAN Archives Research, Volume 7

POLITICAL RHETORIC AND THE MEDIA

THE YEAR IN C-SPAN
ARCHIVES RESEARCH

Volume 8

edited by
Robert X. Browning

Purdue University Press • West Lafayette, Indiana

978-1-61249-820-1 (hardback)
978-1-61249-821-8 (paperback)
978-1-61249-822-5 (epub)
978-1-61249-823-2 (epdf)

Cover image: SeanPavonePhoto/iStock via Getty images

This book is dedicated to

all my C-SPAN colleagues,

who everyday help build

the C-SPAN Video Library

CONTENTS

FOREWORD

Speaking at the 1984 Hackers Conference in Marin County, California, technology guru Stewart Brand famously asserted that ". . . information wants to be free . . ." While Brand's pithy phrase has been widely cited in the subsequent (and ongoing) digital revolution, relatively few people place his quote in the context in which it appeared (note my careful use of ellipses). Brand's full quote, as cited in Levy (2014), was

> On the one hand information wants to be expensive, because it's so valuable. The right information in the right place just changes your life. On the other hand, information wants to be free, because the cost of getting it out is getting lower and lower all the time. So you have these two fighting against each other.*

Brand was pointing out a growing paradox in technology in which the societal value of information continued to be as high as ever, but the cost of its redistribution was dropping dramatically. Focusing on the value of information has often led some in society to try to lock it down tightly to maximize their own benefit. Others have focused on maximizing society's overall benefit and argued that as information becomes cheaper to distribute, it should be spread as widely as possible.

Since its founding a few years after Brand spoke, the C-SPAN Archives has come to exemplify this latter approach: In the decades since its founding in 1987, Robert X. Browning and his team, initially at Purdue and now as part of C-SPAN, have worked to ensure that scholars and the public could better interrogate the statements and actions of their elected representatives. Especially since the debut

---

* Levy, S. (2014). Hackers at 30: "Hackers" and "information wants to be free." *Wired.* https://www.wired.com/story/hackers-at-30-hackers-and-information-wants-to-be-free/

of the C-SPAN Video Library in 2007, the network has been committed to spreading its video resources as widely as possible online, including digitizing its massive back catalog of recordings. Today, C-SPAN is joined by the Purdue Center for C-SPAN Scholarship & Engagement (CCSE), which encourages research and teaching using the C-SPAN Video Library and which sponsored the conference on which this book is based.

Like many other scholars, I have used the C-SPAN Video Library extensively in my research and teaching. As the 10 essays in this volume demonstrate, a wide variety of academic projects can be supported by this information infrastructure, including studies focusing on gender, oral histories, campaign and election coverage, rhetoric and framing of important public debate, journalism, visual symbols, and nonverbal communication.

However, the amazing success of C-SPAN's Video Library is demonstrated not only by the essays in this volume—and the countless other academic studies that have relied on data gleaned from the C-SPAN Archives—but also from all of the use it has seen from those outside of academia. With a collection now approaching 300,000 videos, the Archives reports more than a quarter *billion* views of its videos . . . and counting. For a project focused first and foremost on the inner workings of government, that is a truly staggering reach.

It seems especially appropriate that this archive was created by a professor at Purdue—a public university. Higher education institutions—especially public universities—are funded by the public to create and spread knowledge. Especially in the case of land-grant universities like Purdue, a key part of their founding mission was to provide service to their communities.

The C-SPAN Archives has embodied that mission with the high quality, professionalism, and wide accessibility of its project. This sentiment was echoed by the committee that presented the Archives with a George Foster Peabody Award in 2010 for "creating an enduring archive of the history of American policymaking, and for providing it as a free, user-friendly public service." In this case, at least, Brand's paradox has been solved by a dedicated team who have taken this tremendously valuable information . . . and worked tirelessly to make it available to the public for free.

Tim Groeling
UCLA Department of Communication
Director, UCLA Communication Archive Digitization Project

PREFACE

This eighth volume in The Year in C-SPAN Archives Research series is a blend of historical and rhetorical studies. Each essay uses the C-SPAN Video Library as the basis for analysis and advances our understanding of politics, communication, and history. The result is insights into a wide range of topics based on C-SPAN's video coverage. Together these eight volumes illustrate both different approaches to studying politics, but also different conclusions about political and communication phenomena.

The book begins with three studies by historians who each examine a portion of the media coverage of politics and campaigns. Katheryn Cramer Brownell begins by looking at the history of cable as it expanded its news coverage against the backdrop of the three major broadcast networks. It was during this period that C-SPAN was created, followed by the growth of Ted Turner's CNN. She uses a congressional hearing on early network projections to tell the story of cable and broadcast competition, with Turner holding a dollar sign to counter the broadcast networks' claims that they provide a public service.

Heather Hendershot then uses the 1972 Democratic Convention that nominated Senator George McGovern to illustrate the three themes of her title: television, chaos, and reform. Rather than the carefully orchestrated television conventions of modern day, the 1972 convention was unruly and not on time. McGovern's keynote speech did not air until the following morning, thus missing the guaranteed primetime audiences that conventions were designed to deliver to. The reforms of the McGovern-Fraser Commission meant that many "amateurs" rather than party regulars were delegates and those managing the convention had much less experience.

Jesse Jackson's 1984 and especially his 1988 campaign are the subject of Allison Perlman's historical essay. She contrasts Jackson's coverage on nascent network C-SPAN with that of the other news networks. The latter treated Jackson as the

Black candidate and gave him limited coverage. C-SPAN covered Jackson as one of the candidates and gave him equal coverage. She praises C-SPAN for its balance and candidate coverage in this early stage of its history.

Together these three essays provide a historical look at an early period of cable history and in the case of the 1972 Democratic Convention, a transition period from old style politics to grassroots politics. It is ironic that today, the conventions have become carefully orchestrated television events and the traditional networks have essentially dropped coverage. It is only C-SPAN that provides gavel-to-gavel coverage of what was once "must-see TV."

An effective time-based use of the C-SPAN Video Library is offered by Jennifer Hopper, who examines Senator Ted Kennedy's framing of health care over time. She is able to trace the evolution of his rhetoric and thinking on health care as he evolved from advocacy for an employer mandate to his support for President Obama's initiative just before Kennedy died. Through the clips that she identifies, one can see the changes in important health care advocate views.

Only one president has been impeached twice. Stephanie Wideman and her colleagues look at the visual symbols in President Donald Trump's second impeachment trial. Key tables show the number and frequency of visual aids used by each presenter during the trial. Presenters used the "going public" approach to the use of visuals in the trial. Their finding of the powerful impact of these visuals as public assessments can have far-reaching impacts.

In "Congressional Hearings as Public Spectacle," Joshua Guitar examines hearings from a rhetorical perspective. Expectedly, he looks at some of the more dramatic hearings, such as the Kavanaugh confirmation as well as other less well-known dramatic incidents. Interesting is his observation that spectacle often favors the executive branch over the locus of the legislative branch.

Jared McDonald and Zachary Scott look at how gender shapes emotional political rhetoric. They examine how caring and authority rhetoric are used by Democratic and Republican politicians and the variations observed in men versus women. Their results are not totally expected. In careful analysis, they find differences in governance and campaigning modes. This research ought to be reviewed by other scholars.

Newly Paul utilizes the oral histories of women journalists to tell the story of how these women overcame obstacles in their professional careers. There are women who were sports journalists when few were in that field. There are women who also had to overcome the obstacles of race in a white man's world. Not only are the accounts compelling, but they contain important lessons as well.

Jacob Miller-Klugesherz applies moral foundations theory to agriculture policy. Every five years there is a new Agriculture Authorization Act. We often think of these debates as the province of agriculture state representatives, who dominate the programs, the dollars, and the allocations. Beans for you. Corn for me. Wheat and cotton for others. Miller-Kluresherz takes a different approach and looks at the moral foundations of the agriculture rhetoric using clips from the C-SPAN Video Library.

A great deal of research on audience reactions and nonverbal behavior has been undertaken by Erik Bucy and his colleagues. In this essay, they describe some of this research and propose the creation of a data co-op to house the coding and directions so that others can continue this research in the same manner. It is a way to both replicate and expand upon their techniques and approach.

These 10 essays collectively advance our understanding of history, communication, and politics. They set an example of how the C-SPAN Video Library can be used. Others will follow in their footsteps with new studies and approaches. That is the value of the C-SPAN Video Library. It keeps growing as new programs are added daily and as new scholars recognize its potential for research.

ACKNOWLEDGMENTS

This volume would not be possible without the help and involvement of many people. It started with the October 2021 research conference held virtually at Purdue University in the midst of the COVID-19 pandemic. Sponsored by the Center for C-SPAN Scholarship & Engagement (CCSE) in the Brian Lamb School of Communication, it brings together scholars from around the nation to present their research using the C-SPAN Video Library. Marifran Mattson, head of the Lamb School, leads our efforts and is always a source of ideas and inspiration. Connie Doebele, the first managing director of CCSE, worked right up to the date of the conference on many, many details. She was assisted throughout by the new managing director, Andrea Languish. The CCSE interns, Chevelle Tallman, Jaden Weiss, and Nuri Crosby, assisted with the conference logistics.

Others who helped were Cherie Drake Maestas, head of the Purdue political science department, who is always supportive of our activities. Purdue College of Liberal Arts dean David Reingold has been an enthusiastic supporter of CCSE. Donna Wireman in the Lamb School helped with many details. Rachel Ravellette and Christy Eden helped with publications. The college business office was indispensable in helping with the financial details.

David Mark and Howard Mortman participated in our virtual luncheon sessions. Others who served as facilitators or presenters were Matthew Bergbower, Alan Cloutier, Jen Hall, Alison Novak, Brian Rosenwald, Carly Schmitt, Terri Towner, and Zach Warner.

The Purdue University Press, under the direction of Justin Race, provides able assistance in the design, publication, marketing, and distribution of this series. Katherine Purple, Bryan Shaffer, Chris Brannan, Becki Corbin, and Andrea Gapsch worked with me throughout the production of this book. Kelley Kimm carefully edited the book, making it a better product than I could create myself.

The leadership of C-SPAN helps each year by providing funds for the research grants awarded to the paper presenters. Brian Lamb, Robert Kennedy, and Susan Swain have been stalwart supporters of the Archives for 35 years, and of the Lamb School, and the CCSE. They also provide encouragement and advice for all our endeavors.

Robert X. Browning

1

SHIFTING TELEVISION NEWS VALUES IN CABLE AMERICA

Kathryn Cramer Brownell

On February 27, 1984, Ted Turner sensed an opportunity as he walked into a congressional hearing in a three-piece navy suit (C-SPAN, 1984b). He sat at a long table with executives from the news divisions at the Big Three networks—Columbia Broadcasting System (CBS), National Broadcasting Company (NBC), and American Broadcasting Company (ABC). Turner was determined to distinguish his business—Cable News Network (CNN)—from their operations, which increasingly were under scrutiny that day by a panel of legislators. On Turner's left side, George Watson, the vice president of ABC News, spoke of the responsible coverage of the Iowa caucus happening at that very moment, and he assured the congressional committee that the network would not project any winners in the upcoming New Hampshire primary until all polls had closed.

Such a pledge spoke to the very issue being discussed that day: election news coverage. The four men were on Capitol Hill to testify about the controversial projection of Ronald Reagan as the winner of the 1980 election before polls had closed on the West Coast. The panel of legislators did not challenge the credibility of the information that the broadcasting networks delivered that year. But they did question the timing. By reporting a presidential victory for Reagan before the polls closed, "early projections result in voters feeling like their vote, the lynchpin in this democracy, is worthless," Rep. Timothy Wirth (D-CO) contended as he opened the hearings. He professed a deep concern that the drive for ratings and the push to be first "may be ruining the good news judgement while alienating voters by telling them what they have done before they have done it" (C-SPAN, 1984b).

On Turner's right-hand side, Ralph Goldberg, an executive at CBS News, addressed this broader question during his opening remarks. He defended the network's history of tabulating votes—increasingly with more sophisticated computers over the past three decades—as well as its more recent use of exit polling to help understand voter turnout and demographics (Chinow, 2010). He highlighted the "outstanding record" of CBS with its "accurate and timely news reporting." Rather than apologizing for projecting Reagan's victory before polls had closed, he announced, "We believe it is our role as journalists to report and not withhold information" (C-SPAN, 1984b).

Once all three of the network vice presidents had stated their case, Wirth turned it over to the man known as "Captain Outrageous." Turner leaned into the microphone and unleashed his fury on the men sitting just inches away from him, assailing the networks for abusing their power in society. "Study after study [has] criticized network television for its banal and harmful characterization of women and minorities, for the lack of quality children's programming. For sensationalism and lack of objectivity in news reporting and generally making a mockery of all the institutions that have made this country great, including the military, business, family, religion, government, and so forth." He declared that the "networks remain insensitive to the public interest and these social interests in their uncontrollable desire for ratings and revenue." For Turner, the discussion of election coverage was "just one more example of their network arrogance," and it revealed the deep need for an alternative, which, he noted, the cable dial provided (C-SPAN, 1984b).

Significantly, Turner was not alone in his criticism of the networks that day. Al Swift, a Democrat from Washington, became visibly agitated as he complained that the "Big Three" have become "insensitive" to their viewers, who were upset but had "no means to express that dissatisfaction to you through the marketplace" because of the network broadcasting oligopoly—upheld by Federal Communications Commission (FCC) regulatory policies. "How in the world is the American public going to get your attention and express something to you in clear cut terms to which you would respond?" (C-SPAN, 1984b).

Ted Turner relished this criticism and the national spotlight of a televised congressional hearing. "You hit on it," he told Swift, shaking his head. Then he held up a hand-written dollar sign as he called out "all this B.S. about journalism." To

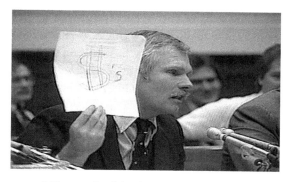

Ted Turner testifying before Congress. (Courtesy of C-SPAN.)

Turner, "journalism isn't what carries the day, it's dollars, and dollars translate with ratings" (C-SPAN, 1984b).

Concerns about election projections generated a discussion of the role of television news in American political life more broadly. For Turner, and many others in the cable industry, portraying the broadcasting industry as elitist and arrogant had become central to promoting cable television as an essential alternative to advance both democracy and consumer choice—two things they argued would reinforce one another. Years later, Wirth recalled Turner's performance as "hilarious" because it so powerfully pierced the network executives' argument about "the public's right to know." Instead, Wirth remembered how Turner exposed the economic factors shaping "what you decide the news is" (Wirth, 2000). Over the next decade, cable television's rapid expansion—made possible by politicians like Wirth and entrepreneurs like Turner—would deliver an expanded and segmented television marketplace, ultimately generating tremendous debates about how growing market diversity and consumer demand influenced the polity and the political process, for better or worse.

The C-SPAN Video Library provides insights into these conversations. Indeed, from the beginning, C-SPAN founder Brian Lamb wanted the public affairs network to bring transparency to the workings of Congress *and* the media landscape—something he had done in his earlier career by launching a newsletter, *The Media Report*, and working as a columnist for *Cablevision* (Brownell, in press). Along with covering congressional proceedings and hearings, C-SPAN featured call-in programs where journalists and pollsters discussed the nuts and bolts of their jobs. Indeed, many call-in shows had a specific format that taught media literacy. The host would pull out a newspaper and encourage viewers to look at their local paper and call in to discuss how stories were positioned and framed. During the 1984 New Hampshire primary, Susan Swain took viewers on a journey through a day in the life of the conservative *Manchester Union Leader* newspaper (C-SPAN, 1984a). Later that year on Election Day, Lamb provided a tour of the production facilities of *USA Today*. "Our objective is to watch this newspaper being put out, not to bring you election results," he emphasized (C-SPAN, 1984c). Lamb wanted to show the public how journalists gathered and reported information, demystifying the process of election coverage by the media.

As the cable dial expanded over the next decade to bring new sports, entertainment, and news options, C-SPAN remained committed to programming that discussed the changing media landscape — and these programs illuminate the ways in which journalists, politicians, and media consultants adapted their practices to the opportunities and challenges of the 24/7 news cycle. By the late 1990s, extensive programming delved into the issue of television news and its economic and civic role, ultimately providing a window into the shifting cultural values underpinning the news as profits and the public interest intersected in ways that frequently advanced the former at the expense of the latter.

————

Ted Turner's very operation challenged a fundamental belief that had upheld the broadcasting television regulatory system over the previous three decades: that news programs cost the broadcasting networks money. Network executives prided themselves on the high price tag of their news productions — it was hard evidence of their commitment to the civic good and helped justify the tremendous profits their entertainment divisions raked in as a regulated monopoly. And so, these ideas appeared regularly in advertisements, congressional testimony by network executives, and hearings with FCC commissioners. As historian Michael Socolow (2010) argues, "The idea of a charitable news service has served to deflect attention from the accumulation of corporate profit" (p. 676). During the 1960s, as reporters covered controversial issues like the civil rights movement and the Vietnam War, this perception also helped to bolster the prestige and credibility of television journalism by advancing the notion that a commitment to balance and fairness — not a desire for ratings and revenue — drove the functioning of newsrooms (Bodroghkozy, 2013; Goodwin, 2022).

In reality, however, network news did make money, something Turner reminded legislators repeatedly during the 1984 hearing. In fact, CNN's very operations had also punctured this myth. Launching in 1980 with just a $20 million investment—which Turner obtained by selling his local broadcasting station in Charlotte, North Carolina—Turner refused to pay celebrity anchors (Napoli, 2020; Parsons, 2008; Ponce de Leon, 2015). He promised to make "the news the star" and celebrated CNN's accessibility and adaptability to cover unexpected political events, including offering live coverage of events like the death of John Lennon in 1980 and the assassination attempt on President Reagan the following year (Applebaum, 1981). But it also emulated the fiscally lucrative strategy deployed by local news programs over the previous decade: including softer news like weather and sports into their reporting (Allen, 2001). And it did so unapologetically, first introducing segments—and then eventually entire programs like *Moneyline*, *Showbiz Today*, and *Larry King Live*—dedicated to business, sports, and entertainment news (Ponce de Leon, 2015, pp. 176–177). In the process, CNN reshaped the very definition of what national news could be—that is, whatever viewers wanted.

Turner also celebrated a concept that network news operations had long been reluctant to highlight: the money made from advertising. He charged cable operators 15 cents per subscriber to carry CNN (if they also carried WTBS—20 cents if not), and similar to the broadcast networks, both CNN and local operators also made money by selling advertisements (Schwartz, 1980). CNN also held advertising seminars for local cable operators and pushed for an industry-wide collaboration to conduct market research about its subscribers (Brownell, in press). Turner did not resort to creative tactics to obscure his profits. He had no need to lend the appearance that the news was corporate philanthropy, as broadcast networks did (Socolow, 2010). Making money was openly discussed and celebrated. By the end of the 1980s, Turner had fought back against potential competitors—notably ABC's effort to partner with Group W Cable and launch the competitor Satellite News Channel (Parsons, 2008). He forged strategic partnerships with cable operators to become "the little network that could," as one 1988 *New York Times* profile put it—turning a consistent profit each year (Leiser, 1998).

The following year, as the business practices of the entire cable industry came under scrutiny, cable industry leaders pointed to CNN as proof that deregulated market competition could also enhance civic life by providing more information and choice for viewers. During a 1989 Senate hearing, Senator Albert Gore Jr. (D-TN), publicly attacked the cable providers for engaging in monopolistic behavior to the detriment of television consumers. In Gore's eyes, cable companies had become the new threat as they were "hell-bent on domination," and regularly would "fleece the consumers as much as they possible can" (C-SPAN,

1989). In response, John Malone, the president and CEO of TCI, defended his company and the cable industry, celebrating the "quality and diversity of the programming" they could "bring to the American public." Malone argued that the explosion of programming demonstrated that deregulation—brought about by the 1984 Cable Communications Policy Act—worked. He noted that the "industry has been very, very successful" in providing programming diversity with "over one hundred twenty national and regional cable networks" (C-SPAN, 1989).

Gore disagreed, and over the next three years led the legislative push to reregulate the industry. It culminated in the Cable Television Consumer Protection and Competition Act of 1992, which passed over a presidential veto that October—a huge financial defeat for the cable industry (Robichaux, 2005). But the presidential campaign that same year also signaled just how integral cable television—and CNN in particular—had become in the political process. Both Ross Perot and Bill Clinton made its *Larry King Live* talk show a central part of their bids for the presidency (O'Mara, 2015). Journalists covered the rise of what they called "the new media," debating extensively the impact of talk shows, tabloids, and local media on the political process that year (C-SPAN, 1992). Hosting a forum, New Media in the 1992 Election, Ellen Hume, the executive director of the Joan Shorenstein Barone Center at Harvard University, questioned a panel of journalists, editors, and talk show hosts about how the turn to cable talk show hosts like Larry King shaped the ongoing election. "Is this trend good or bad for the public?" she asked. "Does it make any difference?"

After winning the presidency by prioritizing a cable television strategy, President Bill Clinton acknowledged just how much the news landscape had shifted. During his first White House Correspondents' Association Dinner he teased journalists about his ability to go on CNN, bypass the networks and mainstream press, and "speak directly to the American people" (C-SPAN, 1993). Although delivered as a joke, Clinton's comments reflected a serious discussion happening in newsrooms, press offices, and campaign headquarters alike: What did the future of television news look like as cable television became the dominant way people received information about the world around them? What happened to the news itself when the veil of the corporate good had been lifted and marketplace achievements were widely celebrated?

These debates intensified over the next few years with creation of two alternative 24/7 news networks: MSNBC and Fox News. In 1994, NBC had started its move into cable news with a network called America's Talking. Developed by Roger Ailes, the short-lived network emphasized commentary and engagement with viewers through call-in programs (Sherman, 2014, pp. 141–157). The network struggled, with Ailes increasingly sparring with NBC executives. And so in May 1995, when NBC announced plans with Microsoft to embark on an interactive 24/7 news venture, Ailes was purposefully excluded. On July 15, 1996, MSNBC took over the America's Talking spot on the cable dial.

When Ailes angrily left NBC, Rupert Murdoch—who had launched the Fox Broadcasting Company as an audacious challenge to the Big Three a decade earlier—saw an opportunity to tap into the growing world of cable news. Eager for the prestige that he believed came with entering the television news industry, Murdoch put Ailes in charge of a network designed to appeal to conservatives by promising "fair and balanced" coverage—an explicit nod to the growing belief in conservative circles about the problems of liberal media bias (Hendershot, 2010; Hemmer, 2016; Rosenwald, 2019). He also shocked the television industry by offering to pay $10 a subscriber for operators to carry the channel—an announcement that scared off competing programming ideas for 24/7 news at ABC (Sherman, 2014, p. 183).

As a result, by the end of 1996, the expanded news options on the dial escalated commentary about the values and practices of newsrooms operating 24/7 and the flood of information this nonstop coverage created. The Close-Up Foundation tackled the issue in a 1997 conversation with high school students televised on C-SPAN (C-SPAN, 1997a). During the discussion, *USA Today* correspondent and media critic Matt Roush explained that all news operations—both cable and broadcasting—were "fighting for an identity in terms of filling all this appetite for news programming." But he also raised a concern about the *kind* of news people were getting. Particularly, he expressed concern about the "tabloidization of the news," even as he recognized that "important stories are being covered."

During the program, CBS News Washington Bureau chief Al Ortiz acknowledged that cable news had reduced the audience for the networks' flagship broadcasts, but he also celebrated the expansion of access to information that the news landscape now provided. He answered a firm yes to the question *Is more better?* He anticipated that the network news role in the future will be to "explain the events, and [try] to give it the kind of perspective and thoughtfulness that you can put in with a few hours of work that you can't do with the covering of fast-breaking news" (C-SPAN, 1997a).

Ted Koppel presented a similar view while accepting the Fred Friendly Award for journalism later that year (C-SPAN, 1997b). The anchor for the ABC News program *Nightline* firmly rejected the notion that "television news as a whole is diminished," even as the competition intensified and increasingly "anyone can be a journalist" with portable cameras and access to the internet. Indeed, he saw the moment as the "greatest opportunity" the networks faced "in our collective history." The American public, he anticipated, "is going to be inundated by gibberish of thousands of anonymous voices in the hundreds of chat rooms" and the hundreds of cable channels. "Some of that information may be brilliant, but how will anyone know?" he asked. "Whose version of the news can you trust?" But, Koppel stated, the networks have built up "more credit, more familiarity, more trust than any of our new competitors can possibly hope to accumulate," and maintaining this required a programming commitment to quality, rather than becoming too "frivolous" and avoiding pressures "to sink into the swamp."

And yet, over the next year, the constant coverage of the Monica Lewinsky scandal pushed all news organizations into the tabloid waters as the line between entertainment and politics—and public and private—disappeared. David Halberstam called it "the worst year for American journalism," as the fast-paced news cycle and constant chatter allowed partisan punditry, rumors, and conspiracy theories to generate tremendous ratings while also alienating the public and undermining the very credibility of the news industry (Greenberg, 2015, p. 423).

An event held by the Hollywood Radio and Television Society addressed these developments directly, bringing media consultants, political advisers, journalists, producers, and news executives into a conversation about press excesses (C-SPAN, 1998a). Los Angeles radio talk show host Michael Jackson led a conversation about the question *How much is too much?* Dee Dee Myers, who had worked in the Clinton war room during the 1992 campaign and as a press secretary for the administration, lamented the rapid spread of lies and the challenge of distinguishing "misinformation from real information." Lisa Caputo, the former press secretary to the First Lady, agreed, explaining that the growth of 24/7 news, in combination with the internet, had made the news cycle itself disappear, with journalists struggling to keep up on what events to even cover and report. "It's created a sort of . . . centrifuge of news coverage to the point where the press are finding it difficult to keep up with the story and for competitive purposes, they're trying to outdo one another." Rather than corroborating sources, she emphasized, news divisions just would go with a story, and apologize later if the facts were wrong.

Vice president of news for WCBS-TV in New York and former *New York Post* editor Jerry Nachman called attention to the sensationalized content of the stories: how Barbara Walters talked about the "potential forensic value of dried semen stains" on 20/20 and Ted Koppel discussed "oral sex, whether it's sex or whether its adultery" on *Nightline*. Such approach to the news, Nachman, argued, constituted a "paradigm shift" over what stories got on the air and the "semi-serious conversations" offered as "commentary" about them. But he also called attention to a fundamental paradox of the media landscape that he and so many others on the panel criticized. Ratings on shows related to the Clinton scandal skyrocketed, even as the majority of Americans responded in polls that coverage of it was excessive. "What do you do with a public that keeps saying, you rotten pieces of shit, but give me more?" he asked (C-SPAN, 1998a).

Later that year, John Malone and Walter Cronkite—two titans of cable television and network news, respectively—directly addressed this question of market choice, viewer demands, and the civic obligation of corporate news companies (C-SPAN, 1998b). The former CBS anchor asked Malone about the tensions between the "mercenary" interests of executives and the journalists working in the newsrooms, especially with the consolidation of ownership that had happened in companies like Malone's TCI. Diversity on television "protects our free society," replied Malone as he, once again, pointed to the explosion of options on the cable dial, especially in regard to cable news networks. "There is no one power broker that can control the media in any market, let alone the national market, to get away with compression or slanting of the news." When programs did this, he argued, the marketplace would serve as a corrective force.

As a counterpoint, Cronkite expressed his concern as to whether market forces could deliver on the civic function of the news, what he called the "very heavy responsibility in our democracy of keeping the people informed adequately enough so that they can perform their role in democracy at the voting polls." While he lauded the growth of consumer options on the cable dial, he also worried deeply about the day when viewers could "punch up and get nothing but golf, for we will have a lot of really good golfers but they aren't going to know what the hell is going on in the rest of the world" (C-SPAN, 1998b).

As *New Yorker* columnist Ken Auletta moderated the conversation, he pushed Malone on this very issue. "There is a belief in journalism that you have an obligation to tell the viewers . . . we think you should sit down and eat your spinach because this is important information about what happened in the world today, and even if it doesn't earn a profit, this is part of the obligation. . . . Do you buy that?" Absolutely not, responded Malone. He called that perspective "elitist" and said that "we underrate the public." In fact, he postured that the public was "probably more informed today than we think," because of the innovations brought by cable news and its "efficient" and "interactive" platforms, including those like MSNBC that worked to engage viewers online as well as on the cable dial. "Consumer is king," emphasized Malone. "The consumer will ultimately demand convenience, accuracy . . . and quality." The determining factor in the future of news is "what the consumer wants" (C-SPAN, 1998b).

Two year later, however, the coverage of the 2000 election made it clear that meeting consumer demands for speed and efficiency could hurt the democratic process. Political scientists, analysts, and pollsters knew that the presidential election between Vice President Al Gore and Governor George W. Bush would be a tight race—one that would come down to battleground states like Florida. Amid catchy graphics—including CNN's "countdown to the next poll closing"—and extensive commentary with pundits predicting the outcomes, the cable and broadcast news programs focused in on the critical state of Florida (Kloer, 2000a). Between 7:50 and 8:02 on election evening, ABC, CBS, NBC, CNN, MSNBC, and Fox News all projected Al Gore as the winner. Two hours later, the call was retracted, and CNN's Jeff Greenfield admitted on the air, "Oh, waiter! One order of crow" (Marks, 2000). Several hours later, the networks made another mistake, declaring Bush the winner of Florida between 2:16 a.m. and 2:20 a.m. before retracting that call less than two hours later.

Voters woke up confused, and over the next few weeks conspiracy theories started to circulate. Conservatives believed that the "liberal media" tried to sway the election for Gore, while Democrats saw the management of the Fox News election desk—and the first to call Florida and the presidency for Bush—by Bush's first cousin John Prescott Ellis as a clear violation of journalistic integrity by a Right-leaning cable network (Sherman, 2014). Scholars have noted that a central problem in the 2000 coverage was not a liberal or conservative bias, but a lack of clarity about how election desks and exit polling worked, where networks actually received their information—notably that all the major TV newsrooms that year used the same data from the Voter News Service to make their projections—and the "limitations of predictive models in a close election" (Wardle et al., 2001).

The pooling of resources was not new. Since 1964, the three networks had shared election data, banding together to form the News Election Service (NES). But as the 1984 hearing on election coverage had demonstrated, the networks also all had individual exit poll operations to corroborate and help analyze the data and project winners. Such resources were expensive, however. In 1990, with election evening costs and pressures to cut budgets both rising, the networks and

CNN joined the Voter Research Survey to conduct research on elections—including exit polling, analysis, and projections—a venture that saved each of them $9 million a year. Two years later, the VRS and NES merged to form the Voter News Service (VNS), beginning what one journalist called "the age where networks artificially compete, using identical information supplied simultaneously but reaching their own conclusions on their own timetable" (*Election Night Coverage*, 2001, p. 150).

Such a merger embodied the demands of 24/7 news programing in an era of corporate restructuring with an emphasis on the bottom line, efficiency, and the prioritization of interpretation of the news over the reporting of it (Ponce de Leon, 2015; Pressman, 2018). In the days that followed the 2000 election, however, academics, practitioners, and the broader public reflected on what happened, and according to a man who had worked with both CBS News and Fox News, the botched coverage made clear the problems that had plagued media operations over the previous years. "It's definitely been damaged," explained political editor Vaughn Ververs to a student asking about the media's reputation in the aftermath of the 2000 election. "People have suspicion of the media in a lot of ways to begin with, not that they don't trust them, but they see them, I think for what they are, and that is becoming more publicity-driven and dramatically-driven rather than news driven" (C-SPAN, 2000).

This trend became even more pronounced during the 39-day legal and political battle to determine a winner in Florida as ratings soared and voter cynicism and partisan polarization intensified (Kloer, 2000b; Prior, 2007). One *New York Times* article discussed the long-term impact of what it called a "political story of a lifetime crashing through the door" (Carter, 2000.) According to Bill Carter, the election dispute "created the prospect of a presidency forever dogged by questions of legitimacy and could give the political talk shows a new, richly partisan, and potentially enduring subject to mine for the intensely headed conversation they aim to sell." While critics lamented the danger of such programs that had become "a divisive irritant in the political process," Carter noted that Sean Hannity was "gleeful." The cohost of *Hannity and Colmes* at Fox News exclaimed during one show, "This could go on forever." Tim Russert, NBC anchor and host of *Meet the Press*, also saw the contested election as a "story made for television" that would play out for the next four years (Carter, 2000). But, such heightened political debate on television potentially had dangerous consequences for the democratic process. Indeed, MSNBC's Chris Matthews expressed an unease at what he predicted would become a "government-in-exile" mentality on political talk shows, while CNN analyst Jeff Greenfield underscored how "this is one case where the newsman's profession is at war with other, very serious things" (Carter, 2000).

In the end, the broadcast and cable networks all apologized for their mistakes and reformed their projection practices for election night coverage even as they also tapped into ratings the broader partisan drama generated. In February, news executives once again traveled to Capitol Hill to discuss their election coverage. But the cast and conversation were very different from 17 years earlier. In 1984, Tim Wirth ended the three-hour conversation by reminding the networks of their "significant public trust responsibility," highlighting that "it is our job to make sure that responsibility in the public trust is carried out," and promising "to watch this issue very, very carefully" (C-SPAN, 1984b). And in fact, he even led the effort that year to deregulate the cable industry to bring more consumer choice to television viewers in hopes that an expanded media marketplace would advance the public interest.

By 2001, these ideas about the importance of market competition had become deeply ingrained in both parties, and it showed during the hearings about election coverage (Geismer, 2022). Chairman of the House Energy Committee W. J. "Billy" Tauzin (R-LA) emphasized that the hearings were not a "penalty" but rather an effort to find out how newsrooms operated and how such a mistake could have happened: to clarify the process rather than to reform it (C-SPAN, 2001). "I hope you have not felt you were here under duress. You came here voluntarily. You know that. I asked each of you to come. You came. I appreciate it, and I will give you one commitment in return. I will fight to the death to protect your right to keep doing this wrong if you really want to do it wrong. That's the truth . . . I will fight vigorously any attempt to legislate in the area of your content. That is wrong for us to even talk about doing. We won't do it."

Despite the recognition of the problems inherent in cable newsroom competition and the acknowledgment that television news failed the American people, Tauzin concluded that the marketplace would motivate the necessary changes in the newsrooms. And he was half right. In the years that followed, the marketplace continued to change cable news. But, instead of pushing it toward a serious reporting-driven product, the pursuit of ratings intensified and cable news expanded commentary designed to cultivate viewer outrage. Tapping into cynicism emerged as a profitable business model (Prior, 2007; Young, 2020). This may have engrossed viewers, but at a cost to a more informed citizenry, just as Walter Cronkite feared.

1. SHIFTING TELEVISION NEWS VALUES IN CABLE AMERICA

REFERENCES

Allen, C. (2001). *News is people: The rise of local TV news and the fall of news from New York*. Wiley-Blackwell.

Applebaum, S. (1981, February 2). CNN fame grows in press circles. *Cablevision*, 16–17.

Bodroghkozy, A. (2013). *Equal time: Television and the civil rights movement*. University of Illinois Press.

Brownell, K. C. (in press). *Cable America: How a different approach to television transformed American democracy*. Princeton University Press.

Carter, B. (2000, November 13). TV talk shows see hope in the never-ending 2000 election. *New York Times*, C1. https://www.nytimes.com/2000/11/13/business/media-tv-talk-shows-see-hope-in-the-never-ending-2000-election.html

Chinow, I. (2010). *Battle of the brains: Election-night forecasting at the dawn of the computer age* [Dissertation, University of Maryland].

C-SPAN (Producer). (1984a, February 21). *A day in the life of* The Union Leader [Video]. https://www.c-span.org/video/?124250-1/day-life-the-union-leader

C-SPAN (Producer). (1984b, February 27). *Early election projections* [Video]. https://www.c-span.org/video/?124198-1/early-election-projections

C-SPAN (Producer). (1984c, November 6). *Election night coverage* [Video]. https://www.c-span.org/video/?124866-1/election-night-coverage

C-SPAN (Producer). (1989, November 16). *Cable Telecommunications Act, Day 1, Part 1* [Video]. https://www.c-span.org/video/?9959-1/cable-telecommunications-act-day-1-part-1#

C-SPAN (Producer). (1992, October 2). *The new media in the 1992 campaign* [Video]. https://www.c-span.org/video/?32993-1/media-1992-campaign

C-SPAN (Producer). (1993, May 1). *1993 White House correspondents' dinner* [Video]. https://www.c-span.org/video/?40370-1/1993-white-house-correspondents-dinner

C-SPAN (Producer). (1997a, May 8). *Future of television news* [Video]. https://www.c-span.org/video/?81042-1/future-television-news

C-SPAN (Producer). (1997b, June 10). *Broadcast news industry competition* [Video]. https://www.c-span.org/video/?86636-1/broadcast-news-industry-competition

C-SPAN (Producer). (1998a, February 12). *Press excesses* [Video]. https://www.c-span.org/video/?100468-1/press-excesses

C-SPAN (Producer). (1998b, September 15). *The state of television news* [Video]. https://www.c-span.org/video/?111881-1/state-television-news

C-SPAN (Producer). (2000, December 4). *Predicting the 2000 election* [Video]. https://www.c-span.org/video/?160979-3/predicting-2000-election

C-SPAN (Producer). (2001, February 8). *Network news coverage of the 2000 election* [Video]. https://www.c-span.org/video/?162507-1/network-news-coverage-2000-election

Election Night Coverage by the Networks: Hearing Before the Committee on Energy and Commerce, One Hundred Seventh Congress, First Session, February 14, 2001. (2001). U.S. Government Printing Office.

Geismer, L. (2022). *Left behind: The Democrats' failed attempt to solve inequality.* Public Affairs.

Goodwin, S. (2022). *Making the news: The development of network television news and the struggle for Black freedom in the 1950s and 1960s* [Dissertation, University of Oxford].

Greenberg, D. (2015). *Republic of spin: An inside history of the American presidency.* W. W. Norton.

Hemmer, N. (2016). *Messengers of the Right: Conservative media and the transformation of American politics.* University of Pennsylvania Press.

Hendershot, H. (2010). *What's fair on the air: Cold War right-wing broadcasting and the public interest.* University of Chicago Press.

Kloer, P. (2000a, November 8). Competitive gimmickry makes race "televisual." *Atlanta Constitution,* E.20.

Kloer, P. (2000b, November 10). Ratings soar as viewers remain riveted to election coverage. *Atlanta Constitution,* E.5.

Leiser, E. (1988, March 20). The little network that could. *New York Times,* 30–38. https://www.nytimes.com/1988/03/20/magazine/the-little-network-that-could.html

Marks, P. (2000, November 8). A flawed call adds to high drama. *New York Times,* B1. https://www.nytimes.com/2000/11/08/us/the-2000-elections-the-media-a-flawed-call-adds-to-high-drama.html

Napoli, L. (2020). *Up all night: Ted Turner, CNN and the birth of 24-hour news.* Abrams.

O'Mara, M. (2015). *Pivotal Tuesdays: Four elections that shaped the twentieth century.* University of Pennsylvania Press.

Parsons, P. (2008). *Blue skies: A history of cable television.* Temple University Press.

Ponce de Leon, C. (2015). *That's the way it is: A history of television news in America.* University of Chicago Press.

Pressman, M. (2018). *On press: The liberal bias that shaped the news.* Harvard University Press.

Prior, M. (2007) *Post-broadcast democracy: How media choice increases inequality in political involvement and polarizes elections.* Cambridge University Press.

Robichaux, M. (2005). *Cable cowboy: John Malone and the rose of the modern cable business.* Wiley.

Rosenwald, B. (2019). *Talk radio's America: How an industry took over a political party that took over the nation.* Harvard University Press.

Schwartz, T. (1980, May 25). TV News, starring Ted Turner. *New York Times*, 1. https://www.nytimes.com/1980/05/25/archives/the-tv-news-starring-ted-turner-ted-turner-and-his-24houraday.html

Sherman, G. (2014). *The loudest voice in the room: How the brilliant, bombastic Roger Ailes built Fox News—and divided a country.* Random House.

Socolow, M. (2010). "We should make money on our news": The problem of profitability in network broadcast journalism history. *Journalism*, *11*(6), 676. https://doi.org/10.1177/1464884910379707

Wardle, C., Kenski, K., Orr, D., & Jamieson, K. H. (2001). The Voter News Service and the 2000 election night calls. *American Behavioral Scientist*, *44*(12), 2306–2313. https://doi.org/10.1177/00027640121958339

Wirth, T. (2000, April 20). Interviewed by P. Maxwell [Video]. Oral Histories, Hauser Collection. Cable Center, Barco Library, Denver, CO. https://www.cablecenter.org/53-the-oral-history-project/w-z-listings/188-timothy-wirth-oral-history

Young, D. G. (2020). *Irony and outrage: The polarized landscape of rage, fear, and laughter in the United States.* Oxford University Press.

2

TELEVISION, CHAOS, AND REFORM

Revisiting the McGovern Campaign via the C-SPAN Video Library

Heather Hendershot

I n a 2007 episode of C-SPAN2's *Book TV*, political scientist Bruce Miroff describes the Democratic convention in Miami Beach where South Dakota senator George McGovern was nominated for president in 1972 as "a puzzling and prophetic mixture of exuberant triumph and disarray." The campaign itself was "marked by mounting crises, by painful stumbles, and then of course, by landslide defeat" (C-SPAN, 2007). Following this, the bulk of Miroff's discussion centers on the long-term fallout of McGovern's campaign—in particular the ongoing Democratic Party concern that a presidential candidate who is "too liberal" will necessarily suffer a humiliating defeat along the lines of McGovern's. Miroff is hitting the key points from his book *The Liberals' Moment*, and given his disciplinary home base one would not expect him to discuss issues of campaign media or news coverage too much. And yet, he provides clues to help us think in that direction. For example, he points to all the dirty tricks the Nixon campaign used in 1972, and, building on this, it is important to remember that while many of those tricks were covert, Nixon's team also depended heavily on the most public of tactics: negative publicity, usually planted in the print and electronic media.

The inflammatory notion that McGovern favored "acid, amnesty, and abortion," for example, was exploited by Nixon's campaign, though it was all fabrication or misdirection: McGovern took heat from feminists for abortion rights *not* having been included in the Democratic platform that year; he favored leniency around pot, not acid; and though McGovern did favor amnesty, Nixon himself had also approved of amnesty for draft resisters before the 1972 campaign (Miroff,

2007; Noah, 2007, 2012). As a media historian, I would emphasize here not only the fact that the anti-McGovern triple-A slogan was dishonest but also that it was a slur spread by his opponents on bumper stickers, posters, billboards, and campaign buttons, and in TV and radio ad spots. It was, in other words, not just a political tactic but specifically a *mediated* tactic.

The Miroff presentation is but one of many artifacts held in the C-SPAN Video Library that provide research material to shore up arguments about the McGovern campaign as a mediated event (and one that misfired), though not all the C-SPAN lectures, interviews, original materials (that is, convention and campaign archival artifacts), and panel discussions consider it directly as such. The following pages will go to the roots of that mediated campaign, which are to be found at the 1968 and 1972 nominating conventions, and then will move on to the 1972 campaign itself.

First, some background. The quadrennial presidential conventions used to be crucial centerpieces of network TV news. The 1948 conventions were the first covered by TV and had been barebones affairs. By 1952, the networks had sunk significant resources into convention coverage, fighting tough ratings battles, and taking the opportunity to show off shiny new technologies—lighter cameras, color cameras, new headsets for correspondents—anything to get a leg up over the competition. For their part, the political parties became increasingly responsive (often resentfully so) to the presence of cameras and reporters. The networks wanted to get an angle on stories and ask tough questions; the parties would have preferred their events presented to viewers as *their shows* that they had invited the networks to air (Frank, 1991). As far as the Republican and Democratic National Committees were concerned, just pointing cameras at the dais constituted ideal coverage. The news teams wanted to *report*, while the Democratic and Republican National Committees would have preferred something closer to stenography.

This context helps elucidate the crisis of the 1968 convention (crucial background for understanding the chaos of the 1972 convention), where Mayor Richard Daley deviously attempted to prevent the networks from providing live coverage outside the convention hall in the streets. The gathering of 10,000 anti-Vietnam protesters undeniably constituted a major, newsworthy story, but Daley feared negative coverage of his police by the networks and did all that he could to censor their reporting. Of course, American TV viewers still saw the street action, just not live. In particular, late on the third night of the convention they watched videotaped footage of Chicago police beating and arresting pro-testers in front of the Conrad Hilton Hotel.[1] The images would be replayed on the nightly news in the days following the event, and still images appeared in news-papers and magazines across the country.

It is these images that have dominated media historians' accounts of the 1968 convention, along with a few live televised crises from inside the Chicago Am-phitheater, such as Daley expressing his rage when Sen. Abraham Ribicoff, in the course of nominating McGovern on live TV, referred to "Gestapo tactics in the streets of Chicago," or CBS anchorman Walter Cronkite referring to the security men who had slugged correspondent Dan Rather as "a bunch of thugs." The dominant memory of Chicago is of street violence, and, inside the convention hall, of a handful of reactions to Daley-sanctioned violence. These are the images that have circulated during the past 50 years, recounted in scholarship and recy-cled in documentary film and television productions, ranging from WGBH's 1983 *Vietnam: A Television History* to Ken Burns's and Lynn Novick's *The Vietnam War* (2017). The 1968 Chicago police even make a cameo appearance in the C-SPAN (2011) episode "George McGovern, Presidential Contender," an installment of a limited run, live call-in series titled *The Contenders.*

There are no similarly resonant—or, if you will, mythologized—images or mo-ments from the 1972 Democratic National Convention (DNC), and the '72 con-vention has appeared to historians as a less impactful media event than 1968's convention. Indeed, media historians have shown no interest in the '72 conven-tion (see, however, Crouse, 1973) and only slightly more in the '68 event, a situa-tion I strive to rectify in my book on network coverage of Chicago (Hendershot, 2022). In '68, angry delegates decried the fact that they were enduring a "closed convention" where the candidate had been predetermined by the party's lead-ers. In '72, various reforms in the delegate selection process struck hard at the old machine players. Mayor Daley and his delegation were even ejected and re-placed by Jesse Jackson's Illinois delegates. The attendees were no less angry than those of four years earlier, but many of them were convention newcomers who did not understand the procedural basics. The result was chaos that rivaled that of '68, though without the violence. The TV cameras once again caught it all. At times, the images clearly conveyed a party in crisis.

How did things reach this point and spin out of control so badly? So much had happened on the floor of the Chicago Amphitheater in 1968 that it was easy to lose track of the procedural ins and outs from the rostrum—the thank-you speeches, formulaic votes, and Robert's Rules of Order–type actions that appear in the DNC's 640-page official transcript of the event but created not even a ripple in TV news coverage and were thus left unseen by home viewers.

One such detail was the decision to create the Commission on Party Structure and Delegate Selection, which would revise the delegate selection process, rework party structure, and increase grassroots participation. This would eventually become known as the McGovern–Fraser Commission, after its directors, George McGovern and Minnesota representative Donald M. Fraser. The commission's consultant committee included Richard C. Wade, a famed urban historian and University of Chicago professor who leaned liberal; he had managed the Upstate New York campaign for RFK's 1964 senatorial run and also served as adviser to Adlai Stevenson and McGovern (Grimes, 2008). For McGovern–Fraser, Wade outlined two choices for delegate selection: the creation of national party guidelines or sticking with the current system of allowing states to decide for themselves, which had enabled procedural chaos not only in Chicago, but also going back to Truman's nomination in 1948, when pro-segregation southern states had walked out with Sen. Strom Thurmond (Sánchez, 2020).[2] The Democrats were now the party of civil rights, and yet southern states could still arrive at conventions with all or mostly white delegations, and they had enough votes to create trouble for the national party. Obviously, national guidelines were in the cards.

The story is complicated, but suffice it to say, McGovern–Fraser has long been seen as the force that democratized the party by allowing for representation at conventions by people who previously had been kept out by state party voting systems: women, people of color, the young. In a key revision, historian Jaime Sánchez has argued that the committee was not simply about *ideological* reform, as it is so often remembered, but even more importantly about *institutional* reform. The national party in effect saved itself from the states by creating uniform delegate selection standards. The most straightforward way of explaining this is to observe that in 1964 and 1968 the Democratic convention had been packed with southern delegates who were unwilling to support the nominee of their own party, going for Barry Goldwater and George Wallace, respectively, rather than LBJ and Humphrey. It had to be stopped. One might add, somewhat contra Sánchez, that this was not an either/or scenario of ideological vs. institutional reform. It was ultimately very much both.

The southern delegates were the ones who had staged the big, spectacular protests, with their walkouts and threatened walkouts over the years, and if TV viewers understood that there was a "delegate problem," they were more likely to understand it as a political problem than an institutional one. Issues like delegate selection, credentials battles, and unit rule voting were covered by the networks, but such procedural matters could quickly devolve into inside baseball. Rather than diving into such minutiae, it was easier for anchormen Walter Cronkite, David Brinkley, and Chet Huntley to explain voter suppression vs. states' rights: who is allowed to vote for convention delegates, and who should decide, the states or the national party?

The disenfranchisement of Black voters made for good drama, and therefore good TV. Teddy White observed correctly that "the impression this open convention made on America outside, in this new age of television, would be, politically, of as much weight in the campaign of 1972 as what anyone at the convention said or did" (White, 1973, p. 159). The new rules seemed to indicate that this year viewers would witness nothing like the Mississippi crisis of 1964 or the Georgia crisis of 1968. In 1964, Black Mississippi challenging delegates had failed to seize seats at the convention. At the same time, their representative, Fannie Lou Hamer, became an icon of that moment, even though President Johnson had succeeded in shutting down her live televised testimony. In 1968, Julian Bond emerged as the icon of disenfranchised Black delegates from Georgia, and those challengers achieved a partial victory in Chicago, a chaotic event captured live by the networks. The cameras often cut to Bond, who was not only accomplished and articulate but also young and handsome, in stark contrast to his opponent, Georgia governor Lester Maddox. The political drama was real, but it was boosted by the strength of a good guy–bad guy narrative that seemed tailor-made for network news.

By 1972, revisions in the rules would theoretically help party leaders control convention coverage, in part, by preventing the need for challenges against white supremacist voting policies of state delegations. Further, from the media spin angle, a positive element for 1972 was Black presidential contender Shirley Chisholm, whose very presence, party officials must have hoped, would help to defuse any brewing complaints regarding Black disempowerment. TV interviews with Chisholm would, theoretically, convey an evolution since Hamer and Bond: the Black outsider was now an insider. Perhaps predictably, things did not play out so smoothly. In fact, 1972 would lay bare the fact that crises of disenfranchisement were not confined to southern states. Daley—mayor of the most segregated city in America, a northern city—was the key operative in attempting to ensure that the Illinois delegation was filled by machine-approved, mostly white candidates.

Even if Georgia had gotten the most airtime for delegate selection conflicts in 1968, Illinois had been just as culpable. In 1972 the McGovern–Fraser reforms would bring this all to the surface, and to American TV screens, when Daley—the party player, the kingmaker, the man nicknamed "Mr. Democrat" by politicians and DNC operatives—was shut out. As per McGovern–Fraser recommendations, at the Miami convention in 1972 "Blacks, women, Spanish-speakers, and people between the ages of eighteen and thirty had to be represented as delegate candidates in proportion to their population in each congressional district. The new rules also required that delegate selection be done in public, with the time and place of the sessions publicized in advance" (Cohen & Taylor, 2001, p. 521). This last rule hit the southern delegations particularly hard, as the segregationists had succeeded in the past by keeping their state party meeting times and locations secret from people of color.

Daley responded that the new rules simply were not valid under Illinois law. And so, his machine selected a slate of 59 candidates, which Chicagoans could vote for or not, with no attention paid to the party's new diversity rules. Independent Chicago alderman William Singer, with Rev. Jesse Jackson, selected an alternative delegate slate confirmed via caucuses held throughout Chicago, with "informal, voice-vote elections, where voting was conducted over the heckling of machine representatives who had infiltrated the meetings. The Daley slate and the Singer-Jackson slate represented two extremes of the cultural chasm that had split the Democratic Party four years earlier" (Cohen & Taylor, 2001, p.522). As usual, Daley's slate won in a citywide election, capturing the vote of white ethnics and others who followed the lead of their precinct captains. There was a complicated legal fight, and ultimately the national party's Credentials Committee voted 71 to 61 to seat the Singer–Jackson alternative slate. Daley and his people complained that this violated the will of the 900,000 Chicago voters who had gone for the machine's slate. Except they didn't call it the "machine's slate" and implied that open elections were standard operating procedure in Chicago.[3] Daley's narrative, suggesting that democracy had been defeated by quotas and radical leftists, gained substantial traction in the national media.

The Singer–Jackson slate thereby seemed extremist, while the Daley slate appeared to be the product of fairness and moderation. Even Chicago's best anti-Daley newspaperman, Mike Royko, disapproved of how the alternative Jackson slate had been selected, wisecracking that "anybody who would reform Chicago's Democratic Party by dropping the white ethnic would probably begin a diet by shooting himself in the stomach" (Royko in White, 1973, p. 165). Daley was ultimately both loser and winner: loser because his own party shut him out, a grand humiliation that took him completely by surprise, winner because he played the indignant victim so well. He was ice-cold toward candidate McGovern and took the "I told you so" line when he lost to Nixon in a landslide. Teddy White, who had been a voice of liberal moderation back in 1964, and who was by 1968 more of a centrist and even a booster for the "New Nixon" of that year,[4] was appalled by the ouster of Daley in 1972: "Whatever one's sympathies, how, now, could one avoid wondering what the political effect would be, on the television audience, of the sight of Black people jumping up and hugging each other with glee as Dick Daley was humiliated, or the sound of Spanish-speaking ladies jubilating over their triumph at this session" (White, 1973, p. 166). White's condescension is galling (and he wasn't really "wondering"), but he was probably on the mark about the effect that the televised proceedings would have on the so-called silent majority of home viewers. All the McGovern–Fraser positive spin seemed to unravel at once with Daley's ejection from the Miami convention.

Between the Chicago and Miami conventions, the national party had worked carefully to present its reforms to the public in a positive light—and to convey those reforms via magazine and TV interviews with high-profile Democrats. In 1969, on NBC's *Meet the Press*, DNC chairman Sen. Fred Harris argued that what Americans were witnessing was "not a movement of [party] fracture . . . but rather of reinvention" (Harris quoted in Sánchez, 2020, p. 11). In 1970, McGovern wrote in *Harper's* that "amidst the madness in Chicago" few had noticed the vote for procedural reform, but now he and his compatriots were "in the process of invigorating our party with a massive injection of democracy. The day of the bosses is all but over" (McGovern, 1970). And in June 1972, McGovern and Humphrey appeared on ABC's *Issues and Answers* to convey party unity, confirming they would support whoever the party's nominee was. The problem was, there were three other candidates, all of whom declined to pledge support for the nominee in advance. The national party's public relations efforts were already faltering, with little more than a month before the convention.

By the time candidates and delegates assembled in Miami, the image of party unity could no longer cohere. Part of the problem was that democratization brought in new inexperienced delegates who didn't understand convention procedures any more than they understood the importance of at least *trying* to look like a unified party on national television. In 1968, the McCarthy delegates understood both procedural issues and the televisual impact of their protest, which they tried to work to their advantage, with uneven success. The youth, women,

Blacks, and other newcomers to the 1972 convention in Miami didn't know the procedural ins and outs or care about most of that image stuff. If the Singer–Jackson victory against Daley played out as a radical left-wing takeover of the Democratic Party on national TV, the late-night debates on the dais over feminism, Black empowerment, and gay rights were also a crisis for a party trying to defeat a conservative incumbent with strong approval ratings.

As one member of the Platform Committee put it, critiquing the newcomer delegates, "Their struggle is between the wild wing and the mild wing; what they're doing is selling out their true believers on things like pot, amnesty, and abortion. There won't be any riots in Miami because the people who rioted in Chicago are on the Platform Committee—they outnumber us by three or four to one" (Wattenberg quoted in White, 1973, p. 161). The longhairs were on the convention floor now. Even Yippies Jerry Rubin and Abbie Hoffman had endorsed McGovern ("M'Govern Endorsed by 2," 1972).

Consider three books written from rather different political orientations, by powerhouse authors chronicling the impact of the neophytes at the 1972 convention. In *The Making of the President 1972*, Teddy White supported the cause of women's rights but saw the homosexual activists' cause as "nonsense" (1972, p. 182). In *St. George and the Godfather*, Norman Mailer felt pretty much the reverse on those two issues (1972, pp. 53, 57). And in *Fear and Loathing on the Campaign Trail '72* Hunter S. Thompson didn't even mention the gays and understood the feminist activists correctly as pawns in McGovern's tactical maneuvers. That is, the gonzo journalist was the one who just focused on the convoluted political game, producing what McGovern operative Frank Mankiewicz described 25 years later on a C-SPAN panel discussion show, with only a little exaggeration, as "the most accurate and least factual account of that campaign" (C-SPAN, 1997).

None of them could altogether clearly explain the procedural crises with South Carolina and California, but Thompson nailed it when he said that *even the networks*, well versed in procedural minutiae, couldn't understand that McGovern needed to *lose* the South Carolina credentials challenge in order to later *win* the California credentials challenge: "What an incredibly byzantine gig! Imagine trying to understand it on TV—not even Machiavelli could have handled *that*" (Thompson, 1973, p. 288; c.f. Navasky, 1972). The one thing that all three had a handle on, though, was the fact that it was a disaster for McGovern, and the newly reformed party in general, for home viewers to see these sorts of crises play out on TV, and that the only break the nominee got was when the most radical stuff happened outside of prime time. What a blessing, from the perspective

of the McGovern campaign, that the gay rights plank was only debated and ultimately rejected by delegates at 5:00 a.m. The newspapers mentioned it, and the
bleary-eyed NBC and CBS correspondents reported it live, but most Americans
missed it completely ("'Gay' People Bitter," 1972).[5]

From the media angle, McGovern's luck was the worst on the final day of the
convention, when he was scheduled to give his acceptance speech. White observed that "even at Chicago in 1968, with all the violence, bloodshed, and dissension, the party had pulled itself together well enough to let Hubert Humphrey
speak to the nation when the nation was ready to listen" (White, 1973, p. 184).
Humphrey's speech had started at 10:30 p.m. Chicago time—11:30 p.m. on the
East Coast and 8:30 p.m. on the West Coast—airing at the same time *The To-
night Show* would have been broadcast in the East. In Miami in 1972, by contrast,
McGovern's acceptance speech began at 2:48 a.m. It was a little before 6:00 p.m.
in Guam, making that the only place where U.S. citizens watched the speech at a
reasonable hour. (Nixon of course was up late watching in San Clemente. [White,
1973, p. 239].) A prime-time speech would have reached 17.4 million homes, but
the senator's ill-timed speech hit about 3.6 million. Today, interested viewers
could seek out such a speech on C-SPAN or YouTube. In 1972, though, when
you missed a TV event, you missed a TV event. A few clips aired on the news
later, and that was it.[6]

One might think it didn't matter much; the candidates were so different, and
it's not as if a diehard liberal or conservative would have been likely to switch
allegiances based on either half-hour speech. But it did matter. The DNC had
made all of its revisions not only to seize national control of the party away from
the states and to make the convention more open but also to regain control over
its own mediated image. Network coverage of Chicago had shown a party out
of control and rife with dissension, even if one subtracted the 3% to 5% of coverage that had centered on street violence. Four years later in Miami, the party still
seemed out of control. McGovern's speech had aired absurdly late because feminists, Black activists, the young—all the new delegates who weren't seasoned
political operatives—exploited procedural rules to make symbolic nominations
for the vice presidential slot. Each nomination was allotted a 15-minute speech.

The riotous nominations had the momentum of a runaway train. Finally, the
nominations were done, and the roll call began, with the chairman of each state
standing up and announcing its delegates' votes. It was a foregone conclusion
that McGovern's choice, Thomas Eagleton, would win, yet symbolic votes came
in for Dr. Spock, the Berrigan brothers, Jerry Rubin, and Ralph Nader—even a

few for Roger Mudd, Chairman Mao, and Archie Bunker. (The most oddball vote in 1968 had been for Alabama football coach Paul "Bear" Bryant.) These scattered protest votes in 1972 made the newly "open" party look silly. McGovern's late-night speech was also a media disaster because this should have been a golden moment to reach a wide audience for an entire half hour of free airtime. If the crisis of 1968 was that "the whole world was watching," the crisis of 1972 was that it was not.

Interviewed on C-SPAN almost 20 years later, McGovern said that the 3:00 a.m. speech was "a dreadful mistake, I think possibly the most costly single mistake that we made in 1972, even more costly perhaps than the vice presidential selection." He added, "It was the first opportunity for me as a junior senator from South Dakota to make an imprint on 75 or 80 million Americans who were watching the convention at 9:00 or 10:00 in the evening when I should have been giving that speech. . . . All we had to do was to call the national chairman Larry O'Brien and say, 'Look, let's put the acceptance speech on now and hold all this other business until after I speak.'" McGovern described it as "the best speech I ever gave in my life." The interview was the introduction to C-SPAN's airing of the speech, and McGovern closes out wrenchingly with, "I'm going to be glad to see it in prime time!" (C-SPAN, 1988b).

One might speculate that if millions more had seen the convention speech, as they would have if it had been shown at a reasonable time, it could have helped to reframe McGovern as a candidate who was both critical of current American policies *and* patriotic. Kathleen Hall Jamieson argues that broadcast spots of five minutes or less tend to "entice the unsuspecting viewer," whereas half-hour productions such as biographical campaign films and election eve programs "attract true believers" (Jamieson, 1996, p. 321). The one exception is the half-hour nomination acceptance speech, because conventions draw voters from both parties, not only because people watch such programming, theoretically at least, out of a sense of civic duty but also because conventions preempted other programming during the network era; if you wanted to watch TV, the convention was the only game in town. A half-hour opportunity in prime time to actually pull in new voters, even the much-coveted "undecided voters," makes the convention speech a prized moment. Excerpts from that precious half hour are typically included in TV spots, and of course, McGovern did include excerpts, but he had lost his initial golden opportunity. Notably, Humphrey had delivered a very good acceptance speech in 1968, but the convention had been so chaotic (both on the floor and in the streets) that his campaign reused as little convention imagery as possible and did not recycle much of the speech. The 1972 convention had also been an unruly spectacle, but without the violence, and the McGovern campaign had nothing to lose in recycling bits and pieces of the otherwise unseen McGovern acceptance speech.

Although one often hears (as per Miroff's description) that McGovern was too liberal, his actual speech reveals a politician who was a carefully measured liberal populist. He points to the numerous small donations received by his campaign, and he emphasizes his desire to end the war with not a "secret" plan (a dig at Nixon) but a public plan: he will halt the bombing on the day of his inauguration. He graciously gives a good word to all the others who had vied for the nomination, even George Wallace—a move that could have been awkward, but McGovern pulled it off, saying: "I was moved . . . by the appearance in the Convention Hall of the governor of Alabama, George Wallace. His votes in the primaries showed clearly the depth of discontent in this country, and his courage in the face of pain and adversity is the mark of a man of boundless will, despite the senseless act that disrupted his campaign. And, governor, we pray for your full recovery so you can stand up and speak out for all of those who see you as their champion" (C-SPAN, 1972). Wallace had recently survived an assassination attempt, and this gave McGovern a hook upon which to hang his profession of empathy.

The pro-segregation Wallace was, of course, the polar opposite of McGovern regarding civil rights issues, and southern Democrats had for some time been migrating to the Republican Party, which welcomed them with open arms. McGovern's reaching out in his acceptance speech could only have happened at this transitional moment in the Democratic Party, which is to say that the moment was tightly sutured to the hard GOP shift right that had been signaled by Sen. Barry Goldwater's nomination in 1964, was advanced by Nixon's election in 1968, and became the party's unequivocal destiny with Nixon's reelection in 1972—even if we take Reagan's 1980 election as the culmination of the death of moderate Republicanism. McGovern's carefully scripted references to Wallace indicated his eagerness to retain any southern votes still available to him, and the speech is thereby symptomatic of this moment in which the South defected from the Democratic Party, but equally importantly, the candidate's nod to the *primary votes* for the right-wing populist Wallace resonated with his own liberal populism.

It was the calculated move of a politician (and his speechwriters) to sidestep all that was undesirable in the candidate Wallace, but McGovern was also spinning the primary votes for the Alabama governor as a voicing of discontent, as a shout-out from the little people—a classic populist gesture. Consider that in the Wisconsin primary McGovern had won 30% of the votes by "tapp[ing] deep wells of economic discontent" and garnering support from "liberals, conservatives, blue-collar workers, farmers, suburbanites and the young," while Wallace had also appealed to "the little man" and "came in second, with twenty-two percent of the vote." *Time* magazine concluded that "adding the Wallace and McGovern totals, fifty-two percent of [Wisconsin] voters cast ballots for anti-Establishment candidates." Both candidates focused on taxes and inflation ("Message of Discontent," 1972).

Viewing McGovern's acceptance speech 50 years later on C-SPAN, we see a candidate who is more complex than the caricature of the immoderate leftist who ruined the party. He is a liberal, but also conveys himself as a team player for the party. He's a populist and an antiestablishment candidate who would alienate the hawks by virtue of his Vietnam stance but was also more than a single-issue candidate, not simply a dove opposing Vietnam, even if the hardest of cold warriors would inevitably perceive only that aspect of his candidacy. He was critical of the status quo but optimistic about change. Arguably, McGovern's most radical move in his 1972 speech is to close out by quoting lyrics from Woody Guthrie's "This Land is Your Land," a heartfelt song about equality and inclusion that was considered a sort of left-wing alternative to the national anthem. Watching the speech, in sum, reveals a nuanced picture of McGovern, rather different from the now-petrified, simplified image of him as the candidate who ruined future prospects for liberal Democratic presidential candidates. Notwithstanding his gutsy closing moments, McGovern did not come across as radical, in large part because he was a careful, measured speaker, not a bellowing fist-pounder, though that was the image that Nixon successfully hammered home in the months that followed.

The Nixon team's attacks clearly worked, but the McGovern campaign ultimately failed for a number of reasons. The one most often singled out is that his first vice presidential candidate, Thomas Eagleton, was forced out of the race when it was revealed that he had a history of mental problems and had received electroshock therapy. A running mate switch mid-campaign was a massive crisis, and choosing a poor candidate in the first place (in a world in which mental illness is stigmatized) made McGovern look bad as well. But the ill-timed acceptance speech was also a huge snafu, a point driven home on numerous panel discussion programs aired later on C-SPAN.

C-SPAN's open discussion format often results in people going "off script" and making more revealing comments than those made in one-on-one interviews.[7] A revealing 1997 panel discussion on the '72 campaign includes Frank Mankiewicz,

Morris Dees, and Hunter S. Thompson, and ends with an audience Q&A session in which panelists get into intricate, wonky policy issues about polling and direct mail campaigns. There's also a question about news bias against Nixon, which is shot down with vigor by the panelists—still furious about the media's having ignored lies in Nixon campaign ads, which they note contrasted sharply with McGovern's more honest ads. Here, a declining Thompson still manages to pull out all the stops in suggesting that Nixon "was a lying dog and had every reason to fear the press," while Mankiewicz sharply observes that any sympathy for Nixon had to be balanced against the deviousness of his suggestion upon learning of the shooting of Wallace that his men should immediately break into the would-be assassin's home and plant McGovern campaign literature there (C-SPAN, 1997).

In addition to the panel shows, for both teachers and researchers the most useful C-SPAN material on the 1972 convention and election is probably the rebroadcasts of material from the time, specifically advertisements, campaign films, and nominating and acceptance speeches. Of course, all who work on media and American political campaigns are aware of the Museum of the Moving Image's Living Room Candidate website, which offers viewers campaign ads going back to 1952, but C-SPAN holds additional materials such as the half-hour biographical campaign films that used to circulated on TV between the conventions in the summer and the election in the fall, and, equally valuable, the half-hour election night campaign films. These are widely forgotten artifacts of the network era of mass audiences, before the rise of narrowly targeted, micromanaged advertising that dominates in the age of niche media and, more specifically, social media.

The McGovern campaign hired Charles Guggenheim to make its ads and documentaries. Guggenheim had made the JFK memorial film for the '64 Democratic convention, and also the '68 memorial film for Bobby Kennedy. Even Hunter S. Thompson, alienated by most aspects of political campaigning, and particularly TV ads, was impressed by Guggenheim's work for McGovern in '72, writing that the candidate's "thirty-minute biography was so good that even the most cynical veteran journalists said it was the best political film ever made for television . . . and Guggenheim's sixty second spots were better than the bio film" (Thompson, 1973, p. 252). The TV spots are indeed excellent, and some run a full four minutes, unthinkably long for a post-network ad spot. As for the biographical film (see Guggenheim, 1972c), it is a careful balancing act, conveying both patriotism and critique. The first part of the film includes images of parades and American flags, but then McGovern narrates his encounters with a range of people struggling to make ends meet. The father of a family of four complains about tax loopholes for millionaires and says, "The poor man is paying for the nation. . . . A lot of people want to be millionaires . . . because they don't have to pay taxes." His wife clips coupons and explains how every week her budget is tight "down to the nickel." Nixon's wage and price controls were "a total failure," McGovern explains, and then continues with segments centered on the financial challenges of farmers and the elderly; a laid-off engineer who feels a loss of self-esteem now that his wife is the breadwinner; and, finally, disabled Vietnam vets seeking to improve their lives. McGovern laments the plight of Americans "caught in the whipsaw of our war-based economy." The overall message is strongly liberal, but one must also note a total disengagement from the student moment, civil rights, Black power, and the women's liberation movement. There is not a single person of color interviewed or even prominently visually featured in the film; a solitary Black boy is shown waving a flag at a parade.

The failure of the McGovern campaign can be chalked up to a few key factors: the Eagleton crisis; the loss of control of the TV image as the Miami convention spun out of control, coupled with the early morning acceptance speech; the break with Daley in Miami and concomitant loss of him as a campaign ally; and the dirty tricks of the Nixon campaign. Taken together, these factors tell the big story. On the other hand, one can also take a more fine-grained approach to understanding his defeat by examining how Guggenheim's films positioned the candidate. In particular, Guggenheim found a positive angle on the openness of the convention. In fact, one of his four-minute ads focused entirely on the little-d-democratic nature of the convention as a strong point. One interviewee, a respectable looking young lady with a modest bouffant, observed, "A lot of people said, oh, you lost prime time by being up all night. Well, that to me was great, and every delegate that was there stayed there and stayed with it." The point here, also made by other delegates in the ad, was that these newcomers were not in Miami to party: they were there to work. Another interviewee singled out the fact that delegates were making peanut butter and jelly sandwiches on the convention floor because they couldn't afford to eat in the hotels, and, anyway, "it wasn't a convention to play" (Guggenheim, 1972a).

Like the other Guggenheim ads, this one was shot mostly with a handheld camera to convey immediacy and authenticity. One shot even includes lens flare, the halo effect from sunshine that before *Easy Rider* (1969) and other countercultural films was understood by cinematographers as "ruining" a shot. Jamieson argues in *Packaging the Presidency* that the cinema vérité style that dominated

McGovern's campaign ultimately worked against him, as his statements were often extemporaneous, whereas Nixon was consistently tight, scripted, professional, and above all *presidential* in his ads (Jamieson, 1996, p. 322). That may be true; Guggenheim's style was risky. That vérité was even used in McGovern's convention-centered ad points strongly to the campaign's strong desire to spin its convention as a huge success because it spoke not just to the young but also to the *sensibilities* of the young, sensibilities that could theoretically be shared by voters of all ages. That didn't play out, obviously, in the voting booths in November. Still, McGovern leaned into his convention imagery about as hard as Hubert Humphrey had avoided his own four years earlier.

The most moving Guggenheim spot was a four-minute ad titled "Young Vets" (Guggenheim, 1972d), which opens with a male voice-over explaining that the men pictured have "shattered lives and broken dreams. And they're looking for all the help and understanding they can find." Following this, the vets express some complaints about wheelchair accessibility and the complications of seeking government assistance, all under the veil of a "lost feeling." McGovern responds by explaining how he was able to get through school on the GI Bill after three years as a World War II bomber pilot, and he goes on to advocate for government programs to educate and employ vets. One vet responds that the government should offer vets jobs: "Some of them can't use their arms and fingers, but that doesn't make them a nonproductive individual." McGovern has reached a tricky moment here; he's having an honest discussion with the young men—an honesty conveyed not only by the dialogue itself but also by the style, a single camera swishing back and forth, a zoom lens moving in and out, and a few barely noticeable cuts (this is a meticulously edited piece, though designed to look spontaneous). The senator responds, "You love your country, there's no question about that. But I bet you're about halfway mad at it, aren't you?" This is a delicate tightrope act; the candidate wants to be honest with his constituents, but he doesn't want to seem unpatriotic, or to make the disabled men appear as such. The veteran's response to the "halfway mad" query is really rough, and worth citing in its entirety:

Believe me, when you lose the control of your bowels, your bladder—your sterility, you'll never father a child—when the possibility of you ever walking again is cut off for the rest of your life, you're twenty-three years old, you don't want to be a burden on your family. You know where you go from here? To a nursing home. And you stay there until you rot. Why isn't there places like this that the government could set up? Nobody thinks of a disabled veteran, or a disabled anybody, but another disabled person. If you fall out of your wheel-chair, you know who's the first one to come try to get you some help? A guy in a wheelchair. And not somebody who's walking. (Guggenheim, 1972d)

McGovern answers that "it's one of the most unconscionable facts in this country today . . . that there are people who are desperately in need of help that can't qualify for it under the present system," and the veteran interjects "to stay alive." McGovern closes out with, "That's right. I love the United States. But I love it enough so I want to see some changes made. The American people want to be-lieve in their government. They want to believe in their country. And I want to be one of those that provides the kind of leadership that would help restore that kind of faith. . . . The president can help set a new tone in this country. He can help raise the vision and the faith and the hope of the American people. And that's what I'd like to try to do" (Guggenheim, 1972d).

McGovern has tried to end on a high note, a hopeful note. To produce an honest ad about the frustrations of Vietnam vets, and then to convey optimism and love of country was an almost impossible task. McGovern attempted it by suggesting that he could make changes, and by suggesting that one of the young men loved his country but was "about halfway mad at it," a painful understate-ment. Again, the style of natural lighting and you-are-there handheld camera work also worked to convey the candidate as honest and in touch with voters, especially young voters.

In McGovern's half-hour "election eve" film (see Guggenheim, 1972b), a recur-rent genre for presidential candidates in the network era (accessible now thanks to C-SPAN's *American History TV*), Guggenheim mixes the vérité style with a more conventional documentary approach featuring swelling dramatic music and a narrative voice-over. The end of the film, though, includes excerpts from the shorter ads, ads that Guggenheim had drawn from for his half-hour biograph-ical film (see Guggenheim, 1972c). The most wrenching footage Guggenheim shot during the whole campaign was the rap session between McGovern and Vietnam vets. Here in this final film, though, Guggenheim uses only short clips of the vets and minimizes and tempers the impact of that footage with soaring, inspirational music. The idea was to amplify the candidate's patriotism in order to balance out his criticisms.

Needless to say, it didn't work. Nixon was ahead in the polls, and he remained there, successfully painting McGovern as an extreme left-winger. McGovern gave him fodder for this line of attack by virtue of being critical of America at all, by even implying in the four-minute ad that a veteran might be "halfway" angry and that people "wanted" to believe in their government. In his C-SPAN book talk, Bruce Miroff quotes Sen. Herman Talmadge of Georgia, saying, "What was wrong with George in the campaign was that he gave the impression that he was mad at the country. He was condemning her policy in Vietnam, and he was complaining about the poor and talking about women's rights. . . . If you get up there and preach day and night against America, you're not going to be elected" (C-SPAN, 2007). Miroff hastens to add that "McGovern was *not* preaching against America" but that he was *caricatured* as unpatriotic. Indeed, campaign ads such as "Young Vets" bent over backward to convey concern, critique, and compassion. Further, when bits of the vet interviews were recycled in the biographical and election eve half-hour films, they were infused with music and carefully worded voice-overs to compensate for the realism and cinema vérité edge conveyed in the shorter ads. But Nixon's spin machine had successfully pushed home the idea that McGovern was anti-American, and Guggenheim's efforts to present a somewhat more moderate image were too little, too late.

As media studies scholars and teachers, we should consider all of the McGovern campaign media—not only the shorter ads, but also material such as the longer biographical and election eve films and the convention speech itself, all held by the C-SPAN Video Library. Only by doing so can one craft a holistic picture of the campaign's media use. The 1972 convention and campaign can thereby be understood as both political and televisual events, on their own and also in relationship to the events of 1968. More than a reaction against the chaos of 1968, the 1972 DNC was a continuation of the crises of that convention, also suffused with chaos, though of a different valence. Following McGovern's nomination, the campaign thought it could tap into the wild energy of the delegates and convey that energy in its ads and films. But as former North Carolina governor and 1972 Democratic presidential contender Terry Sanford noted in a 1988 C-SPAN interview, the milk had already soured: "We gave the public the impression that the Democratic Party had gone wild" (C-SPAN, 1988a), and there was no going back. To make matters worse, Sanford added, all those new delegates were not the sort of "regular Democrats" who "would build a consensus when they went back home." Between that tactical failure and the Nixon campaign's effective negative advertising and dirty tricks, no amount of brilliant media could rebalance the scales for McGovern.

NOTES

1. CBS's coverage of the second, third, and fourth days of the Democratic convention are available for viewing at the Paley Center for Media, New York City. Excerpts from the third day of CBS's coverage are available in the C-SPAN Video Library. NBC's full coverage is available from the Vanderbilt Television News Archive.

2. Recall also the 1924 Democratic convention, which lasted 16 days; votes were cast 103 times before a candidate was selected. "The convention is often called the 'Klanbake' because one of the front-runners, . . . William G. McAdoo, was supported by the Ku Klux Klan. The Klan was a major source of power within the party, and McAdoo did not repudiate its endorsement. The other front-runner [was] New York Governor Al Smith, a Catholic who represented the party's anti-Klan . . . wing . . . and his faction failed by a slim margin to pass a platform plank condemning the Klan" (Shafer, 2016). See also Murray (1976). "After 1936, blacks shifted their allegiance to the Democratic Party in spite of the Party's poor record in regard to blacks. And as their numbers began to increase in the conventions their influence in the conventions grew" (Walton & Gray, 1975, p. 277).

3. Daley and his followers allowed only that there was an "organization" in Chicago; in a 2005 C-SPAN symposium, Richard J. Daley and American National Politics, Daley's system was praised as "representative democracy" by Adlai Stephenson III (C-SPAN, 2005). Dan Rostenkowski argued that the old system allowed for "talent" to be nurtured outside of a political system driven by mass media. For all the unfairness of the machine, this argument has some merit. Within the machine system, unlimited media spending was simply not an issue. If you were on the slate, you had a good chance of being elected. While not fair to those outside the machine, the system also did not privilege the most wealthy, telegenic, or sensationalist candidate.

4. White was roundly attacked by the Left for his 1968 book. He saw it as a blame-the-messenger situation, because Nixon had won, but the book reveals an author completely taken in by the "New Nixon," a candidate whom White (1969) esteemed as newly "carefree, jovial . . . hoisting drinks" with the press, "quite candid in his talk," and offering a basically positive law-and-order message (p. 150). See also Buckley (1969).

5. ABC reduced its coverage from gavel-to-gavel for the 1968 convention and continued this in 1972. Both years, ABC gave nightly 90-minute summaries. My focus is on CBS and NBC because ABC was the underdog network, the weakest player in terms of both news and entertainment programming in this era.

6. At the GOP convention in August of 1972, by contrast, over 20 million homes tuned in for Nixon's 10:30 p.m. acceptance speech (White, 1973, p. 186).

7. Media and the 1968 Chicago Democratic Convention (see C-SPAN, 2018), for example, is an excellent 2018 C-SPAN panel that includes David Farber, Bernardine Dohrn, Frank Kusch, and Hank DeZutter.

REFERENCES

Buckley, W. F. (1969, September 22). The making of the president 1968 (Program Number 169) [TV series episode]. In *Firing line*. Transcript retrieved from the Hoover Institution, Stanford University, *Firing Line* collection. https://digitalcollections.hoover.org/objects/6103

Cohen, A., & Taylor, E. (2001). *American pharaoh: Mayor Richard J. Daley—His battle for Chicago and the nation*. Back Bay.

Crouse, T. (1973). *The boys on the bus*. Random House.

C-SPAN (Producer). (1972, July 13). *Senator George McGovern 1972 acceptance speech* [Video]. https://www.c-span.org/video/?3437-1/senator-george-mcgovern-1972-acceptance-speech

C-SPAN (Producer). (1988a, July 16). *Dem. Convention 1968: Retrospective interview* [Video]. https://www.c-span.org/video/?3426-1/dem-convention-1968-retrospective-interview

C-SPAN (Producer). (1988b, July 17). *Democratic Convention 1972: Retrospective interview* [Video]. https://www.c-span.org/video/?3433-1/democratic-convention-1972-retrospective-interview

C-SPAN (Producer). (1997, April 8). *McGovern 1972 presidential campaign* [Video]. https://www.c-span.org/video/?80213-1/mcgovern-1972-presidential-campaign

C-SPAN (Producer). (2005, April 20). *Richard J. Daley and American national politics* [Video]. https://www.c-span.org/video/?186812-3/richard-j-daley-american-national-politics

C-SPAN (Producer). (2007, November 6). *The liberals' moment* [Video]. https://www.c-span.org/video/?202321-1/the-liberals-moment

C-SPAN (Producer). (2011, December 2). *George McGovern, presidential contender* [Video]. https://www.c-span.org/video/?301280-1/contenders-george-mcgovern-1972

C-SPAN (Producer). (2018, June 6). *Media and the 1968 Chicago Democratic Convention* [Video]. https://www.c-span.org/video/?446354-2/media-1968-chicago-democratic-convention

Frank, R. (1991). *Out of thin air: The brief wonderful life of network news*. Simon & Schuster.

"'Gay' people bitter after Plank defeat." (1972, July 12). *Washington Post*, A14.

Grimes, W. (2008, July 25). Richard Wade, 87, urban historian, dies. *New York Times*. https://www.nytimes.com/2008/07/25/nyregion/25wade.html

Guggenheim, C. (Producer). (1972a). *Convention* [Presidential campaign commercial]. Retrieved from The Living Room Candidate. http://www.livingroomcandidate .org/commercials/1972#

Guggenheim, C. (Producer). (1972b, November 6). *McGovern 1972 election eve program* [Video]. C-SPAN. https://www.c-span.org/video/?418053-1/mcgovern-1972 -election-eve-program

Guggenheim, C. (Producer). (1972c, August 1). *1972 McGovern for president film* [Video]. C-SPAN. https://www.c-span.org/video/?463998-1/1972-mcgovern-president-film

Guggenheim, C. (Producer). (1972d). *Young vets* [Presidential campaign commercial]. Retrieved from The Living Room Candidate. http://www.livingroomcandidate.org /commercials/1972#

Hendershot, H. (2022). *When the news broke: Chicago 1968 and the polarizing of America*. University of Chicago Press.

Jamieson, K. H. (1996). *Packaging the Presidency: A history and criticism of presidential campaign advertising* (3rd ed). Oxford University Press.

Mailer, N. (1972). *St. George and the Godfather*. Arbor House.

McGovern, G. (1970, January 1). The lessons of 1968. *Harper's*, 43–47.

"A message of discontent from Wisconsin." (1972, April 17). *Time*. https://content.time. com/time/subscriber/article/0,33009,944457,00.html

"M'Govern endorsed by 2 on radical Left." (1972, April 24). *New York Times*, 29. https:// www.nytimes.com/1972/04/24/archives/mgovern-endorsed-by-2-on-radical-left .html

Miroff, B. (2007). *The liberals' moment: The McGovern insurgency and the identity crisis of the Democratic Party*. University Press of Kansas.

Murray, R. K. (1976). *The 103rd ballot: Democrats and the disaster in Madison Square Garden*. Harper & Row.

Navasky, V. S. (1972, July 23). A funny thing happened on the way to the coronation. *New York Times Magazine*, SM9. https://www.nytimes.com/1972/07/23/archives/a -funny-thing-happened-on-the-way-to-the-coronation-a-funny-thing.html

Noah, T. (2007, November 11). McGovern redux [Review of the book *The Liberals' Moment*, by Bruce Miroff]. *New York Times*. https://www.nytimes.com/2007/11/11 /books/review/Noah-t.html

Noah, T. (2012, October 22). "Acid, amnesty, and abortion": The unlikely source of a legendary smear. *New Republic*. https://newrepublic.com/article/108977/acid-amnesty-and-abortion-unlikely-source-legendary-smear

Sánchez, J., Jr. (2020). Revisiting McGovern-Fraser: Party nationalization and the rhetoric of reform. *Journal of Policy History*, 32(1), 1–24. https://doi.org/10.1017/S0898030619000253

Shafer, J. (2016, March 7). 1924: The wildest convention in U.S. history. *Politico*. https://www.politico.com/magazine/story/2016/03/1924-the-craziest-convention-in-us-history-213708/

Thompson, H. S. (1973). *Fear and loathing on the campaign trail '72*. Grand Central.

Walton, H., Jr., & Gray, C. V. (1975). Black politics at the national Republican and Democratic conventions, 1868–1972. *Phylon*, 36(3), 269–278.

White, T. H. (1969). *The making of the president 1968*. HarperCollins.

White, T. H. (1973). *The making of the president 1972*. HarperCollins.

3

WITH THE EXCEPTION OF C-SPAN

Television and the Jesse Jackson Campaigns

Allison Perlman

"With the exception of C-SPAN," wrote *New York Amsterdam News* columnist Abiola Sinclair (1987), "the white media has generally been ignoring Jesse Jackson, or playing him down" (p. 32). Though, Sinclair noted, at the time Jackson was the front-runner to secure the Democratic nomination, the press refused to acknowledge his popularity, and instead drummed up criticisms of Jackson that had been ubiquitous when he had run for president in 1984. This coverage of Jackson, for Sinclair, was part and parcel of the mainstream press's relationship to the Black community in its tendency to alternate between negative coverage and no coverage whatsoever.

This emphasis on how, and whether, the press covered Jackson's run for the Democratic presidential nomination in 1984 and 1988 informed subsequent analyses of Jackson's presidential runs. To read assessments of Jackson's 1984 and 1988 bids is to encounter excoriations of the role of the media. Mfanya Tryman (1989) for example, has insisted that the media pigeonholed Jackson in 1984 as the "black Presidential candidate," and repeatedly framed him as unelectable in 1988. Arnold Gibbons (1993) has suggested that journalists were overly harsh on Jackson and subjected him to stricter standards than other candidates. Gibbons further noted, as have others, that Jackson's 1984 run was marred by continual allegations of anti-Semitism in the press, which further hindered his candidacy. Cedric Robinson (2019) has asserted that the press marginalized Jackson's campaign, misrepresenting it as a "racial political insurgency" rather than a broader based campaign focused on "the plight of American workers and farmers and the conduct of capital at home and abroad" (p. 19). Adolph Reed (1986), in contrast, has attacked the press not for its harshness but for its lenience in its uncritical acceptance of Jackson as a spokesperson for the Black community that, accordingly, enabled his visibility in the primary process. Others have flagged how the press framed Jackson as unelectable (Broh, 1987; Walters, 1988) or have interrogated how media coverage informed voters' perceptions of his candidacy (Gandy & Coleman, 1986).

Sinclair's qualification—"with the exception of C-SPAN"—notably acknowledged how the cable network strayed from the practices of commercial media in its coverage of the presidential primaries more broadly, and of Jackson's candidacy specifically. If a goal of C-SPAN since it first went on the air in 1979 was to provide viewers with unmediated access to the workings of government—delivered initially through its coverage of congressional sessions and hearings—its campaign coverage furthered this mission by its capacious programming of campaign events. C-SPAN's refusal of explicit editorial comment or media frames was of especial utility to a candidate like Jackson, whose position as a "serious" Black contender for a major party's nomination, and whose policy views pushed the boundaries of legitimate debate in the 1980s, had proven a challenge to extant practices deployed by the political press corps. C-SPAN's coverage of Jackson's speeches and debate performances allowed the candidate to speak for himself; it would be up to viewers to assess the efficacy of his policy prescriptions, the wisdom of his diagnoses of contemporary problems, or the viability of his campaign to secure the Democratic nomination.

Thus, one way to understand C-SPAN's coverage of the primaries in the 1980s, and of Jackson's campaigns in particular, is as an *antidote* to the commercial press, one that provided comprehensive coverage of campaign events and debates, rather than the selective and, to some, slanted reporting on offer on the broadcast networks. This coverage provided Jackson a platform from which not only to discuss a wide panoply of issues but to address concerns raised in other outlets about his electability and experience.

And, as this essay demonstrates, C-SPAN's programming operated not only as a *corrective* but as an interlocutor and critic. C-SPAN's call-in shows and forums provided sites to articulate criticisms of the commercial media and to discuss and disrupt ideas calcifying within their coverage. These programs furthered the "with the exception of C-SPAN" position of the network, as its own programming and editorial decisions seldom were enfolded into the critiques of the media—explicit or implicit—made within these shows. That is, if the very format of C-SPAN registered disapproval of how the media covered politics, its programming also gave voice to overt criticisms of the press corps's coverage of the Jackson campaign and spoke the unspoken racist assumptions on which it was predicated.

In anchoring its analysis in C-SPAN's coverage of the Jackson campaigns, this essay demonstrates how the network not only offered a fuller depiction of Jackson's candidacy's scope and reach but also, by chance and by editorial choice, provided a platform for concurrent criticisms of how the mainstream press reported on his campaign. The more extensive coverage of Jackson's campaign events furthermore illuminates how the candidate himself routinely redressed these critiques of his candidacy at events covered by C-SPAN cameras. Focusing our gaze on the C-SPAN coverage thus allows us to see how the problem of the media—with the exception of C-SPAN—was a live concern during Jackson's campaigns in addition to a key plank of retrospective assessments of them.

THE CANDIDATE

When Jackson declared his candidacy for the Democratic Party's nomination for president in 1983, he already was a nationally recognized civil rights leader. Across the late 1960s and 1970s, Jackson rose to prominence for his activism in Chicago as well as for his participation in national struggles for racial justice. During this period, Jackson made savvy use of the media not only to advocate for and promote his campaigns for racial equality, but to position himself as the leading spokesperson for civil rights. To track Jackson across this period, however, is to encounter shifting, and sometimes contradictory, political positions on strategies to redress U.S. racism and the role of partisan electoral politics in securing racial justice.

Jackson's civil rights activism began in 1960 in Greenville, South Carolina, when he participated in a sit-in to desegregate a public library. Jackson later would become a chief lieutenant in Martin Luther King Jr.'s Southern Christian Leadership Conference's (SCLC) 1966 Chicago desegregation campaign. He subsequently helmed Chicago's Operation Breadbasket Program, which originally aimed to abolish discriminatory hiring practices in Black neighborhoods (Beltramini, 2013). This would also be the focus of Jackson's Operation PUSH (People United to Save Humanity), formed after he broke with the SCLC, which similarly pressured large corporations to sign pledges to hire more Black workers, up-grade facilities in Black neighborhoods, and put funds in Black banks (Landess & Quinn, 1985; Marable, 1985).

Jackson's media celebrity arose after the death of King in 1968. He had been at the Lorraine Hotel in Memphis when King was murdered and appeared on a range of local and national news programs in the wake of King's death. As Na-thaniel Clay, PUSH communication director, noted, "Jesse did not become the Jesse we know until after King died" (Hunt, 1988, p. 16). Jackson spoke at a memo-rial session of the Chicago City Council the day after King's death, covered live on television, in a blood-stained turtleneck, reported to be soiled with King's blood. The dramatic spectacle of Jackson's shirt made him both a focus of national me-dia attention and a controversial figure amongst SCLC staffers, who saw it as a willful misrepresentation of Jackson's proximity to King in the aftermath of the shooting and a cynical use of a devastating tragedy to usurp the national spot-light (Landess & Quinn, 1985, pp. 4–7).

Jackson's political activism and media celebrity would only expand in the sub-sequent decade. Jackson was a leader of the Poor People's Campaign of 1968, the mobilization that King had been working on when he was killed, that brought a multiracial coalition of poor people to Washington, D.C., to resurrect the War on Poverty (Wright, 2007). In Chicago the following year, Jackson led a pro-test of 2,000 people in the state capital of Illinois to protest hunger and malnu-trition and draw media attention to the plight of poor people in Chicago (Stone, 1988, pp. 101–105). Jackson further cemented his standing as a civil rights leader in Chicago and led campaigns, for example, against the racism of the Chicago Transit Authority, discriminatory hiring practices for skilled construction work-ers, and the violence of poverty for many Chicago residents. This work garnered Jackson both local and national media attention, where he stressed themes of Black unity and racial pride (Hunt, 1988).

While across the 1970s Jackson would maintain a strong presence in the na-tional media—he became a favored guest of talk shows for his charisma and el-oquence—he increasingly would function as a spokesperson for a politics of personal responsibility. Jackson increasingly focused on the role of teachers and parents in assuring that Black children receive a quality education; though he also continued to flag structural problems that maintained discrimination, the mainstream press overwhelmingly reported on his message of personal responsi-bility. In addition, if in the early part of the 1970s Jackson had amplified the need for Black unity and Black pride, by the end of the decade he spoke of transcending race, especially in redressing economic injustice (Hunt, 1988).

And throughout the 1970s, though he was never elected to public office, Jackson turned to electoral politics. In 1971, Jackson unsuccessfully ran for mayor of Chicago as an independent. In so doing, he sought to educate and mobilize Black voters and disrupt the slate-voting practices that had defined local electoral politics. In this, his campaign also aimed to get more Black aldermen elected in the city. During the campaign, despite the endorsements he garnered, Jackson could seem uncommitted or not entirely serious about his candidacy, leading some supporters to suspect it was more of a media stunt than a genuine run for public office (Stone, 1988, pp. 111–112).

The following year, Jackson challenged Chicago mayor Richard Daley's Illinois delegation at the Democratic National Convention in Miami. In the wake of the 1968 election, the Democratic Party had changed the rules for delegate selection, including a requirement that state delegations be representative of a state's demographics and that delegates were to be chosen on an open basis. Daley had flagrantly ignored this rule and selected delegates loyal to him. Jackson's slate of delegates won out over Daley's, Daley himself choosing to sit out the convention as a result. At the convention, Jackson helped secure George McGovern's nomination by actively working against the candidacy of another Black leader, Shirley Chisholm (Stone, 1988, pp. 120–125).

Jackson furthermore was a key figure in national conversations about Black electoral strategy. Jackson's candidacy for president would emerge out of a decade and a half of Black candidate electoral successes at the local and state levels. Black mayors were elected in Cleveland (Carl Stokes in 1967), Gary, Indiana (Richard Hatcher in 1967), Newark (Kenneth Gibson in 1970), Los Angeles (Tom Bradley in 1973), and Atlanta (Maynard Jackson in 1973). By 1977, over 200 Black mayors had been elected in cities across the nation. While their elections enabled far more Black workers and leaders in city government and the public sector, they faced substantial obstacles, by choice or by circumstance, in addressing the problems facing the Black working class and poor. As Adolph Reed (1999) has argued, "The institutions that black officials administer are driven by the imperatives of managing systemic racial subordination, but the expectations that they cultivate amongst their black constituents define the role of black administrative representation in those institutions a de facto challenge to racial subordination" (pp. 131–132). That is, Black mayors were able to people local government with Black employees but not to dismantle how its institutions functioned as levers of sustained racial discrimination.

The cast and function of Black electoral politics informed debates across the 1970s about paths toward national political power. Across the 1960s, Black challengers to the presidency had run as third-party candidates, frequently on socialist or liberal-left party tickets. These bids had failed to secure substantial Black votes or to force some semblance of accountability from white presidential candidates in the major political parties (Marable, 1985). In 1971, poet and activist Amiri Baraka, Detroit congressperson Charles Diggs, and Richard Hatcher coordinated meetings amongst Black politicians, organization leaders, and prominent figures to discuss paths to attain national political power (Davies, 2017, p. 178). These meetings led to the 1972 National Black Political Convention in Gary. The goal of the conference was to unite various strands of Black politics—cultural nationalist, integrationist, Black capitalist, revolutionary nationalist—into, in the words of historian Peniel Joseph (2013), a "pragmatic coalition" (p. 173) with a political platform that functioned as an electoral bloc. The conference produced the National Black Political Agenda, which included provisions such as a "steeply progressive income tax" to redistribute wealth, a guaranteed minimum income, an increase in the minimum wage, substantial reduction in national defense and space budgets, and increased funding for social programs, education, housing, and economic development, community control over schools, and support for Third World liberation struggles, inclusive of Palestinian rights. In other words, as Tim Adam Davies (2017) summarizes, the agenda "was unmistakably dominated by Black Nationalist and Black Power sentiment" (p. 179).

The unity produced by the convention soon frayed, especially around strategies for mobilizing Black political power. At the center of the conflict was whether the Black coalition should form an independent political party or work within the Democratic Party (Davies, 2017, pp. 178–181). Jackson had been part of a network—that included Carl Stokes, John Conyers, and Percy Sutton—who wanted to run a Black presidential candidate to assure Black concerns were addressed in the 1972 election (Pierce, 1988, pp. 6–7). Jackson had used his syndicated column Country Preacher to advocate for a Black candidate and female running mate and to stress the political power of Black voters (Pierce, p. 7). At the convention in Gary, Jackson at once called for the formation of a new political party (Johnson, 2007, pp. 120–22), though later worked to defeat a resolution to create a new political party, ultimately arguing it was too early to take this step (Moore, 2018, p. 130; Pierce, pp. 9–10).

Rev. Jesse Jackson. (Courtesy of C-SPAN.)

Similar tensions would emerge amongst Black political and civil rights leaders in 1984. They were divided on the wisdom of running a Black candidate for president in the primaries or pooling support around the white candidate best positioned to defeat incumbent Ronald Reagan in the general election. Jackson and his allies argued that a Black candidate could galvanize the Black electorate and force the Democratic Party to consider issues of particular import to the Black community. Furthermore, whether Jackson would be the best candidate was also an open question. Jackson had broken with Black elected officials in 1980 by supporting Jimmy Carter over the more liberal Ted Kennedy and even had flirted with the Reagan campaign; his embrace of Black capitalism and entrepreneurialism as a vehicle for racial justice put him at odds with other Black freedom struggle leaders, many of whom were skeptical of private enterprise as an appropriate remedy to racial discrimination (Marable, 1985). Thus, that he did not receive the support of a number of Black political leaders once he announced his candidacy for the 1984 race spoke not only to divisions over tactics but to skepticism amongst some over his leadership (Simien, 2016).

One could see the Jackson campaigns of the 1980s, as Paulette Pierce (1988) has argued, as a direct continuation of the 1972 conference, Jackson's Rainbow Coalition a manifestation of a long-standing political strategy to secure power and address the needs of Black Americans. One also could narrate Jackson's runs for the Democratic nomination in the 1980s as the apotheosis of Bayard Rustin's call for a tactical shift in the Black freedom struggle from protest to politics. Rustin (1965) argued that the problems facing Black Americans—such lack of gainful employment, substandard housing, inadequate educational opportunities—could only be addressed through political power. Rustin urged the forging of a "coalition of progressive forces" built on interracial alliances. And for Rustin, the best path forward was to work within the Democratic Party to transform it into a "vehicle for social reconstruction." While, as Rustin noted, it had become fashionable to pin white liberals as the greatest obstacle to racial equality, it was conservatives—for Rustin, Barry Goldwater and Thomas Eastland; for Jackson in 1984, Reagan himself—who would enshrine or tolerate racial discrimination in law and who were the most threatening enemies to civil rights.

Jackson's campaigns also could be seen as a recommitment and elaboration on Jackson's devotion to economic justice. That some members of the Black political class initially steered clear of Jackson's campaign, as Manning Marable (1992) has argued, opened up key campaign positions to liberal-leftists and social democrats; accordingly, in 1984 Jackson would become, in Marable's assessment, the most left-wing national spokesperson since Eugene Debs. In his campaigns, as Cedric Johnson (2007) has noted, Jackson relied on a network of Black Power and New Left activists, many of whom had been key figures in the political mobilizations of the 1970s. And in both policy prescription and campaign strategy, Jackson's 1984 primary run was as an insurgency campaign. If, as Robert C. Smith (1990) has summarized, Jackson's reliance on activists, academics, and clergy in 1984, as well as his campaign's deployment of "constituency desks" to build a multiracial coalition, shaped the campaign's politics, his lack of staffers experienced in national politics and of financial resources meant that the Jackson campaign lagged other candidates in its fundraising, press relations, and scheduling. In contrast, in 1988, Jackson recruited experienced campaign professionals, most of whom were white, and eliminated constituency desks from his campaign apparatus. While his positions on key issues would remain fairly constant across the campaigns, in 1988 the Jackson campaign would more resemble that of his opponents than it had in the previous election.

Jackson would rely on "free" media—such as news coverage and debate coverage—across both campaigns as he had less money is his campaign coffers than his main rivals. By the time of his campaigns, he already was a national figure who had savvily used the media both to shine a light on issues of racial justice and economic injustice and to secure his own status as a civil rights leader. Yet he launched his campaigns in a transforming media ecosystem that portended key shifts in how the media would cover political campaigns. Cable networks like C-SPAN would function as a corrective, both for their coverage and for their implicit and explicit criticisms of other media outlets.

THE CONTEXT

The 1984 and 1988 primaries occurred amidst a substantive transformation of the role of media in presidential campaigns. In the wake of the 1968 election, the Democratic National Committee had assembled a commission to reconfigure how the Democratic nominee for president was to be selected. The Commission on Party Structure and Delegate Selection, commonly known as the McGovern–Fraser Commission, issued a series of recommendations in 1972 to democratize the selection of delegates and to assure diverse participation at the national convention. McGovern–Fraser intentionally diminished the long-standing role of party elites as delegates and privileged state primaries and caucuses. Over the course of the next decade and a half, the Democratic Party would continue to alter its delegate selection rules in the face of electoral defeats for the White House, and would increasingly re-elevate the role of party elites, in the form of superdelegates, in the nominee selection process (Atkeson & Maestas, 2009; Kaufmann, et al., 2003; Leduc, 2001; Sánchez, 2020). The allocation of delegates would be an issue of consternation in both the 1984 and 1988 campaigns for Democratic nominees, including Jackson.

Importantly, the increased emphasis placed on primaries also increased the import of the media during the nomination process. As Kathleen Hall Jamieson (2000) has argued persuasively, one of the crucial functions that the media play in campaigns is in their coverage of primaries, when journalists establish not only who is a credible and electable candidate, but how credibility and electability ought to be defined. Indeed, in the wake of the McGovern–Fraser reforms, the press increasingly functioned less as an observer of primary campaigns than as an active player in shaping the political fortunes of those running for the nomination.

In addition, the 1984 and 1988 elections took place alongside sizable changes in the U.S. media environment. An impact of many of these shifts—outside purchases of the major broadcast networks, increased subscriptions to cable services, the rise of independent broadcast stations, the launch of the Fox Broadcasting Company, deregulation and the repeal or diminishment of public interest obligations (Auletta, 1992; Brainard, 2004; Haggins & Timberg, 2018; Holt, 2011; Perlman, 2016)—was a transformation in commercial network news practices. Seeking desirable audiences to sell to advertisers, news coverage of elections focused on the cultivation of drama and conflict, spectacle and entertainment. Campaigns had to adjust to this environment by cultivating both appropriately televisual candidates and campaign surrogates capable of controlling the spin on campaign developments. In addition, the broadcast networks greatly reduced their coverage of political conventions, limiting live coverage to a few hours in prime time.

C-SPAN, created by Brian Lamb in the late 1970s initially to carry unmediated access to congressional sessions, intervened in this media climate and enhanced its reputation for fairness and neutrality. C-SPAN was supported by cable operators, who were persuaded that carriage of C-SPAN not only would provide much needed content to their systems but would provide legitimacy to the burgeoning cable television sector, help with local franchise agreements, and secure a favorable congressional environment. C-SPAN's content would unmask the workings of government and politics without commentary, framing, or opinion; viewers were to draw conclusions themselves based on the unedited access that the network provided. C-SPAN also would host call-in shows, imagined as a "New England town hall for the modern age" (Frantzich & Sullivan, 1996, p. 108) that would model democratic deliberation and discussion.

The 1984 election season extended C-SPAN's coverage to include campaign coverage. At the time, C-SPAN was carried by over 1,300 cable systems and reached 17 million people, or roughly one-half of all cable subscribers ("It Belongs," 1984). C-SPAN and CNN, which had debuted in 1981, received plaudits in the print press for their campaign coverage, especially for their offering of gavel-to-gavel coverage of both political conventions and their decision to air an 18-minute film about Ronald Reagan—a positive, idealized portrait of the president that introduced him to the convention—even as the broadcast networks deemed it as "not news" and refused to air it ("The Gavel Passes," 1984; "Reagan Film Controversy," 1984). C-SPAN also provided coverage of primary campaign events across the nation and went on the road during the general election season, visiting 14 cities to document campaign events (Garisto, 1984; "News Finds," 1984) and, in the words of Lamb, "take the pulse of the electorate" ("Cross-Country," 1984, p. 32). C-SPAN's coverage of the 1988 campaign was even more robust, offering extensive coverage of primaries and caucuses, debate coverage followed by call-shows, gavel-to-gavel coverage of the conventions trained on the action at the podium, and a weekly series, *Road to the White House*, that curated and re-aired key events from the previous week ("And Now," 1988; "Covering the Zone," 1988; Frantzich & Sullivan, 1992, p. 178; "Low Ratings," 1988; "Night of Number Two's," 1988).

Jackson pursued the Democratic nomination in the midst of these substantive transformations in the role of the press during elections as well as amidst increased scrutiny over how media outlets covered campaigns. By design, C-SPAN functioned as an antidote to the broadcast networks both in the extensiveness of its coverage and in its explicit refusal to provide commentary on or evaluations of campaign events. To view the Jackson campaign through the lens of C-SPAN's coverage is to reconfigure how the media mattered to his candidacy. In addition, it is to witness how Jackson and his surrogates implicitly and explicitly responded to mainstream coverage of his campaign, a critique further propelled by the network's coverage of panels and talks of assessments of the media's performance.

THE COVERAGE

C-SPAN's commitment to unmediated coverage of politics distinguished it from other television networks. If other media coverage of the Jackson candidacy applied frames that worked to the candidate's disadvantage, C-SPAN's approach ostensibly offered a view of Jackson unmarred by editorial comment or the excision of clips or comments removed from their broader context. By and large, most of C-SPAN's coverage was of Jackson himself. To view it is to see how in both campaigns Jackson simultaneously staked positions to the left of the mainstream Democratic Party in the 1980s, validated his candidacy through appeals to his moral leadership, and positioned his campaign as a necessary fusion of social movement activism with electoral politics. In addition, to examine the C-SPAN coverage is to see how Jackson himself squared the circle of both being and transcending his position as "the Black candidate." C-SPAN also provided a platform to propel criticisms of how other media outlets covered the campaigns more broadly and Jackson's candidacy specifically.

C-SPAN coverage of Jackson's 1984 and 1988 campaigns specifically took seven forms overall: campaign events (speeches, rallies) covered in their entirety; forums in which Jackson appeared with other candidates running for the nomination; debates between the candidates in the lead-up to primaries and caucuses; Jackson press conferences; convention coverage; call-in shows primarily with campaign surrogates; and forum discussions between journalists and political consultants about the campaign. In addition, in 1988 C-SPAN inaugurated its weekly *Road to the White House*, which offered up to three segments covering

Rev. Jesse Jackson campaigning. (Courtesy of C-SPAN.)

different campaigns, a series that tempered the network's commitment to un-
obstructed coverage with more explicitly mediated and edited perspectives on
campaign events. The discussion that follows flags particular Jackson telecasts
as representative of larger themes that recur across the C-SPAN Video Library
coverage of his campaigns.

And while, as discussed in greater detail below, the C-SPAN coverage offered
a robust view of Jackson's candidacy, it also gave a unique window into his campaign events. In telecasting entire campaign events, C-SPAN allowed viewers to
hear the range of diverse endorsements secured by Jackson from both national
elected officials and local figures—inclusive of teachers, students, clergy, and activists—who affirmed the singularity of Jackson's positions on a range of issues,
domestic and foreign. In addition, these telecasts provided unvarnished access to
these events, inclusive of the range of sites in which they took place and of the fact
of late candidate arrivals and the improvisations they elicited. They also exposed
the repetitions in campaign rhetoric that recur across campaigns as Jackson, like
all candidates, drew on consistent metaphors and anecdotes in his public appearances. If the coverage allowed for a fuller view of Jackson as a candidate, it also
enabled viewers insight into the mechanics of the modern campaign.

Jackson's campaign foregrounded four primary themes. At the core of Jackson's political project was the Rainbow Coalition, an appeal to voters across racial and ethnic lines to find common cause in a fight for economic justice and
political power. As he outlined in his campaign launch event in 1983, the fate of
women, people of color, and workers were profoundly intertwined, their freedom hinging on one another. Explicitly repudiating Reaganism, Jackson further-

more insisted that the lives of people of color, workers, farmers, and women had been imperiled by the deregulation of environmental and labor protections, the offshoring of U.S. jobs, and an increasingly bellicose and expensive foreign policy that sanctioned, and enabled, violent human rights abuses and led the world closer to nuclear war. Jackson routinely called up the Rainbow Coalition, as he did in a 1987 address at Dartmouth College, in which he likened the nation to a quilt, made strong by the variety of its differently colored pieces, and in which he insisted on the common plight of diverse peoples struggling in the face of the privatization and deregulation of the Reagan era:

 America is not a blanket. One piece of an uncut cloth of a common color. America is more like a quilt. I grew up in South Carolina and my grandmother could not buy a blanket—didn't have credit, couldn't go to Sears, Penney's, or Belk's. She'd reach back and get old pieces of coat and shirt and slip and dress, overalls and sack, put those odd pieces and colors and sizes and textures on the cot, some wool, some linen, some cotton, some silk. While they were apart they were just rags, hardly fit to wipe off your shoes with. But then she would bind those odd pieces and patches and colors with a common cord, to make of those patches and pieces a quilt, a thing of beauty, a thing of warmth. She used what she had, she did not cry about what she did not have. But every patch, every piece, every color was important. Any missing piece or patch or color made the quilt less complete, inadequate, insufficient. America is a quilt. A leader must be able to appreciate the pieces and patches that make us up. We can have unity without uniformity. Americans, of diverse backgrounds, must find common grounds. The point on the compass where all roads meet. The family farmer saying, "We want fair prices, supply management, markets, and return on our land." They're out in rural America, and they don't hear the voice of those in the city saying, "We want fair wages, market to return our jobs." And they don't hear youth saying, "We've done our best but we can't get a scholarship, we can't afford the loan." And they don't hear steelworkers saying, "But then, our pension money was taken from us and invested against our interests in competitive steel mills abroad at uncompetitive wages. And now our money has been used to buy the rope by which we are now hanging." Women are saying, "We want an Equal Rights Amendment, we want pay equity. We shouldn't be punished for childbearing years. We need daycare and Head Start because it's in our national interest for productivity." Those in the wheelchair are saying, "We have an apparent impediment, but everybody has an impediment, because nobody's perfect." When we reach out and connect the family farmer and the urban worker; the male and the female; the black, the white, the brown and find common ground we become a stronger nation. (Riggsa, 2020)

Jackson's Rainbow Coalition thus acknowledged the shared economic precarity across people; it also stressed the necessity for coalitional politics to improve myriad communities' futures.

In both of his bids for the presidency, Jackson also targeted voting laws as a civil rights issue. In 1984, his focus was on the second primary in southern states, which he claimed hindered candidates of color from gaining office. In 1988, Jackson's ire was on the role of superdelegates in the nomination process, positioned by Jackson as an affront to the one-person, one-vote ethos at the center of U.S. democracy. Jackson launched his 1984 campaign by stressing the need to enforce the 1965 Voting Rights Act and to end discriminatory voting rights impediments.

In addition, Jackson also ran an anti-corporate campaign, highlighting the responsibility of U.S. companies for offshoring U.S. jobs, elevating profits over the well-being of their workforce. Jackson's speeches frequently made this point, as when, at the Jefferson–Jackson dinner in Wisconsin in 1988, he analogized the economic violence of plant closures in Kenosha to the political violence facing civil rights activists in Selma. Insisting that slave labor abroad had displaced organized labor at home, Jackson stated that capital follows "profit," not "conscience." He then offered an anecdote that he had used often in his campaign, that the U.S. bought 7 million bicycles from Taiwan, produced for U.S. company Schwinn, for depressed wages to sell back to U.S. consumers for a high profit. "The Taiwanese are not taking jobs from us; GE, GM are taking jobs to them." This was a constant refrain across Jackson's campaigns as he attacked corporations, and the policies that enabled their decision-making, for abandoning U.S. workers to exploit workforces abroad.

In both campaigns, Jackson linked his anti-corporate message to his avowed environmentalism. In a speech in New Hampshire in 1984, Jackson advocated for conservation efforts and solar power, excoriated the building of a nuclear power plant, and laid the blame for the environmental crisis—described by Jackson as "chemical warfare"—on corporate greed and a toothless Environmental Protection Agency that had enabled it. Jackson repeated the charge of chemical warfare in his 1988 campaign, when he noted that if the Russians, rather than corporations, were responsible for the environmental degradation facing the U.S., the nation would consider a substantive response:

 There's nothing magic about it, it's chemical warfare. It's destroying the earth, it's destroying the people. If the Russians made acid of our rain, the Russians poisoned our streams, killed fish, wildlife, and people; the Russians sprinkled our earth and those poisons got down in the ground and poisoned our flow of water, we'd have a summit meeting. Let's fight back. The Russians engage in chemical warfare. I'm going to tell you the earth does not make such political decisions. No one has the right to poison the earth, no one has the right to poison the water, no one has the right to destroy the people. (CSPAN User-Created Clip, 2021b)

In this, Jackson also linked the need for an environmental rights movement to a labor rights movement, emphasizing how unchecked corporate power had led to a range of human rights abuses.

Jackson furthermore stressed a need for a foreign policy that would advocate for denuclearization and diplomacy, redirect money spent on weapons to domestic programs, and recognize and redress the unspoken racism of U.S. policy priorities. Jackson was a vociferous critic of U.S. policy in Central America, advocated for dialogue in the Middle East—he himself met with Palestinian leader Yassir Arafat—and decried the apartheid regime in South Africa. Placing human rights at the center of his foreign policy, he excoriated the U.S. for its uneven attentiveness to whose rights matter, affirming, for example, the boycotts in response to human rights violations in Poland, but questioning why no attention had been paid to the detention of Haitian refugees, the ravages of drought in African nations, or South African apartheid (C-SPAN, 1984). Jackson, especially in the 1988 election, focused on the issue of drugs, insisting that the flow of drugs was both a foreign policy issue in terms of supply, and an economic disinvestment issue in terms of demand. At a rally in D.C. in 1988, Jackson emphasized how the problem of drugs was a problem of lackluster border control and weak leadership in foreign affairs that did not take this threat seriously enough.

In addition to articulating his policy views, Jackson's campaign appearances anticipated and addressed concerns over his lack of qualifications for the office he sought. He routinely stressed his long-standing political activism for a range of causes inclusive of but not limited to African American civil rights. As he stated in an address to students at Dartmouth College in 1987, Jackson has fought, and would continue to fight, for the fates of workers who lost jobs from plant closures, farmers facing foreclosure, union members whose jobs were outsourced to workers overseas, and patients who were denied medical care because they lacked insurance; Jackson positioned their fates as intertwined and requiring redress. Jackson positioned himself as the candidate who had shown moral leadership on these vital issues, but also spoke to his abilities to identify exigent issues, address them, and staff government positions with those similarly committed to equity and justice.

In this, Jackson drew stark contrasts between himself and his opponents, contrasting their governing and policy experience with his record of moral leadership. At a rally in Harlem in March 1984, for example, Jackson outlined his participation in a string of civil rights protests, noting his opponents had been "old enough" to participate, but "they were not there." In December 1987, Jackson told of his support of teamsters in Cincinnati resisting trusteeship of their union, of gay and lesbian protesters in D.C. affirming their civil rights, and of peace activists opposing South African apartheid, support that his competitors refused to provide for fear of the impact on their political fortunes. This insistence was not only an implicit rebuke of the press's credibility discourse that marred his campaign but of the very criteria deployed within it.

Jackson also stressed in his speeches how his platform, and his candidacy itself, was an opportunity for moral renewal. If his platform insisted that the fates of farmers, workers, the uninsured, racial minorities, religious minorities, and sexual minorities were intertwined, to be determined by whether the nation rejects the policies of the Reagan era, his campaign also offered his own electoral success

Rev. Jesse Jackson with bullhorn. (Courtesy of C-SPAN.)

as a moral test of the nation and its commitment to racial egalitarianism and equal opportunity. Jackson positioned the campaign, in the language of a 1984 address, as an opportunity to "redeem the soul of the nation." He routinely placed voting for him in a lineage that included Rosa Parks's decision to defy segregated seating on buses, Greensboro students staging sit-ins to desegregate lunch counters, freedom riders facing mob violence, the 1963 March on Washington, and civil rights activists risking their lives in Mississippi and Alabama to extend voting rights to all. This move—of his linking his campaign to milestones in the Black freedom struggle—was a frequent facet of Jackson's campaign rhetoric.

Jackson and his supporters throughout both campaigns furthermore flagged Jackson's own leadership in civil rights as a qualification for the candidacy, while also emphasizing that his campaign represented the interests of his Rainbow Coalition in the service of a more just American and a safer world community. This discourse positioned Jackson as he had established himself to be: the heir to the struggles of Martin Luther King, the shift to electoral politics the next logical stage in the fight for equality. This shift was evident from the launch of Jackson's 1984 campaign, when prominent Black elected officials—such as Congressperson John Conyers (D-MI), Congressperson Ron Dellums (D-CA), Washington, D.C., mayor Marion Barry, Congressperson Shirley Chisholm (D-NY), and Gary, Indiana, mayor Richard Hatcher—framed Jackson's campaign as a pivotal development in the fight for racial justice and an apotheosis of the securing of Black political power that began in the previous decade. Jackson's campaigns thus offered a national script that positioned a future rooted in economic justice and human rights enabled by past commitments to Black civil rights by figures like Jackson. In this, the campaigns centered the story of U.S. progress in the history of the Black freedom struggle, and thus positioned Jackson as the most capable candidate to redirect the nation after the Reagan revolution back on a path toward greater equity and justice.

The C-SPAN Video Library includes not only an impressive range of Jackson appearances, events, debates, and press conferences, but call-in programs, book talks, and panel discussions that addressed the Jackson campaign. As Stephen Frantzich and John Sullivan (1996) have noted, the call-in format was foundational to C-SPAN's commitment to fostering public deliberation. Debuting on the network in October 1980, the call-in show was to provide citizens direct access to elected officials, decision makers, and journalists. Though distinct from the fly-on-the-wall perspective that C-SPAN adopted in relation to congressional sessions and campaign events, the principles of the call-in shows, as outlined by

Frantzich and Sullivan, hewed to a comparable aspirational neutrality. Hosts were to facilitate dialogue, but not to weigh in or offer opinions or theories or even corrections to misinformation or errors made by guests or callers. Callers were not to be screened to privilege one perspective over another. The ideal of the show was to facilitate conversation between guests and callers unimpeded by the perspective, knowledge, or insight of the C-SPAN host (pp. 146–149).

The C-SPAN Video Library includes four call-in shows each for the 1984 and 1988 Jackson campaigns, that included campaign surrogates, supporters, and advisers, and once with Jackson himself. While the conversations across the programs varied, there were topics and tropes that recurred across many of them. Guests often were asked about Jackson's relationship to the Jewish community and questioned about his relationship to Nation of Islam leader Louis Farrakhan, as well as whether he was a communist. Especially in 1988, the shows increasingly focused on the Democratic Party's relationship to its Black constituency, the treatment of Jackson by the party positioned as a synecdoche for its response to the concerns of the Black community. Other shows highlighted the diversity of political opinion within the Black community, as callers expressed divergent views on Jackson's platform.

Another recurring topic was the role of the media in the Jackson campaign. In a February 1984 show with political consultant John Tapscott and Iowa campaign cochair Jesse Taylor, Tapscott and Taylor, in response to a caller question, addressed how the media had unfairly questioned Jackson's legitimacy as a candidate, harped on controversies that were not controversial, and reduced him to the "Black candidate," ignoring the coalitional politics at the center of his campaign. The media also was a topic in a New Hampshire call-in show with Mary Summers, deputy director of Jackson's New Hampshire campaign, in which Summers excoriates the press for driving a false narrative about Jackson's alleged anti-Semitism and allegations that he was a communist ("And Now, New Hampshire," 1988). Ann Lewis, adviser to the Jackson campaign in 1988, further addressed the role of the media, and especially the mainstream press's inattention to his campaign for the early part of the 1988 primaries.

C-SPAN's telecasts of forums and panels further interrogated the performance of the press in covering Jackson. The C-SPAN Video Library includes a telecast of a press conference to discuss C. Anthony Broh's analysis of the 1984 election, *Horse of a Different Color*, in which he expressly states that commercial television's coverage of Jackson, which positioned him as unelectable, was motivated by an uninterrogated racism:

The point I'm trying to make, then, is that Jesse Jackson was hurt in this sense. That is, the main metaphor, the main way that television looks at a campaign is the horse race. And Jesse Jackson often wasn't part of that, considered part of that race. Now that begs the question of why is that the case, and I personally believe that the reason that that is the case is that Jackson was not considered to have a chance at winning from the very beginning. And why was he not considered to have a chance of winning from the very beginning? My belief is not because he was too liberal; after all [Senator Alan] Cranston got similar kinds of coverage as Jackson did in many areas. But he got a different kind of coverage because he was Black. And that that is the significant factor in American politics, in American presidential politics today. It's the dominating one in mass media, in television coverage. It becomes what I believe is a self-fulfilling prophecy. That self-fulfilling prophecy is that a candidate who is Black can't win, is thought not to be able to win, therefore does not get the typical type of coverage. Not receiving the typical type of coverage, that candidate looks different; it guarantees that that candidate will not win the nomination. And that is the reason I call Jesse Jackson a "horse of a different color." (C-SPAN User-Created Clip, 2021)

A November 1988 panel at Drake University, also carried by C-SPAN, was dedicated to media coverage of the Jackson campaign. Michael Tackett of the *Chicago Tribune* summarizes one of the main takeaways of the conversation, which similarly speaks to the press corps's struggles with covering a Black candidate. Panels of journalists and political consultants in 1987, in anticipation of the 1988 campaign, further spoke to how the press treated Jackson differently than other candidates, underlining that his race accounted for the differing standards journalists—and other candidates—applied to his campaign.

While Jackson was not the Democratic nominee in 1984 or 1988, his campaigns had important consequences for down-ballot races. His 1984 campaign registered nearly 2 million new voters who, in turn, helped elect Black governors in New York and Virginia and Black mayors in cities across the nation. Jackson's impressive showing in the 1988 election—most notably his big wins on Super Tuesday and in the Michigan primary—also secured for him a leadership position in the fall campaign and his allies roles on the Democratic National Committee (Colton, 1989; Walters, 2005). Indeed, as a roundtable on the future of the Democratic Party telecast as part of C-SPAN's *Road to the White House* series underlined, leaders in the party recognized that Jackson would have an influential role at the convention and that he had expanded and energized the party; in addition, they underscored how much Jackson's positions on some issues would be embraced by Democrats broadly, even if especially his foreign policy views did not. In a telling aside, Representative Thomas Foley (D-WA) told a joke about a political cartoon that imagined Jackson's inauguration in January 1989, with a caption that read "What do you think Jesse wants?" Despite the respect that Jackson had earned with fellow Democrats, Foley's joke reminds of a persistent press discourse that routinely refused to take his candidacy for the presidency seriously. It was a takeaway that had been reinforced across other programs telecast by C-SPAN.

By circumstance and by design, C-SPAN's coverage of the Jackson campaigns not only allowed Jackson—through telecasts of his unedited speeches and rallies—to counter mainstream media tropes about his campaign, but also explicitly offered a platform to surrogates, voters, academics, and journalists themselves from which to reflect on the challenges his campaign posed to the press corps and to flag how Jackson's race delimited how the media could see his candidacy, his constituency, and his viability. C-SPAN functioned during these campaigns not only as a corrective to the commercial press but as a site that magnified these criticisms of the media's performance.

CONCLUSION

There are a number of ways to reflect on the significance of Jackson's run for the Democratic nomination in 1984 and 1988. We can position these campaigns as, for example, Jackson (2012) himself and others (Smallwood, 2010) have, as anticipating and enabling the election of Barack Obama in 2008. We also can look to Jackson's runs as precursors to the campaigns of Bernie Sanders in their shared efforts to move both the moral and political calculus of the Democratic Party and re-center progressive politics in its platform. We also can see in the complicated relationship of Democratic nominees to Jackson, captured in programs in the C-SPAN Video Library, a rehearsal of a long-standing and resilient ambivalence over the party's relationship to a rainbow coalition and its imagined impact on the anticipated electoral preferences of white voters.

The materials in the C-SPAN Video Library provide ample material to build out all these narratives and to draw substantive comparisons. Yet, as this paper has identified, another important facet of the C-SPAN Jackson coverage is not only in how it offered programming distinct from other media outlets, but in how it explicitly acknowledged failures of the press to contend with a Black candidate for the president. This critique of the media, also found in academic assessments published immediately after the Jackson campaigns, echoed ingrained criticisms of the press—perhaps most publicly and forcefully articulated in the 1968 Kerner Report—as an institution that propelled racial inequality. This facet of the Jackson campaign strikes as particularly important to remember, as it co-existed alongside other attacks on the media that have had more purchase in the years to follow. The reconfiguration of the media ecology in the 1980s led some to assert that television networks in particular had abandoned their civic obligations in the pursuit of profits and ratings; the same period saw an escalation of another long-standing criticism of the media from the political right, which charged the networks and mainstream newspapers with a liberal bias hiding behind sham pretenses to objectivity. The Jackson campaign, and the castigations on the media's coverage of him—with the exception of C-SPAN—requires a grappling with failures of the political press corps and the racialized logics that guided their assessment of leadership, electability, and credibility throughout both campaigns.

REFERENCES

"And now, New Hampshire." (1988, February 15). *Broadcasting*, 63.

Atkeson, L. R., & Maestas, C. (2009). Meaningful participation and the evolution of the reformed presidential nominating system. *PS: Political Science and Politics*, 42(1), 59–64.

Auletta, K. (1992). *Three blind mice: How the TV networks lost their way*. Vintage Books.

Beltramini, E. (2013). *SCLC Operation Breadbasket: From economic civil rights to Black economic power*. Fire!!, 2(2), 5–47.

Brainard, L. A. (2004). *Television: The limits of deregulation*. Lynne Rienner Publishers.

Broh, C. A. (1987). *A horse of a different color? Television's treatment of Jesse Jackson's 1984 presidential campaign*. Joint Center for Political Studies.

Colton, E. O. (1989). *The Jesse Jackson phenomenon: The man, the power, the message*. Doubleday.

"Covering the zone in Iowa." (1988, February 8). *Broadcasting*, 45–47.

"Cross-country with C-SPAN." (1984, August 20). *Broadcasting*, 32.

C-SPAN (Producer). (1984, March 31). *Jackson campaign rally* [Video]. https://www.c-span.org/video/?124283-1/jackson-campaign-rally

C-SPAN User-Created Clip. (2021a, October 8). *Clip of* Horse of a Different Color

(August 19, 1987); *User clip: Clip, Broh press conference* [C-SPAN user video clip]. https://www.c-span.org/video/?c4981265/user-clip-clip-broh-press-conference

C-SPAN User-Created Clip. (2021b, December 15). *Clip of* Jackson Campaign Speech (November 6, 1987); *User clip: Jackson, 1988, NH clip* [C-SPAN user video clip]. https://www.c-span.org/video/?c4992183/user-clip-jackson-1988-nh-clip

Davies, T. A. (2017). *Mainstreaming Black power*. University of California Press.

Frantzich, S., & Sullivan, J. (1996). *The C-SPAN revolution*. University of Oklahoma Press.

Gandy, O. H., Jr., & Coleman, L. G. (1986). Watch Jesse run and tell me what you see: A first look at student perceptions of the Jesse Jackson presidential candidacy. *Journal of Black Studies, 16*(3), 293–306.

Garisto, L. (1984, September 23). C-SPAN widens its campaign focus. *New York Times*, H28, H37. https://www.nytimes.com/1984/09/23/arts/cable-tv-notes-c-span-widens -its-campaign-focus.html

"The gavel passes to a new generation." (1984, July 23). *Broadcasting*, 33–37.

Gibbons, A. (1993). *Race, politics, and white media: The Jesse Jackson campaigns*. University Press of America.

Haggins, B., & Timberg, J. (2018). The multi-channel transition period: 1980s–1990s. In A. Bodroghkozy (Ed.), *A companion to the history of American broadcasting* (pp. 111–133). John Wiley & Sons.

Holt, J. (2011). *Empires of entertainment: Media industries and the politics of deregulation, 1980–1996*. Rutgers University Press.

Hunt, B. A. (1988). *The use of television by the reverend Jesse Jackson, 1968–1978*. [Unpublished doctoral dissertation]. Northwestern University.

"It belongs." (1984, March 26). *Broadcasting*, 98.

Jackson, J., Sr. (2012). "The rising American electorate is a rainbow": Reflections on the Jackson presidential campaigns of 1984 and 1988. *Souls, 14*, 67–72. https://doi .org/10.1080/10999949.2012.723248

Jamieson, K. H. (2000). *Everything you think you know about politics . . . and why you're wrong*. Basic Books.

Johnson, C. (2007). *Revolutionaries to race leaders: Black power and the making of African American politics*. University of Minnesota Press.

Joseph, P. E. (2013). *Dark days, bright nights: From Black power to Barack Obama*. Basic Civitas Books.

Kaufmann, K. M., Gimpel, J. G., & Hoffman, A. H. (2003). A promise fulfilled? Open primaries and representation. *Journal of Politics, 65*(2), 457–476. https://doi.org/10.1111 /1468-2508.t01-2-00009

Landess, T. H., & Quinn, R. M. (1985). *Jesse Jackson and the politics of race*. Jameson Books.

Leduc, L. (2001). Democratizing party leadership. *Party Politics, 7*(3), 323–341.

"Low ratings cast cloud over convention coverage." (1988, July 25). *Broadcasting*, 27–28.

Marable, M. (1985). Jackson and the rise of the rainbow coalition. *New Left Review*, 3–44.

Marable, M. (1992). At the end of the rainbow. *Race and Class, 34*(2), 75–81.

Moore, L. N. (2018). *The defeat of Black power: Civil rights and the National Black Political Convention of 1972*. Louisiana State University Press.

"News finds its niche on cable." (1984, December 3). *Broadcasting*, 68.

"Night of the number two's." (1988, December 10). *Broadcasting*, 31.

Perlman, A. (2016). *Public interests: Media advocacy and struggles over U.S. television*. Rutgers University Press.

Pierce, P. (1988). The roots of the rainbow coalition. *The Black Scholar, 19*(2), 2–16.

"Reagan film controversy: The news at GOP convention." (1984, August 27). *Broadcasting*, 35.

Riggsa. (2020, July 28). *Clip of* Presidential Qualities (December 11, 1987); *User clip: The national quilt* [C-SPAN video user clip]. https://www.c-span.org/video/?c4895649/user-clip-national-quilt

Reed, A .L., Jr. (1986). *The Jesse Jackson phenomenon*. Yale University Press.

Reed, A. L., Jr. (1999). *Stirrings in the jug: Black politics in the post-segregation era*. University of Minnesota Press.

Rustin, B. (1965). From protest to politics: The future of the civil rights movement. *Commentary*, 25–31.

Robinson, C. J. (2019). White signs in Black times: The politics of representation in dominant texts. In H. L. T. Quan (Ed.), *Cedrick J. Robinson on racial capitalism, Black internationalism, and cultures of resistance* (pp. 183–194). Pluto Press.

Sánchez, J., Jr. (2020). Revisiting McGovern-Fraser: Party nationalization and the rhetoric of reform. *Journal of Policy History, 32*(1), 1–24. https://doi.org/10.1017/S0898030619000253

Simien, E. M. (2016). *Historic firsts: How symbolic empowerment changed U.S. politics*. Oxford University Press.

Sinclair, A. (1987). Post swipe at Jesse just the beginning? *New York Amsterdam News*, p. 32.

Smallwood, J. M. (2010). Run, Jesse, run! In B. A. Glasrud & C. D. Wintz (Eds.), *African Americans and the presidency: The road to the White House* (pp. 113–128). Routledge.

Smith, R. C. (1990). From insurgency toward inclusion: The Jackson campaigns of 1984 and 1988. In L. Morris (Ed.), *The social and political implications of the 1984 Jesse Jackson presidential campaign* (pp. 215–230). Praeger.

Stone, E. (1988). *Jesse Jackson: A biography*. Holloway House.

Tryman, M. D. (1989). Was Jesse Jackson a third party candidate in 1988? *The Black Scholar, 20*(1), 19–29. https://doi.org/10.1080/00064246.1989.11412914

Walters, R. W. (1988). The American crisis of credibility and the 1988 Jesse Jackson campaign. *The Black Scholar, 19*(2), 31–44. https://doi.org/10.1080/00064246.1988.11412808

Walters, R. W. (2005). *Freedom is not enough*. Rowman & Littlefield.

Wright, A. N. (2007). *Civil rights "unfinished business": Poverty, race and the 1968 Poor People's Campaign* [Unpublished doctoral dissertation, University of Texas at Austin].

4

SAME MESSENGER, NEW MESSAGE

Senator Ted Kennedy and the Framing of Health Reform

Jennifer Hopper

INTRODUCTION

In the 1970s, when President Richard Nixon proposed two major health care policy overhauls—the National Health Insurance Partnership plan (1971) and the Comprehensive Health Insurance Plan (1974)—the proposals were formulated, rolled out, and communicated to the public largely in response to the health plan and political activities of Democratic senator Edward Kennedy of Massachusetts. Archival research from the Nixon Presidential Library demonstrates that at every turn, the Nixon team's internal discussion of health care was significantly motivated and shaped by its efforts to take any credit for addressing this policy sphere away from Kennedy and to attack the senator, seeking to steer attention from his health initiatives toward the president's and to counter the significant amount of media and public attention the senator from Massachusetts tended to receive (Hopper, 2020). Moving forward to 2009, as President Barack Obama gave a major address before Congress advocating health reform legislation, he concluded his speech with a discussion of Kennedy and a letter he had received from the senator, who had recently died. The president shared Kennedy's prediction that this would finally be the year the "great unfinished business of our society" would be achieved and heralded Kennedy's "large-heartedness" and "passion . . . born not of some rigid ideology, but of his own experience" when it came to questions of health care (Obama, 2009b).

Over four decades in American politics then, Senator Kennedy loomed large as a figure in health care debates, both shaping policy behind the scenes and as a public face for proposals to expand health benefits to more Americans. He held key positions of power within Congress for influencing health policy, spending many years as chair of the Senate Committee on Health, Education, Labor, and Pensions. During the Nixon administration, Kennedy had advocated a government-run single payer system, but as time progressed, he moved toward embracing more piecemeal changes that built upon the established system of private insurance (Furrow, 2011). When the "unfinished business" of the Democratic Party was addressed with the passage of the Affordable Care Act in 2010, the politics of the possible in health care reform had moved in a distinctively right-leaning direction compared to what party leaders had advocated in the mid-20th century. The ACA rested largely on the private insurance system and mandates requiring coverage, ideas that bore a resemblance to Nixon's 1974 plan and had been promoted by Republicans in the early 1990s. How did we get there? Kennedy was arguably the most prominent American politician on health care issues over 40 years. What can his communication choices over this period tell us about the path of both health politics debates and policy outcomes in this crucial time span for reform?

In this study, I engage in a framing analysis of the communications of Senator Kennedy discussing health care available through the C-SPAN Video Library, which includes hundreds of videos featuring Kennedy talking about health reform from 1987 through the year of his death in 2009. Specifically, I assess how Kennedy framed key aspects of health policy over time, including incremental vs. systemic reform, a single payer system, and the role played by insurance companies and businesses. I then take a brief look at U.S. news media coverage of Kennedy and health care around the time of several of his C-SPAN appearances to help determine what aspects of Kennedy's health care framing appeared in news content reaching an even wider audience. The study concludes with public opinion polling data related to the subjects of Kennedy's framing over time, connecting his political communication to long-term public views around reform. Overall, I find that the framing and rhetoric Kennedy used around health reform evolved in significant ways over the decades, both reflective of and contributing to the ideological rightward turn the health policy debate took during this period. Yet some elements of Kennedy's communication remained consistent over time, such as depicting health care coverage as a basic right that all Americans were entitled to, keeping more progressive frames part of the health care public conversation for the long term.

FRAMING, SENATOR KENNEDY, AND HEALTH CARE

To explore how Senator Kennedy sought to influence how various facets of health care reform would appear and be discussed in public discourse, I make use of the concept of framing. Framing as it will be used in this study entails selecting central organizing themes in order to focus attention on some elements of an issue or event and deemphasize others, promoting a particular interpretation of a story (Altheide, 1976; Bennett, 2005; Callaghan & Schnell, 2005; Entman, 2004; Lakoff, 2004). The framing process makes some aspects of our reality more noticeable than others and helps to set the terms of debate (Kuypers, 2009; Kuypers & D'Angelo, 2010; Reese et al., 2001). Yet politicians do not typically have a free hand to frame issues without alternative interpretations from opponents. Efforts to frame high-stakes issues for the public can produce competition amongst elites or "framing contests," with two sides that compete to successfully interpret events for the news media and the public (Chong & Druckman 2007a, 2007b; Entman, 2004; Hopper, 2017; Jamieson & Waldman, 2004; Schaffner & Atkinson, 2010; Wolfsfeld, 1997; Wolfsfeld & Sheafer, 2006). In Kennedy's case, several of his frames were constructed to respond to critics of reform, and his framing of health policy was at times challenged in news coverage.

To identify public statements by the senator to analyze for his framing strategies and choices, I searched all of the C-SPAN Video Library's content, tagging Ted Kennedy after adding "health" to the search terms, resulting in 307 videos. I then more closely reviewed the results to narrow them down in two ways: First, I only used instances of Kennedy speaking outside of Congress (not in floor debate or congressional hearings); 108 videos fit into this category, including speeches to various groups, press conferences, and rallies. These were some of the lengthiest remarks Kennedy gave about health care reform, and his audience was typically the general public, the news media, or advocacy groups, likely to be the primary targets of carefully crafted messaging and framing efforts.[1] Second, I confined my analysis to the 55 videos within the 108 in which general comprehensive health reform efforts to expand coverage to a wider swath of the population was a major focus (rather than mentioned in passing), and as opposed to more specialized health topics such as veterans' care, Medicare prescription drug coverage, or federal AIDS policy.[2]

In line with Cappella and Jamieson (1998), Entman (1991, 2004), Kuypers (2006, 2009), Kuypers et al. (2010), and Kuypers et al. (2012), I identified major themes in these 55 examples of Kennedy's public statements through qualitative inductive analysis, and then analyzed the senator's words for "framing devices," or phrases, references, and concepts, that repeatedly showed up in the video content. Such framing devices demonstrate how the senator intended those preliminary themes to be framed, or interpreted and understood by audiences. Reviewing the videos chronologically, I then identified shifts in Kennedy's framing of the same topics over time, to demonstrate the development of his communication tactics in this policy sphere over decades of his political career. The definition of the major problems in the U.S. health care system stayed remarkably similar over the course of these 40 years, a helpful constant in focusing on how Senator Kennedy's communication and policy tactics changed over time. The number of uninsured or underinsured Americans, health care costs skyrocketing out of control (for government, businesses, and individuals/households), and poor U.S. health indicators such as illnesses/deaths, infant mortality rates, and life expectancy statistics were all major concerns from the 1970s through the 2000s (and in some cases continue to be of concern in the present day).

This is not a random sample or complete survey of Kennedy's public statements on health care over his nearly 47-year career in the U.S. Senate. However, after reviewing many hours of footage of Kennedy's C-SPAN appearances, many of the senator's frames, themes, and talking points on health care recurred, not only in the same time frame but in some cases across decades. This suggests that the C-SPAN Video Library holdings featuring Kennedy are representative of his general communication choices on health policy. Additionally, by virtue of being televised, the senator's messaging in these cases would reach a larger audience than his public appearances would have ordinarily, and potentially an influential one, as C-SPAN airings might draw greater scrutiny by activists, politicians, and interest groups most invested in this policy realm. As the C-SPAN Video Library does not go back prior to September 1987, in the analysis below I also make use of a major address on health reform Kennedy gave on December 9, 1978, before the Democratic National Committee Workshop on Health Care. This speech provides insight on how Kennedy framed health reform during his single payer advocacy days as well as some indication of how his communication on these elements changed or stayed the same in the years to follow.

Though my research has previously focused on presidential framing of health care (Hopper, 2015, 2017), Kennedy offers a unique opportunity to review how health care communication shifted over a much longer period than a single administration. The Democratic senator's lengthy career allows us to see how health reform was portrayed by one of its most prominent champions over several decades, promoting numerous different kinds of policy reform, and as the broader political environment shifted in terms of the two major parties' political fortunes as well as the ideological cast of public opinion.

There are clear limitations to focusing on a single political actor's health care rhetoric. This study does not presume Kennedy to be the sole U.S. politician to use these frames and does not demonstrate causality between the senator's communication choices and the shifting political environment surrounding health reform. However, because Kennedy was such an undeniably influential politician on health politics and a high-profile national celebrity by virtue of his family legacy, it is reasonable to assume he had an outsized impact on public debates surrounding health care, which in turn have constrained or boosted the prospects for reform over time. Additionally, although Kennedy's influence in this policy sphere is widely recognized, there is no comprehensive scholarly inquiry focusing on the role the senator played in affecting health care debates over the long term. Most of the accounts we have are either pieces of general historical biographies of Kennedy (Gabler, 2020; Littlefield & Nexon, 2015) or larger studies on the evolution of health policy in which he pops up from time to time (Starr, 2013), but not a focused treatment of the ways he may have shaped how we talk about these issues from the past to the present.

Furthermore, the common perception of Kennedy as the "liberal lion" of the Senate makes any conservative shifts in his communication on health care more noteworthy. If this is how Ted Kennedy came to speak about and advocate for health reform, we would expect that other Democratic politicians were likely to be following suit. Schimmel (2016) identifies Democratic presidents like Clinton and Obama shifting rightward on health care, deeming it evidence of "how the American social imaginary has emerged in a way that incorporates elements of Republican limited government ideology not only as a result of Republican efforts, but also of deliberate Democratic appropriation of elements of these ideas and ideals and incorporation into a new conciliatory centrist Democratic rhetoric which strives to appeal to as broad a segment of the American population as possible" (p. 99). Communication shifts can also be more influential when the messenger is unexpected: Berinsky (2012) finds that rumors, for instance, were more effectively dispelled by a surprising source, such as a Republican politician contradicting the existence of "death panels" in the ACA, though the effectiveness of these corrections faded over time. Kennedy first made his mark in health policy by championing a national insurance program, and in 1980 challenged incumbent president Jimmy Carter for the Democratic nomination from the left, making him a novel and remarkable presenter of any messaging more conservative in tone.

This is a study of Kennedy's public communication strategies on health reform, rather than a review of the many, many health-related policies and bills he supported throughout his lengthy congressional career. As will be discussed below, however, at times his preferred frames were directly tied to the specific legislation he championed in the moment.

THE SONG REMAINS THE SAME: CONSISTENT THEMES IN KENNEDY'S FRAMING OF HEALTH POLICY

Before delving into the evolution of Kennedy's framing of health politics over time, we should note that key parts of his messaging stayed remarkably consistent over a long period in American politics (see Table 4.1). In some instances, the senator's framing of health care reform stayed the same even as the substance of the policies he was advocating were different. A close look at Kennedy's health care speeches over four decades reveals the repeated framing of the U.S. as out of step with the rest of the world, lagging behind its industrialized democratic counterparts on health policy, an argument not distinctive to the senator and one still used in the present day by advocates of expanding health care. Back in 1978, Kennedy asserted, "America now stands virtually alone in the international community on national health insurance. . . . No other industrial nation in the world leaves its citizens in fear of financial ruin because of illness" (Kennedy, 1978). In 1992, referring to the U.S. as having the highest health costs in the world, greater than Canada, Germany, and Japan, the senator added, "Surely we cannot say with a straight face that every other industrial nation in the world is out of step except Uncle Sam. Yet alone among these countries we refuse to guarantee health care" (C-SPAN, 1992c). Kicking off a new decade in the year 2000, Kennedy declared, "One of our very highest national priorities must be to secure health care as a fundamental right for all of our people," noting that "every other industrialized

TABLE 4.1 *Consistency in Kennedy's Health Care Frames Over Time*

Frame	Framing devices
U.S. lags behind the world on health care	"No other industrial nation in the world leaves its citizens in fear of financial ruin because of illness" "Alone among these countries we refuse to guarantee health care" "Every year in America we continue to fall behind"
U.S. spending on health care astronomical, cost of a single payer system pales in comparison	"We cannot afford not to have national health insurance" "National health insurance, over 30 years ago, the cost of that was $100 billion dollars; we're spending a trillion 400 billion dollars now"
The proposed health reform is just like Social Security and Medicare	The "great unfinished business" of the Democratic Party "If our senior citizens like Medicare, all Americans will like health care" "We heard all of the same old arguments that we heard in opposition to Medicare, those were echoed on Social Security, we hear them again now on health insurance, and they don't have any more . . . value than they did before"
Health care as a basic human right	"A basic right for all, not just an expensive privilege for the few"

society in the world except South Africa achieved that goal in the 20th century . . . but every year in America we continue to fall behind" (C-SPAN, 2000).

Kennedy's depiction of national health insurance or a single payer system evolved over time (as we will see further along), but there was a constant in how this reform was used throughout the period analyzed: it helped the senator stress the astronomical amount of money spent on health care in the U.S., in whatever era he was speaking. In 1978 he warned, "There are some who say we cannot afford national health insurance. . . . But the truth is, we cannot afford not to have national health insurance," continuing, "If we do nothing, if all we do is drift with

Sen. Kennedy (D-MA) at a health care rally. (Courtesy of C-SPAN.)

the present system, the cost of health care in America will climb from $175 billion this year to $250 billion in 1981" (Kennedy, 1978). A decade later, though he was no longer actively pushing for single payer, the senator used his prior plan to put the "crisis" of sharply increasing health costs into perspective: "What we're spending now is $460 billion on health care—$460 billion. We're talking about my old program, that was $100 billion, you know, 15 years ago which would have provided comprehensive" (C-SPAN, 1988). Kennedy could always usefully update the dollar amounts in this messaging, as health care costs continued to grow. By 2002 he told his audiences, "National health insurance, over 30 years ago, the cost of that was $100 billion; we're spending a trillion $400 billion now" (C-SPAN, 2002b). This framing device sought to take the sting out of critics' charges that the reforms Kennedy backed in each period were too costly—a major attack on his national health insurance plans of the 1970s then, that the country could not afford such a massive expenditure, was later continually employed in service of promoting reform. If opponents could not tolerate those costs back then, they must surely agree that current spending levels necessitated policy change.

Social Security and Medicare were also regular touchstones in the senator's rhetoric on health care. Kennedy used the two pillars of the American welfare state to frame whatever health reform he was advocating at the time as less frightening and threatening than what critics charged. He was aided here in that health reform's critics remained remarkably consistent in their attacks over time, as Democratic health plans were depicted as costly, intrusive overreach by big government and socialized medicine. Kennedy emphasized the role of his party in bestowing these widely supported social programs upon the American people, defining it as the policy legacy of the Democrats, pointing inevitably to comprehensive health care reform as the next step in that legacy moving forward. Speaking in 1978, Kennedy pushed health reform as the aforementioned "great unfinished business" of Democrats, declaring, "our party gave Social Security to the nation in the 1930s. We gave Medicare to the nation in the 1960s. And we can bring national health insurance to the nation in the 1970's" (Kennedy, 1978). In 1991 Kennedy identified "powerful forces" arrayed against health reform efforts, noting, "If they had their way in the 1930s, we would have no Social Security. If they had their way in the 1960s, we would have no Medicare. But they did not have their way then, and they will not have their way today" (C-SPAN, 1991b). Into the 1990s, Kennedy identified affordable, accessible health care to be the "unfinished business of Social Security and Medicare" (C-SPAN, 1991b), arguing, "The red shirt of socialized medicine delayed Medicare for 20 years. That debate is over. If our senior citizens like Medicare, all Americans will like health care" (C-SPAN, 1992b). Referring to Republicans' criticism of Democratic plans in 1992, Kennedy dismissed the "old call to arms about socialized medicine — ask any senior citizen whether they think Medicare is socialized medicine. We won that battle for health care for the elderly a generation ago, and the time has come to win it now for every other American" (C-SPAN, 1992d). Ten years following that statement, Kennedy recalled the difficulty Congress had passing Medicare in the mid-'60s: "Is there anybody in the Congress — Hello? — who is asking to repeal that legislation?" Kennedy continued, "We heard all of the same old arguments that we heard in opposition to Medicare, those were echoed on Social Security, we hear them again now on health insurance, and they don't have any more . . . value than they did before" (C-SPAN, 2002c). Nine of the 55 videos in the C-SPAN Video Library featuring Kennedy speaking about health care outside of Congress include his references to either both Social Security and Medicare or Medicare alone in the context described above. Not only did this frame seek to quell fears about policy change, it also created the expectation that if enacted, the proposed reform program would eventually be beloved by Americans and supported across both sides of the political aisle.

Lastly, Kennedy throughout his career framed health care as a fundamental and basic right, not a privilege. Over the decades encompassed by this study, he continually depicted expanding health care access and coverage as an issue of justice and the humane policy to pursue. In 1978, he called for health care as "a basic right for all, not just an expensive privilege for the few" (Kennedy, 1978), just as in 2008 he expressed renewed hope in achieving "the cause of my life," that "every American . . . will have decent quality health care as a fundamental right and not a privilege" (C-SPAN, 2008).

Won't Get Fooled Again: The Evolution of Kennedy's Framing of Health Care Over Time

A close look at Kennedy's C-SPAN appearances outside of Congress over the years reveals several themes in his framing of health care that evolved with time, as the politics of the possible in health reform shifted with electoral results and changes in public opinion. I identified the categories that follow as areas of Kennedy's communication where the subject matter was the same, but how that issue or entity was framed changed substantively. In Table 4.2, I tie these categories to chronological time periods in the senator's career covered by the C-SPAN Video Library.

From dismissing "band-aids" to the virtues of incrementalism

Under the first Bush administration, Kennedy's addresses framed health care as requiring a complete overhaul, and that more piecemeal efforts to meet the system's problems were at best insufficient and at worst dangerous. Speaking to the National Health Council in 1991, the senator began his address by contending, "The crisis in our health care system continues to worsen; the incremental steps we have taken in recent years to improve access to health care and the patches and band-aid approach have failed. They have kept this deterioration from becoming even greater. But there is no question that we are continuing to fall behind" (C-SPAN, 1991a). A few months later, he went a step further, maintaining, "Incremental action will not do. Band-aids only make the problem worse" (C-SPAN, 1991b), and in early 1992 he asked, "What we ought to be held accountable for—are we [for] band-aids, which is completely unacceptable, or are we for systemic change?" (C-SPAN, 1992a). Referring to the legacy of the actions taken by Presidents Roosevelt, Kennedy, and Johnson on Social Security and Medicare, Kennedy stressed, "[They] didn't wait for a consensus! We've been waiting 11 years now under Presidents Reagan and Bush; no program . . . has come forward" (C-SPAN, 1992a). Kennedy could thus portray the reform proposals of the opposition party as gravely lacking, while simultaneously indicating that only the comprehensive proposals coming from Democrats met the moment's health care crisis in a serious way.[3]

However, beginning with the health care debate that took place surrounding President Bill Clinton's plan in 1993 to 1994, Kennedy shifted away from this re-

TABLE 4.2 *The Evolution of Kennedy's Health Care Frames Over Time*

Evolving framing	1987–1993: Precursor to reform push	1993–1995: Battle for the Clinton plan	1995–2009: Republican control of Congress and then the presidency	2009: Moving toward the ACA*
From dismissing "band-aids" to the virtues of incrementalism	Systemic change required, not band-aids	Build on the strengths of the current system; fix its most serious flaws	Incremental change is good	
The meaning of single payer	Scare tactic to promote more moderate alternative	Current plan is *not* national health insurance	Single payer as desirable but just not practical politics	
Portrayal of insurance companies	"Powerful interests," "status quo profiteers" working against us	Reform preserves a robust role for private insurance, but the current crisis in large part due to their problematic practices	Guilty of abusive practices; insurers interfering with care decisions that should be between doctors and patients, enabled by Republicans	Positive that insurance companies coming to the table in good faith reform discussions
Portrayal of business	Should help inform policy, or end up with reform less palatable than an employer mandate	Employer mandates only fair, to allow businesses to compete on equal footing; small businesses need special help, aid from government	Government asking for minimum obligations from private sector; responsible corporate citizens should be on board	

*Having been diagnosed with brain cancer in May 2008, Kennedy played a less prominent role in much of the ACA negotiations that went on in 2009 than he had in previous health care efforts, which is why much of this column remains empty. However, he became an important symbolic figure in the debate, his staff contributed a great deal to working on the legislation, and his occasional appearances in support of reform, such as at the March 2009 White House Health Care Summit covered here (see C-SPAN, 2009), garnered significant attention and allow us to consider how he viewed this last push for reform while he was still alive.

jection of band-aid solutions to downplaying the impact of proposed Democratic reforms. Perhaps acknowledging how public apprehension tended to contribute to derailing reform efforts, Kennedy sought to reassure listeners that such proposals would *not* represent a seismic shift with potentially unknown or alarming repercussions. A repeated sentiment in Kennedy's C-SPAN video appearances was that his preferred proposal of the time built upon the strengths and what worked in the current system and sought to fix the system's most serious flaws (C-SPAN, 1992c, 1993, 2002b, 2002c). In early 2000, he struck a starkly more conservative note in discussing his preferred parameters for reform, maintaining:

> We should not disrupt the health coverage that 152 million Americans 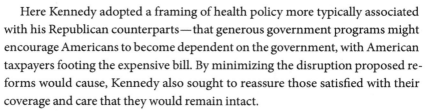 receive now through their employers, otherwise we risk forcing those who already have reliable employer-based health insurance to turn instead to our government-subsidized program. The cost to taxpayers would balloon needlessly and force us to reduce benefits to cut costs. (C-SPAN, 2000)

Here Kennedy adopted a framing of health policy more typically associated with his Republican counterparts—that generous government programs might encourage Americans to become dependent on the government, with American taxpayers footing the expensive bill. By minimizing the disruption proposed reforms would cause, Kennedy also sought to reassure those satisfied with their coverage and care that they would remain intact.

Having suffered the defeat of health reform in the Clinton era and facing Republican control of Congress and then the presidency from the mid-1990s on, Kennedy also pivoted to a full-fledged embrace of the incremental policy responses he had once derided. In this sense, the shift in Kennedy's communication was conservative in terms of largely maintaining the status quo, if not necessarily backing ideologically conservative health reforms. His postmortem was this: "The lesson of the failure of health reform in 1994 is that a sharply divided Congress cannot make far-reaching changes in an election year. Instead of repeating that mistake, we should enact the consensus, incremental reforms that have broad bipartisan support and that are achievable this year" (C-SPAN, 1996a). When Kennedy was successful at achieving such incremental, bipartisan reform, as when the Health Insurance Portability and Accountability Act (also known as the Kennedy–Kassebaum bill) was passed in 1996, he framed it as a step toward more wide-scale reform.[4] At the signing ceremony, he depicted the new law as "a sign of our commitment to carry this battle forward in the months and years ahead, and build on what we have accomplished here," further saying,

"We will never give up the fight to achieve accessible and affordable health care for all Americans—and when I say all, I mean *all*," the emphasis on the final word drawing applause from the friendly crowd (C-SPAN, 1996c). In 2002, he told the National Press Club that he was hopeful for a bipartisan compromise on health care, noting, "I am happy to be now an incrementalist," which provoked laughter from the audience (C-SPAN, 2002a). Here, Kennedy's public persona as a stalwart liberal of the Senate and champion of big progressive proposals like national health insurance perhaps shaped perceptions of his framing of health policy. If even Kennedy was able to find common ground and compromise on the signature issue of his political life, this could make those who refused to negotiate appear even more recalcitrant and obstructionist than they might have otherwise.

The meaning of single payer

Because Kennedy had been so closely associated with national health insurance in the 1960s and '70s, when he later backed other types of reform, he frequently emphasized to his audiences that such proposals (whether pay or play, employer mandates, or expansions of public health programs) were *not* single payer, and at other times he had to explain to left-leaning audiences why he was no longer advocating the progressive plan. Throughout the period analyzed here, Kennedy never denied his past association with or fondness for a single payer solution, but he did refer to it differently over time in promoting whatever policy he was backing at that moment.

For instance, in mid-1992, speaking to representatives of the insurance industry, he framed his preferred pay or play plan as the moderate alternative the group should accept now, lest they regret it when a more radical policy was adopted instead. Using the prospect of single payer as a scare tactic, Kennedy warned, "Pay or play is not a stalking horse for single payer," but

 the real stalking horses for single payer are the variety of lesser alternatives currently being urged in the name of health reform by the Bush administration, HIAA [Health Insurance Association of America], and others. They fail the test of universal coverage and effective cost control, and those failures may well make single payer irresistible a few years down the road if you block action now. (C-SPAN, 1992c)[5]

After comprehensive health reform failed to pass in President Clinton's first term, Kennedy was considerably less brash in his use of the term "single payer" in public debates. When audiences asked about the progressive proposal in several

of his addresses that aired on C-SPAN, the senator's response was typically along the lines of "In my heart of hearts I am still a single payer" (C-SPAN, 2002b), "but we couldn't get groups aboard" (C-SPAN, 1996a). In 2000, he stressed the need for pragmatism in health politics: "I started with the single payer. . . . If you were to go in a perfect world that's where I'd be, but I've been on 14 other bills. I want to get to the outcome of this and I am prepared to deal with the devil if we can get us there" (C-SPAN, 2000). Thus Kennedy transitioned from portraying single payer as potentially just around the corner to a sense of resignation that it was unachievable.

In one of the later C-SPAN videos featuring Kennedy—in an appearance at a 2006 rally opposing some of President Bush's health care proposals—the senator did tell the crowd, "Many of us believe in expanding the Medicare system to cover all Americans. We are serious about dealing with our health care crisis, and we're going to fight for a good program in this Congress" (C-SPAN, 2006). That year Kennedy introduced the Medicare for All Act in the Senate, though it was never voted on. When Kennedy moved away from single payer then, rather than denigrating the substance of that policy, he attributed his move to the improbability of getting it enacted into law. In some sense, the senator provided a steady through line on the positives of a single payer approach from a policy standpoint in Democratic messaging over many years, in a way that might be useful to contemporary advocates of such proposals.

Insurance companies and HMOs emerge as villains

Back in the early 1970s, during his campaign for national health insurance, Kennedy would explicitly attack opponents' plans that relied on private insurance companies—for instance charging that the Nixon administration's 1971 reform plan would gift the industry, which had been an unregulated, unscrupulous actor, with "a windfall of billions of dollars annually" (Hopper, 2020, p. 16). But Kennedy's speeches in the earlier C-SPAN videos analyzed here made far more vague allusions to the enemies of serious reform efforts, without being explicit or clear as to who he was talking about. In the early 1990s, he told audiences, "I do not underestimate the difficulty of the task ahead. Although public support continues to mount for reform, powerful interests are arrayed against us" (C-SPAN, 1991a).[6] In the summer of 1994, he accused "status quo profiteers/profiteering" of holding up reform, those that "make billions of dollars at the cost of working families in the health care system in America today" (C-SPAN, 1994c, 1994d). One could reasonably infer that Kennedy was talking about major sectors of the private health industry, but he did not name them.

In the early '90s, Kennedy also made appearances before groups more hostile to his health care proposals, such as in a 1992 address before the Health Insurance Association of America (HIAA), an invite he told his audience was "a little like asking Daniel to stop by the lion's den."[7] Describing what he saw as the crisis in health care, Kennedy issued a challenge to the insurers, contending, "Whether the private insurance industry is part of the solution depends in no small degree on the decisions you make in the weeks and months to come" (C-SPAN, 1992c).[8] Kennedy's appearance is notable in representing both a prominent politician's willingness to speak before an unsympathetic audience (far more rare today) and a prominent Democrat on health issues reaching out to the industry, something the party was accused of not doing enough of in the 1993 push for reform. Here, as in some of his later speeches, Kennedy took pains to stress that the proposals he backed would "preserve a central role for private insurance" and depended "on a strong private health insurance industry" (C-SPAN, 1992c). This reflected the evolution of Kennedy's thinking on health care over the course of his career. Though in the late '60s and early '70s he vigorously opposed any plans built on private insurance, beginning in the late 1970s/early 1980s with his shift away from single payer, he embraced plans involving competing private insurers (Starr, 2013, p. 20). While Kennedy sought to emphasize the altered approach from his national insurance days, he also sought to minimize the scale of the change to the existing system to put insurers' minds at ease. But alongside these reassurances, Kennedy did not mince words in speeches such as those before HIAA about what he found unacceptable in their business practices and stance toward reform. He told them, "You did not support my single payer proposal in the early 1970s, which is understandable. But you did not even support President Nixon's alternative. . . . In the 1990s when the need for action is much more urgent, you are as hostile as ever to comprehensive reform" (C-SPAN, 1992c). According to the senator, the insurers' behavior had "unquestionably made this crisis worse," as they operated by a "don't insure anyone unless you think they won't get sick" philosophy. Kennedy declared to HIAA:

 Health care is the fastest growing failing business in America, and you bear a major share of the responsibility for that fact. (C-SPAN, 1992c)

Following the missed opportunity of health reform under Clinton and facing Republican congressional majorities in the mid to late '90s,[9] Kennedy doubled down on framing insurance companies as the villain in America's health care predicament, putting their profits over the best interests of patients. A recurring theme involved recounting the "abuses" of insurers denying or delaying people the care they deserved and that should have been covered by the premiums they paid. He equated the insurance industry with another familiar enemy to his audiences, Big Tobacco (C-SPAN, 1998a, 1998c). The senator stressed that insurers were not being held accountable for their sins, immunity the tobacco industry had also enjoyed until recently: "No other industry in America has such protection from liability for the injuries it causes, and the health insurance industry does not deserve such protection either" (C-SPAN, 1998b).

Further, Kennedy framed his Republican opponents as willing enablers and defenders of insurers' misdeeds, depicting a party on the industry's payroll. He closely tied Republican proposals that countered his own to the insurance industry's sway (C-SPAN, 1996b), arguing that insurers used campaign donations to preserve their power and "buy" favorable bills from Republicans, who allowed insurers to craft legislation to their liking (C-SPAN, 1999a, 1999b, 2002c, 2006). George W. Bush's position was similarly categorized by Kennedy, as he argued the president "should be the trustee of Medicare, not the salesman in chief for the insurance industry" (C-SPAN, 2003).

Beginning in 1999 in the videos analyzed here, Kennedy's disparagement of insurance providers was often aimed at health maintenance organizations specifically, though he would also lump them together with insurance companies generally in accusing them of denying Americans proper care. This was also a period in which the senator sought to pass a Patients' Bill of Rights that focused on rectifying the problems such managed care was presenting for customers. Kennedy tied the Bush administration to backing HMOs over the public interest, contending that some sort of bipartisan compromise should have been possible, as had recently been achieved on education policy. Kennedy claimed, "In many respects, the differences in the area of Patients' Bill of Rights were less than we had in the area of education, the only explanation was, on Patients' Bill of Rights, there's the HMO industry. . . . Each and every recommendation that this administration has made has been on the side of the HMO and not the patients" (C-SPAN, 2001b).

One component of Kennedy's negative depiction of the insurance industry from the late 1990s forward was a repurposing of a long-standing conservative argument against Democratic health plans going as far back as the Truman administration, that "socialized medicine" advocated by Democrats would create "socialized doctors" and "socialized, regulated patients" (Hopper, 2017, p. 121), allowing "big government" to get between Americans and their doctors.[10] In 14 C-SPAN videos featuring Kennedy speaking outside of Congress from 1998 through 2009, the senator charged that a major problem with the current health system was that insurance company figures—alternately referred to as "accountants," "number-crunchers," "agents," and so forth—were interfering with the health care decisions that should properly be made between doctors and patients (C-SPAN, 1998a). Kennedy thereby engaged in what some have called "frame shifting," or promoting a new frame of reference that contrasts with how a subject was previously perceived (Zarefsky, 2004). Building on the highly effective messaging of conservatives capitalizing on Americans' fear of a large, soulless entity interfering with some of the most personal health decisions they would make with their trusted family doctors, Kennedy substituted insurance company accountants for government bureaucrats. Republican reform proposals in 1998, according to Kennedy, would do "nothing to guarantee that medical decisions are made by doctors and patients, not insurance industry accountants" (C-SPAN, 1998b). Promoting the Patients' Bill of Rights in 2001, he identified its intent as ensuring that

 medical decisions are going to be made in the interest of the family, of the child or the husband or the parents, rather than a health decision that is being made by a bean counter, in many instances, thousands of miles away, who is not trained, does not have the skill and is only interested in the bottom-line profits of the HMOs. (C-SPAN, 2001a)

However, in one of his final appearances in the C-SPAN Video Library, at a White House Health Care Summit in 2009 discussing policy that would ultimately lead to the Affordable Care Act, Kennedy struck a friendlier tone toward insurers and their inclusion in the process:

 If you look over this gathering here today, you see the representatives of all the different groups that we have met with over the period of years—I mean you have the insurance companies, you have the medical professions, all represented in one form or another. That has not been the case over the history of the past, going all the way back to Harry Truman's time. . . . It'd be hard to think of those interests being together, and being as concerned and providing the leadership that they are, as they are demonstrating that kind of a commitment as we have today. (C-SPAN User-Created Clip, 2021b)

A key strategy of the Obama administration in the push for the ACA was to get special interests known for obstructing reform in the past (particularly in

the 1993–1994 Clinton-led effort) on board at an early point, including insurers, pharmaceutical companies, and hospital associations (Hacker, 2010; Starr, 2013). Kennedy's sentiment that it was noteworthy and positive to see the insurance industry at the table was somewhat out of step with the harsh rhetoric he had directed at them in the decade prior, but very much in line with the way he reached out to groups like the HIAA and American Medical Association, traditionally hostile to reform, in some of his earlier speeches on C-SPAN.

Portrayal of the role of business in health policy

In one of the earliest C-SPAN videos analyzed here, a 1988 address before the National Association of Manufacturers, Kennedy struck a similar tone before business interests as he would with the HIAA. Making the case for employer mandates to provide insurance for their workers, he urged the group to be receptive and involved in negotiations, lest they miss their chance to impact the policy Congress would pass:

> You can either be inside the ballgame or outside. You may be able to defeat it, but eventually we're gonna get it. But if you want to be outside the ballgame and be complaining about it for the rest of the time, so be it, and that'll be the way it is. You may be able to defeat it, but you're not going to be able to defeat it long because we're moving into a crisis. (C-SPAN User-Created Clip, 2021a)

Ultimately, Kennedy warned the business representatives that the resulting policy would be one "you're going to live with for the rest of the time that you're going to be working in your various companies" (C-SPAN, 1998a). In the earliest years covered by the C-SPAN Video Library, Kennedy was more likely to issue forceful challenges to the naysayers of reform, using the presumption that major legislation was around the corner to bring them inside the tent.

As time progressed, Kennedy sought to frame employer mandates, a policy provision he advocated for off and on over his career, as an issue of fairness in the sense of businesses competing against each other. Sensitive to the negative connotations of applying the term "mandate" to this policy, Kennedy asserted in a 1994 interview with C-SPAN: "There is already a mandate, the mandate's on the American employers that are spending about $32 billion a year paying for other employers who are not providing health insurance—that is already existing—so I hope we don't get caught up in too much of the rhetoric" (C-SPAN, 1994b).[11] In

2002, Kennedy made some of his framing strategy transparent, telling his audience of supporters:

 We have to get away from . . . the word . . . "mandate." I admire Republicans for a lot of reasons, but they've got a wordsmith somewhere out there, they have the D5 missile and it was "the peacekeeper." . . . Everything is the "peacemaker" or the "safety" or the "better health" or "better start" . . . and we're stuck with "mandating" companies. (C-SPAN, 2002b)

In the later years analyzed, Kennedy downplayed the extent to which business interests would be asked to contribute to solving the problem of the uninsured and framed what his proposals would require of them as relatively undemanding and painless. This was a major shift from his earlier claims that the private sector could only make reform less painful by resigning itself to the reality that it was inevitable and coming to the negotiating table. Proposing in 2000 that employers contribute to the cost of their employees' coverage, Kennedy depicted the stipulations of his plan as "a minimum obligation that responsible employers should be willing to accept" (C-SPAN, 2000). On more than one issue in this speech Kennedy advocated "a new alliance of government and business," portraying the two institutions as working together rather than at odds, and by calling it "new," potentially implying that the regulatory politics of the past lacked such a partnership.

Asked in that same appearance about the concessions that both corporate and labor interests would have to make to move forward on health policy, the senator rejected the question's premise, arguing that we ought to try to "free" ourselves "from sort of the blame game. We shouldn't have one win and the other lose . . . the idea is that we all win." In 2002 he discussed an employer mandate for employers with over 100 workers, asking them "to be good corporate citizens" (C-SPAN, 2002a). When Kennedy was questioned in this period about the costs such mandates placed on business, he first shifted the focus from financial costs to human costs: "We're paying extraordinary costs every single day with the pain and suffering of those that don't have any health insurance." The senator then returned to financial costs, however, portraying providing insurance as in the best interest of businesses because they faced "extraordinary costs in the fallouts in productivity from these workers . . . because they're sick," and further that we all were "paying more than we should because we're treating people only when they're sicker" (C-SPAN, 2002c). Throughout the Kennedy videos analyzed here, the senator frequently focused on the costs to small businesses in particular of providing insurance to workers, stressing his priority was to make it easier for them and treat them more fairly (C-SPAN, 1988, 1991a, 2002b, 2002c), reflecting the more favorable public sentiment toward small businesses as entities in comparison to larger corporate actors.

News Coverage of Kennedy's C-SPAN Health Appearances

I searched Nexis-Uni for all U.S. news mentions of "Kennedy" and "health care" one day before and two days after the nine videos included in the analysis that featured Kennedy's lengthiest remarks on health care and in which comprehensive health reform was the major focus of the event.[12] Most of these searches revealed no coverage for Kennedy on health care.[13] The Associated Press was the lone outlet to cover his combative appearance before the HIAA in April 1992, though its story was likely published in other outlets as well, potentially extending its reach. The article begins, "A surprised audience of health insurance executives got a dose of castor oil when Sen. Edward Kennedy accused them of contributing to the nation's burgeoning health care crisis" (Diamond, 1992). Kennedy's speech is then quoted throughout the article, listing the litany of misdeeds the senator attributed to the insurance industry. Included in the article, however, were counter-frames to some of Kennedy's contentions, as a representative for HIAA was quoted saying, "We think we've come a long way and done on a lot better than the senator does," and maintaining that the association had been working against preexisting exclusions and redlining in insurance coverage (accusations Kennedy had made against the group) in state-level legislation.

The date range that produced the most coverage for Kennedy was the senator's May 11, 1994, Health Care Reform press conference on C-SPAN, resulting in 15 news articles/transcripts.[14] The greater media attention in this instance is likely attributable to Kennedy introducing his own alternative bill to the Clinton plan at this time, providing journalists with the novelty of an intraparty rivalry over health care, but also Kennedy portraying his plan as an effort at bipartisan compromise potentially signaled to reporters that it had a greater chance of passage. Fourteen of the 15 news items described Kennedy's plan as easing the burden/concerns/fears of, exempting, freeing, offering concessions to, or softening the blow for small/mom-and-pop businesses of an employer mandate to provide coverage to workers. If the senator wanted to convey in this period that his party was pursuing reforms that kept the interests of small business in mind and avoided onerous government requirements, he was largely successful in the news in that regard. Four of the articles, however, included counter-framing by Republican congressmembers calling Kennedy's version "the Clinton plan just repackaged" and/or framing it as entailing "the same heavy mandates, extensive government controls, and high price tags that have already turned the American people away from the president's plan."[15]

Public Opinion and Kennedy's Framing of Health Care

A brief look at some of the public opinion polling from the early 1990s to 2009 can give us some sense of how Americans' views on the health topics discussed here changed or remained the same over time, placing Kennedy's framing choices into greater context. Gallup asked Americans whether they preferred "Congress deal with health care reform on a gradual basis over several years, or should Congress try to pass a comprehensive healthcare reform plan this year" in both the summer of 1994 and the fall of 2009. In both instances, "gradual basis" enjoyed a substantial majority's support, including 68% of respondents in August 1994 and 58% in October 2009 (Gallup, 2021). Such long-term consistency in public support for incremental change and apprehensions about policy overhauls are in keeping with Kennedy's eventual emphasis on downplaying the extent of the change he was advocating for. At the same time, the polling data also shows that Americans were at least somewhat less averse to comprehensive change by the time the ACA debate rolled around.

With regard to employer mandates, a 1993 *New York Times*/CBS News poll illustrated the policy's relative popularity: 54% of Americans supported requiring employers to provide insurance to workers, and the number rose to 63% when the question identified that this was a way of making sure all Americans were covered. At the same time, the survey revealed respondents worried about the "job impact" of the mandate, though those concerns became less acute when people were told about government subsidies to small businesses to aid with the requirements (Toner, 1993), justifying Kennedy making this a point of emphasis. By 2014, Kaiser Family Foundation (KFF) revealed that 60% of Americans had a favorable impression of the employer mandate in the ACA; however, that support could be tenuous. If the foundation then told mandate supporters that employers could react by shifting workers from full- to part-time status, that 60% support level dropped to 27%. But at the same time, amongst those who expressed disapproval of the mandate, when told that most large employers would not be impacted because they already covered employees, the popularity of the mandate increased to 76% (KFF, 2014). While including these implications of the mandate unsurprisingly led some respondents to change their answers, it also sheds light on how a particular framing could potentially shape public impressions of the provision.

Framing insurance companies as bad actors in the U.S. health care system was not out of step with doubts Americans held widely about the industry. A review of Gallup polling from 1999 to 2013 that asked respondents how much confidence they had in HMOs revealed that 2001 and 2002 were the organizations' least popular years, when 47% of the public said they had either very little or no confidence in them (by 2009, the standing of HMOs had improved slightly, with 35% expressing little or no confidence) (Gallup, 2021). In 1999, KFF asked how much of the time respondents could trust health insurance companies, including HMOs, to do what was best for patients and customers: 20% said almost none of the time, 48% said some of the time, and just 29% said almost all or most of the time (KFF, 1999). In 2009, KFF found that 48% had a lot or some trust in their health insurance company to put their interests above the company's interests, while 50% had only a little or no trust in this (KFF, 2009). This reflected a decline in insurers' public standing over time: back in 1997, KFF polling found a full 80% of the public trusted their current health insurance plan to do the right thing for their care just about always or most of the time (KFF, 1997). Asked about the quality of medical services/care provided by health insurance companies generally in 2003, 65% rated it only fair or poor, compared to just 33% who rated it excellent or good. That same poll, for comparison, found that only 19% rated their care by doctors as fair/poor (Gallup, 2021). When Kennedy first began attacking insurers it was perhaps a bit of a tougher sell than it would later become; Democrats' broadsides against the industry over time certainly may have contributed to this diminished standing as well.

Kennedy may have done well to subtly praise single payer throughout his career even as he expressed doubts it could be passed or championed other proposals. KFF used polling averages to show that from 1998 to 2000, 40% of Americans backed "a national health plan in which all Americans would get their insurance from a single government plan," but by 2016 this had increased to 50% (KFF, 2020). This same study showed relatively steady levels of support for Medicare for All plans between 2019 and 2020 of 53% to 56% support.

CONCLUSION

The pragmatic, at times conservative turn in Kennedy's health care communications reflects the lessons the senator appeared to internalize from his long political career. His efforts at achieving broad, left-leaning overhauls of the American health care system had fallen short on numerous occasions, including his quest for national health insurance in the early 1970s and his party's 1993–1994 attempt at reform. In 1974 when President Nixon proposed the Children's Health Insurance Program (CHIP), which included an employer mandate and a government program to cover the remaining uninsured, and as Kennedy came to realize his own national insurance proposal was not going to pass through Congress, he had his staff quietly meet with Nixon aides to hammer out a compromise. In the end, Kennedy almost endorsed the Nixon plan but decided against it because of the opposition of some of his key constituencies, like labor unions. He later expressed great regret about this missed opportunity, believing it might have been the best chance the government would have to pass comprehensive health reform (Stockman, 2012). That year represented a unique policy moment when prominent members of both political parties were seeking to claim credit for addressing the nation's health care problems, and were not tremendously far apart in policy substance (Wainess, 1999). Kennedy eventually called "spurning Nixon's health care plan . . . the biggest policy mistake of his career" (Farrell, 2017, p. 646). As mentioned earlier, when the Affordable Care Act was debated and then ultimately passed into law in 2010, some observers noted its similarity to what Nixon had proposed ("Echoes of Kennedy's Battle," 2009; Freed, 2015; Starr, 2013).

Meanwhile, Kennedy's lasting legislative legacy in health care included high-profile, bipartisan laws that were incremental in expanding coverage and benefits, such as the Kennedy–Kassebaum bill and the Children's Health Insurance Program. Toward the end of Kennedy's life, however, and in the years to follow, partisan polarization and the increasing unwillingness of members of Congress to give the opposition anything that could be construed as a political victory made that Kennedy model of compromise difficult to emulate. Precisely this criticism emerged around Democrats' push for the ACA, that conservatives were granted concessions and yet the policy ultimately won zero Republican support, despite its watering down. The Kennedy approach might have been attractive to Democrats pursuing health reform in the first decade of the 21st century, but it also may have meant they gave up too much in policy for no political gain. Still, the need to mollify moderate Democrats to garner the votes needed for passage might have required this rightward turn, and certainly also made it more difficult for a subsequent Republican-controlled Congress to repeal the law, despite many years of campaigning on ridding the nation of "Obamacare."

It is undeniable that after 70 years of seeking comprehensive health care reform, Democrats passed landmark legislation with the ACA in 2010. In one of his final C-SPAN appearances speaking about health care just months before his death in 2009, Kennedy told President Obama and other leaders gathered for a White House Health Care Summit:

> I'm looking forward to being a foot soldier in this undertaking, and this time we will not fail. (C-SPAN User-Created Clip, 2021b)

The major health care reform overhaul that emerged and passed into law the following year was very far in substance from what Kennedy had advocated for in the early years of his Senate career, but it did reflect the more piecemeal and pragmatic turn his health care communication had taken. As he predicted, it did not fail.

NOTES

1. This is not to say that Kennedy's speeches within Congress did not include such content; however, a review of those videos indicated that his remarks were frequently along procedural lines or reactive to amendments or comments by other senators, making them potentially less relevant than his addresses outside the legislature.
2. For a complete list of the videos included in the analysis, please contact the author.
3. This is in keeping with sentiments Kennedy expressed in the 1970s as well. In that era, he compared his own plans to the Nixon administration's by identifying himself as on the side of "a major overhaul" and Nixon as for "the sort of patchwork, piecemeal effort we have been making for so long" (Hopper, 2020). Certainly his advocacy of a national health insurance program in and of itself reflected a commitment to systemic reform rather than incremental fixes.
4. This is not the only possible framing of such policies. Others have questioned whether incremental expansions of coverage cause universal coverage in the

U.S. to become less likely, removing the impetus for more comprehensive reform (Marmor, 2009; Oberlander, 2019).

5. This was consistent with sentiments Kennedy had expressed decades earlier as well, such as when he warned that were Nixon's 1971 health plan enacted, it would create a crisis that would ultimately require "the government to take over the entire health care system in the nation, lock, stock and barrel" (Hopper, 2019).

6. Kennedy uses nearly identical language just a few months later, declaring "powerful forces are arrayed against us" (C-SPAN, 1991b).

7. The following year, HIAA was the group responsible for funding the "Harry and Louise" ads opposing the Clinton health care plan that were widely credited with helping to defeat reform efforts.

8. To be fair, Kennedy also told the American Medical Association that "physicians are part of the problem and you must also be part of the solution," though the overall tone of that address was friendlier than that to HIAA (C-SPAN, 1993).

9. Numerous scholars point to the failed Clinton reform experience as one deeply scarring to the Democratic Party and its political prospects. Hacker (2010) argues that it led to "fifteen years of inaction and incrementalism but also the Republican control of Congress that continued through 2006." Skocpol (1997) calls it a watershed moment in American health care politics, after which the partisan, institutional, and policy contexts were altered in such a way that the trajectory of health care policy would shift dramatically to the right.

10. For instance, see Ronald Reagan's popular 1961 recording "Ronald Reagan Speaks Out Against Socialized Medicine" for further articulation of this conservative argument that Democratic health reform plans would jeopardize the freedom of doctors and patients and compromise the sacrosanct relationship between the two (Reagan, 2020). President Obama pushing for health care in 2009 noted the longstanding nature of the critiques of his reform plans, saying, "When JFK and then Lyndon Johnson tried to pass Medicare, they said this was a government takeover of health care; they were going to get between you and your doctor—the same argument that's being made today" (Obama, 2009a).

11. See also C-SPAN (2002b) for this same argument.

12. As the purpose here was to see how Kennedy and his frames were portrayed in objective news sources that might reach a larger segment of the population, I did not include in the analysis articles from industry journals, press releases, abstracts, or editorial/opinion commentary. The U.S. news sources available and analyzed through Nexis Uni included print outlets, wire news services such as the

Associated Press, and nightly/cable news transcripts. The nine videos with the most health care content were C-SPAN 1988, 1990, 1991a, 1992c, 1993, 1994a, 1998a, 2002b, and 2002c.

13. There were, however, brief mentions of Kennedy in two articles between March 11 and March 13, 1991, and one article on March 24, 1993.

14. For a complete list of articles, please contact the author.

15. For instance, Senator Nancy Kassebaum (R-KS) quoted in Rich (1994).

REFERENCES

Altheide, D. L. (1976). *Creating reality: How TV news distorts events.* Sage Publications.

Bennett, W. L. (2005). *News: The politics of illusion* (6th ed.). Pearson Longman.

Berinsky, A. J. (2012). *Rumors, truth, and reality: A study of political misinformation. Massachusetts Institute of Technology* [Unpublished manuscript].

Callaghan, K., & Schnell, F. (2005). *Framing American politics.* University of Pittsburgh Press.

Cappella, J. A., & Jamieson, K. H. (1998). The role of the press in the health care reform debate of 1993-1994. In D. Graber, D. McQuall, & P. Norris (Eds.), *The politics of news, the news of politics* (pp. 110–131). CQ Press.

Chong, D., & Druckman, J. N. (2007a). Framing theory. *Annual Review of Political Science, 10,* 103–126. https://doi.org/10.1146/annurev.polisci.10.072805.103054

Chong, D., & Druckman, J. N. (2007b). A theory of framing and opinion formation in competitive elite environments. *Journal of Communication, 57*(1), 99–118. https://doi.org/10.1111/j.1460-2466.2006.00331.x

C-SPAN (Producer). (1988, January 28). *Access to health care* [Video]. https://www.c-span.org/video/?1117-1/access-health-care

C-SPAN (Producer). (1990, December 11). *Expanding access to health care* [Video]. https://www.c-span.org/video/?15470-1/expanding-access-health-care#!

C-SPAN (Producer). (1991a, March 12). *Health system reform by the year 2000?* [Video]. https://www.c-span.org/video/?17040-1/health-system-reform-year-2000

C-SPAN (Producer). (1991b, October 17). *Pepper Distinguished Service Award 1991* [Video]. https://www.c-span.org/video/?22115-1/pepper-distinguished-service-award

C-SPAN (Producer). (1992a, January 23). *U.S. urban issues* [Video]. https://www.c-span.org/video/?23949-1/us-urban-issues

C-SPAN (Producer). (1992b, February 6). *Health care reform response by senate Dem-*

ocrats [Video]. https://www.c-span.org/video/?24241-1/health-care-reform-res ponse-senate-democrats

C-SPAN (Producer). (1992c, April 27). *Health care reform* [Video]. https://www.c-span .org/video/?25767-1/health-care-reform

C-SPAN (Producer). (1992d, August 4). *Democratic health care proposal* [Video]. https://www.c-span.org/video/?30564-1/democratic-health- care-proposal

C-SPAN (Producer). (1993, March 24). *Presidential health care proposal issues* [Video]. https://www.c-span.org/video/?39677-1/presidential-health-care-proposal

C-SPAN (Producer). (1994a, May 11). *Health care reform* [Video]. https://www.c-span .org/video/?56743-1/health-care-reform

C-SPAN (Producer). (1994b, June 7). *Health care reform* [Video]. https://www.c-span .org/video/?57676-1/health-care-reform

C-SPAN (Producer). (1994c, June 22). *Health care reform* [Video]. https://www.c-span .org/video/?58134-1/health-care-reform

C-SPAN (Producer). (1994d, June 30). *Health care reform* [Video]. https://www.c-span .org/video/?58397-1/health-care-reform.

C-SPAN (Producer). (1996a, June 17). *New progressive agenda* [Video]. https://www .c-span.org/video/?74067-1/health-care-reform

C-SPAN (Producer). (1996b, August 1). *Health care reform* [Video]. https://www.c-span .org/video/?74067-1/health-care-reform.

C-SPAN (Producer). (1996c, August 21). *Health insurance reform signing* [Video]. https://www.c-span.org/video/?74511-1/health-insurance- reform-signing.

C-SPAN (Producer). (1998a, March 9). *Health care issues part 1* [Video]. https:// www.c-span.org/video/?101878-1/health-care-issues-part-1

C-SPAN (Producer). (1998b, June 24). *Democratic response to health care proposal* [Video]. https://www.c-span.org/video/?107873-1/democratic-response-health-care -proposal

C-SPAN (Producer). (1998c, July 10). *Senate minority leader* [Video]. https://www .c-span.org/video/?108512-1/senate-minority-leader

C-SPAN (Producer). (1999a, July 13). *Managed health care* [Video]. https://www.c-span .org/video/?150334-1/managed-health-care

C-SPAN (Producer). (1999b, July 13). *Senate minority leader news conference* [Video]. https://www.c-span.org/video/?150280-1/senate-minority-leader-news-con ference

C-SPAN (Producer). (2000, January 19). *Policy speech* [Video]. https://www.c-span .org/video/?154802-1/policy-speech

C-SPAN (Producer). (2001a, May 15). *Health care legislation* [Video]. https://www
.c-span.org/video/?164279-1/health-care-legislation

C-SPAN (Producer). (2001b, August 2). *Patients' bill of rights* [Video]. https://www
.c-span.org/video/?165501-1/patients-bill-rights

C-SPAN (Producer). (2002a, January 16). *Outlook for 2002* [Video]. https://www.c-span
.org/video/?168218-1/outlook-2002

C-SPAN (Producer). (2002b, April 28). *Future of health care* [Video]. https://www
.c-span.org/video/?169804-1/future-health-care

C-SPAN (Producer). (2002c, June 18). *Health care issues* [Video]. https://www.c-span
.org/video/?170665-1/health-care-issues

C-SPAN (Producer). (2003, April 28). *Medical issues* [Video]. https://www.c-span.org
/video/?176362-1/medical-issues

C-SPAN (Producer). (2006, February 1). *Health care reform rally* [Video]. https://www
.c-span.org/video/?191000-1/health-care-reform- rally

C-SPAN (Producer). (2008, August 25). *Tribute to Senator Kennedy 2008 convention*
[Video]. https://www.c-span.org/video/?280553-7/tribute-senator-kennedy-2008
-convention

C-SPAN (Producer). (2009, March 4). *White House Health Care Summit closing* [Video].
https://www.c-span.org/video/?284447-3/white-house-health-care-summit-closing

C-SPAN User-Created Clip. (2021a, October 17). *Clip of* Health Care Legislation (May
15, 2001); *User clip: Beancounter thousands of miles away* [C-SPAN user video clip].
https://www.c-span.org/video/?c4982134/user-clip-beancounter-thousands-miles

C-SPAN User-Created Clip. (2021b, October 17). *Clip of* White House Health Care Summit Closing (March 4, 2009); *User clip: Final 2009 WH summit* [C-SPAN user video
clip]. https://www.c-span.org/video/?c4982202/user-clip-final-2009-wh-summit

Diamond, J. (1992, April 28). Kennedy confronts insurers in health care speech. Associated Press.

"Echoes of Kennedy's battle with Nixon in health care debate." (2009, August 26). *News-
week*, https://www.newsweek.com/echoes-kennedys-battle-nixon-health-care
-debate-211550

Entman, R. M. (1991). Symposium framing United States coverage of international
news: Contrasts in narratives of the KAL and Iran Air incidents. *Journal of Communication, 41*(4), 6–27. https://doi.org/10.1111/j.1460-2466.1991.tb02328.x

Entman, R. M. (2004). *Projections of power: Framing news, public opinion, and U.S.
foreign policy.* University of Chicago Press.

Farrell, J. A. (2017). *Richard Nixon: The life.* Doubleday.

Freed, G. L. (2015). Nixon or Obama: Who is the real radical liberal on health care? *Pediatrics Perspectives, 136*(2), 211–214. https://doi.org/10.1542/peds.2015-1122

Furrow, B. R. (2011). Health reform and Ted Kennedy: The art of politics . . . and persistence. *New York University Journal of Legislation and Public Policy, 14*, 445–476.

Gabler, N. (2020). *Catching the wind: Edward Kennedy and the liberal hour, 1932–1975.* Crown.

Gallup. (2021). *Healthcare system.* Gallup Poll. https://news.gallup.com/poll/4708 /healthcare-system.aspx

Hacker, J. S. (2010). The road to somewhere: Why health reform happened—Or why political scientists who write about public policy shouldn't assume they know how to shape it. *Perspectives on Politics, 8*(3), 861–876. https://doi.org/10.1017 /S1537592710002021

Hopper, J. (2015). "Obamacare" and the politics of health care reform rhetoric. *International Journal of Communication, 9*, 1275–1299. https://ijoc.org/index.php/ijoc /article/viewFile/3187/1367

Hopper, J. (2017). *Presidential framing in the 21st century news media: The politics of the affordable care act.* Routledge.

Hopper, J. (2019, November 8). *Keeping up with Kennedy: President Nixon's efforts to co-opt and sell health care policy* [Paper presentation]. 51st Annual Meeting of the Northeastern Political Science Association, Philadelphia, PA.

Hopper J. (2020, September 13). *President Nixon, Senator Kennedy, & the battle for the health reform spotlight* [Paper presentation]. 116th Annual Meeting of the American Political Science Association, San Francisco, CA.

Jamieson, K. H., & Waldman, P. (2004). *The press effect: Politicians, journalists, and the stories that shape the political world.* Oxford University Press.

Kaiser Family Foundation (KFF). (1997, October 30). *Kaiser/Harvard national survey of Americans' views on managed care.* https://www.kff.org/health-costs/report /kaiserharvard-national-survey-of-americans-views-on-2/

Kaiser Family Foundation (KFF). (1999, September 30). *Race, ethnicity, and medical care: Improving access in a diverse society.* https://www.kff.org/racial-equity-and-health -policy/report/race-ethnicity-and-medical-care-improving-access/

Kaiser Family Foundation (KFF). (2009, April 1). *April 2009 health tracking poll.* https://www.kff.org/health-reform/poll-finding/april-2009-health-tracking-poll/

Kaiser Family Foundation (KFF). (2014, December 18). *Public easily swayed on attitudes about health law, poll finds.* https://khn.org/news/public-easily-swayed-on -attitudes-about-health-law-poll-finds/

Kaiser Family Foundation (KFF). (2020, October 16). *Public opinion on single-payer, national health plans, and expanding access to Medicare coverage.* https://www.kff.org/slideshow/public-opinion-on-single-payer-national-health-plans-and-expanding-access-to-medicare-coverage/

Kennedy, E. M. (1978, December 9). *Democratic National Committee workshop on health care.* https://www.emkinstitute.org/resources/democratic-national-committee-health-care

Kuypers, J. A. (2006). *Bush's war: Media bias and justifications for war in a terrorist age.* Rowman & Littlefield.

Kuypers, J. A. (Ed.). (2009). *Rhetorical criticism: Perspectives in action.* Lexington Books.

Kuypers, J. A., Cooper, S. D., & Althouse, M. T. (2012). George W. Bush, the American press, and the initial framing of the war on terror after 9/11. In R. E. Denton Jr. (Ed.), *The George W. Bush presidency: A rhetorical perspective* (pp. 89–112). Lexington Books.

Kuypers, J. A., & D'Angelo, P. (Eds.). (2010). *Doing news framing analysis: Empirical and theoretical perspectives.* Routledge.

Lakoff, G. (2004). *Don't think of an elephant! Know your values and frame the debate.* Chelsea Green Publishing.

Littlefield, N., & Nexon, D. (2015). *Lion of the Senate: When Ted Kennedy rallied the Democrats in a GOP congress.* Simon and Schuster.

Marmor, T. R. (2009). Senator Edward M. Kennedy: Making common cause with adversaries while committed to health reform. *Health Affairs, 28*(6), 1049–1051. https://doi.org/10.1377/hlthaff.28.6.w1049congress-health-care

Obama, B. (2009a, August 15). *Remarks by the president in town hall on health care Grand Junction Colorado* [Speech transcript]. Obama White House Archives. https://obamawhitehouse.archives.gov/the-press-office/remarks-president-town-hall-health-care-grand-junction-colorado

Obama, B. (2009b, September 9). *Remarks by the president to a joint session of Congress on health care* [Speech transcript]. Obama White House Archives. https://obamawhitehouse.archives.gov/the-press-office/remarks-president-a-joint-session-congress-health-care

Oberlander, J. (2019). Lessons from the long and winding road to Medicare for all. *American Journal of Public Health, 109*(11), 1497–1500. https://doi.org/10.2105/AJPH.2019.305295

Reagan, R. (Speaker). (2020, May 19). Socialized medicine [Audio podcast episode]. In *Words to live by*. Ronald Reagan Presidential Foundation and Institute. https://

www.reaganfoundation.org/programs-events/webcasts-and-podcasts/podcasts /words-to-live-by/socialized-medicine/

Reese, S. D., Gandy, O. H., Jr., & Grant, A. E. (2001). *Framing public life: perspectives on media and our understanding of the social world*. Lawrence Erlbaum Associates.

Rich, S. (1994, May 10). Kennedy changes health plan; Senator's version softens Clinton's key provision that small firms insure workers. *Washington Post*, A.1.

Schaffner, B. F., & Atkinson, M. L. (2010). Taxing death or estates? When frames influence citizens' issue beliefs. In B. F. Schaffner & P. Sellers (Eds.), *Winning with words: The origins and impact of political framing* (pp. 121–135). Routledge.

Schimmel, N. (2016). *Presidential healthcare reform rhetoric: Continuity, change, and contested values from Truman to Obama*. Palgrave Macmillan.

Skocpol, T. (1997). *Boomerang: Health care reform and the turn against government*. W. W. Norton.

Starr, P. (2013). *Remedy and reaction: The peculiar American struggle over health care reform*. Yale University Press.

Stockman, F. (2012, June 23). Recalling the Nixon-Kennedy health plan. *The Boston Globe*. https://www.bostonglobe.com/opinion/2012/06/22/stockman/bvg57mguQxOV pZMmB1Mg2N/story.html

Toner, R. (1993, September 22). Poll on changes in health care finds support amid skepticism. *New York Times*. https://www.nytimes.com/1993/09/22/us/clinton-s -health-plan-poll-changes-health-care-finds-support-amid-skepticism.html

Wainess, F. J. (1999). The ways and means of national health care reform, 1974 and beyond. *Journal of Health Politics, Policy, and Law, 24*(2), 305–333. https://doi.org /10.1215/03616878-24-2-305

Wolfsfeld, G. (1997). *Media and political conflict: News from the Middle East*. Cambridge University Press.

Wolfsfeld, G., & Sheafer, T. (2006). Competing actors and the construction of political news: The contest over waves in Israel. *Political Communication, 23*(3), 333–354. https://doi.org/10.1080/10584600600808927

Zarefsky, D. (2004). Presidential rhetoric and the power of definition. *Presidential Studies Quarterly, 34*, 607–619. https://doi.org/10.1111/j.1741-5705.2004.00214.x

5

VISUALIZING THE INCITEMENT OF INSURRECTION

A Content Analysis of Visual Symbols Used in Donald J. Trump's Second Impeachment Trial

Stephanie Wideman, Whitney Tipton, and Laura Merrifield Wilson

On January 6, 2021, pressure to hold outgoing President Trump accountable for his rhetoric peaked when a violent mob of the president's supporters attacked the U.S. Capitol after attending a pro-Trump rally, where President Trump delivered a fiery speech imploring his supporters to "fight." In this case, the insurrection was televised, and a nation weary from years of intense partisan divide and political rhetoric watched as the U.S. Capitol was violently desecrated by mobs of Americans calling for lawmakers to stop the vote on the certification of Joe Biden's presidential victory. In the aftermath of the insurrectionists' clash with Capitol police, five people were left dead and the nation and world were left with many questions, not the least of which was Who will be held accountable? Congress responded in the form of the second impeachment of Donald Trump by the U.S. House of Representatives. The House sent a single article of impeachment for "incitement of insurrection" against the U.S. government to the Senate. This move set the stage for a trial historic in that it is the first time a U.S. president was to be impeached a second time, as well as being the first post–presidential term impeachment.

The focus of the trial would be on accountability. For presidential researchers, the relationship between democracy and the media requires analysis of the ability of presidential rhetoric to obfuscate accountability. Jacobs and Schillemans (2016) highlight this role by explaining that "media can stimulate actors to reflect on their behaviour, trigger formal accountability by reporting on the behaviour of actors, [and] amplify formal accountability" (p. 1). However, in the case of President Trump's rhetoric, the very ability of the media and our government to hold Trump accountable was immediately called into question. Higgins (2019) attributes this query to President Trump's reliance on the mediatization of politics, claiming his reliance on this phenomenon results in a type of "'pseudo-presidency,' which confounds orthodox forms of political accountability" (p. 129). The trial commenced on February 9, 2021, with the prosecution playing a 13-minute video documenting the insurrection. "House impeachment managers recounted their experiences on January 6 in emotional terms" as they "sought to make senators relive their own near-misses with the mob that invaded the U.S. Capitol" (Kapur, 2021). The video provided even more visual evidence than was previously available to the public, including frantic officer calls for backup and a visual demonstration that tracked just how close the rioters came to encountering congressional members. Of particular spectacle was the video of Vice President Mike Pence being escorted out of the Capitol seconds before rioters chanting "Hang Mike Pence" reached his location.

The emotional experience of witnessing the failed insurrection in real time, and then viewing the subsequent trial a month later, constructed a particularly virulent rhetorical exigence. Pundits immediately pointed out that the potential for a conviction was pretty unlikely. Getting two-thirds to convict seemed implausible in the current political environment. However, whether this trial had the potential to hold Trump's presidential legacy accountable, or even act as a form of catharsis for a politically exhausted populace, remained to be seen. In that effort, the dominant reliance on imagery throughout the proceedings promotes examination of the role of visuals, both moving and still images, as a form of political argument in the process of impeachment, as well as the effort to shape public opinion on accountability. To that end, we conducted the following examination of the communication and political science literatures, followed by the use of content analysis of materials from the C-SPAN Video Library, to identify the ways in which visual rhetoric shaped the impeachment trial itself, as well as the public's view of the proceedings and the changing nature of the rhetorical presidency.

LITERATURE REVIEW

The Rhetorical Presidency

The concept of the "rhetorical presidency," or the argument that the real power of the presidency comes from a president's ability to communicate policy issues directly to the people, also known as the bully pulpit, offers great explanatory power to a wide range of disciplines. Prominent of these fields are the disciplines of political science and communication, as a president's use or misuse of the bully pulpit has implications for both the form and function of a government. For instance, in political science Tulis (1987) argues the rhetorical presidency is a 20th-century phenomenon wherein presidents utilize the available media of the day to bring policy clarity directly to the people. At the same time Tulis recognized the power of the bully pulpit, he warned of the potential danger that could come from pathos (emotion) being so readily imbued in our political discourse.

In the field of communication and rhetorical studies, fear of pathos has dissipated by recognizing the ubiquity of political emotion as inescapable force in presidential discourse (Erickson, 2000; Smith, 2007; Stuckey, 2010). In their foundational work, *Deeds Done in Words*, Campbell and Jamieson (1990) trace the roots of the rhetorical presidency to the framers of the Constitution. Essentially, they argue that the founders' reliance on the interaction between the three branches of government necessitates the study of that interaction through the lens of communication. It is within the interaction of the three branches that the communicative lens is situated. Essentially, if all branches are equal in power, then any policy decisions must be made through a series of negotiations fueled by complex persuasive messages. In fact, "there is widespread agreement that whatever the specific history of the rhetorical presidency, presidents in the contemporary era are quite willing to go over the heads of Congress and to attempt to mobilize the public as a routine means of governance" (Stuckey, 2010, p. 40).

Much of the development of our understanding of the potential of the rhetorical presidency has been shaped by the availability of media technology. Tulis (1987) marks the beginning of our modern rhetorical presidency as the Wilson administration and its use of radio, the first electronic mass media. References to FDR's Fireside Chats, the Nixon vs. Kennedy televised presidential debate, the advent of the 24/7 cable news cycle, and the Obama and Trump campaigns' use of social media reveal the important role of media in shaping presidential rhetorical style. "The presidency was once a carefully scripted and carefully controlled site of speech production. Today's media environment has not lessened efforts at control, but it has rendered these efforts increasingly more difficult" (McCormick & Stuckey, 2013, p. 3). Further, Stuckey (2010) reminds us we must continue to contend with the past and future of the rhetorical presidency as it is shaped by media:

> While the "rhetorical presidency," has been both accepted as a heuristic justifying the study of presidential speech on one hand and disputed as to its accuracy and utility on the other, this model assumes a white male president who governs within a pre-cable, pre-internet political context. (p. 38)

This study attempts to answer Stuckey's call and theorizes on the impact of a form of nonverbal persuasive communication that is virtually omnipresent in our cable news and social media-driven era: visual rhetoric.

The Visual Turn

Any attempt to theorize the utility of a visual rhetorical presidency requires that we track visual rhetoric's rise through rhetorical and argumentation studies. "Ours is a visual age. The image seems to have taken over the written word as we are confronted more than ever before with visuals in our everyday lives," (Foss, 1982, p. 55). What is important in this argument is not whether verbals or visuals reign supreme, but the acknowledgment that visual communication has gained relevance and brought with it a need for a better understanding of how we got here.
Mitchell (2005) argues:

> We do not live in a uniquely visual era. The "visual" or "pictorial turn" is a recurrent trope that displaces moral and political panic onto images and so-called visual media. Images are convenient scapegoats, and the offensive eye is ritually plucked out by the ruthless critique. (p. 343)

Advancements like the 24/7 news cycle and the dominance of social media have brought with them a reliance on the visual image. To account for the potential rhetorical impact, rhetorical studies have shifted to a renewed respect for the role of emotion, as disseminated in visual images, in shaping public discourse. Hariman and Lucaites (2002) attribute this shift to a recognition of the nature of constitutive rhetoric:

Like the art of rhetoric generally, visual media have been thought to be either irrelevant or dangerous with respect to democratic deliberation and the public use of reason.

Although part of a pervasive logocentrism in the Western academy, such objections also reflect assumptions about intentionality and influence that recently have been displaced by theoretical claims about the constitutive function of public discourse. (p. 364)

Constitutive rhetoric is derived from the work of Charland (1987), who drew from Kenneth Burke's concept of identification as permitting "a rethinking of judgment and the working of rhetorical effect, for [the rhetor] does not posit a transcendent subject as an audience member . . . but considers audience members to participate in the very discourse by which they would be persuaded" (p. 133). Essentially, meaning is created not by the rhetor alone, but instead through a complicated interaction between rhetoric and audience. It is in this process where the negotiation between Aristotle's rhetorical proofs relies heavily on pathos. Hariman and Lucaites (2002) situate this power within the arena of politics and our collective civic education:

The daily stream of images in the public media, although merely supplemental to reporting the news, define the public through an act of common spectatorship. All viewers seem to see the same thing. When the event shown is itself a part of national life, the public seems to see itself, and to see itself in terms of a particular conception of civic identity. (p. 365)

A visual turn in rhetorical studies

Early visual analysis borrowed from theoretical frameworks in semiotics, aesthetic theory, and visual design. Rhetorical scholars created a place for the visual in communication studies by arguing:

Not every visual object is a visual rhetoric. What turns a visual object into a communicative artifact—a symbol that communicates and [can] be studied as rhetoric—is the presence of three characteristics. . . . The image must be symbolic, involve human intervention and be presented to an audience for the purpose of communicating with that audience. (Foss, 2004, p. 144)

At the foundational level visual rhetoric is understood through the term "image." Image is a purposefully ambiguous concept, without clear or definite boundaries, the meaning of which is continually complicated by subject, spectator, and author. Analytical preference suggests the power of the image comes from its ability to entice the spectator to interact with it. It is commonplace to view the image as a window or a portal into another world; similarly, the power of the study of visual rhetoric is to allow the analyst to see the image as a frame or lens for interpreting and engaging that world.

In the United States, "research into visual rhetoric has flourished in colleges and universities for over half a century now," with these 50-plus years of scholarship resulting in a vocabulary of visual terminology (Olson, 2007, p. 1). Students are often introduced to visual rhetoric within the following classification: visuals can operate rhetorically in three primary ways—iconically, indexically, or symbolically (Sellnow, 2018, pp. 30–31). Icon images are images that visually remind you of something else by means of resemblance. Index images communicate by referring to other meanings by general association. Images operate symbolically by connecting themselves to socially constructed symbols and meanings. These classifications situate the visual well within the purview of rhetorical studies and can be extended to the conceptualization of the visual in argumentation studies.

A visual turn in argumentation studies

"Despite widespread agreement on the importance of visual rhetoric, the role of visual rhetoric within argumentation studies is questioned primarily due to a presumption that a visual cannot argue in the same sense as verbal arguments" (Wideman, 2017, p. 91). Scholars such as Fleming (1996) have asserted that including the visual as a form of argument would unjustifiably expand argumentation studies due to an image's lack of a capacity to engage in oppositional argumentation. Basically, they are saying a visual artifact cannot respond to propositional claims. However, Fleming's argument dismisses the capacity of images to interact with audiences as seen within the concept of constitutive rhetoric.

A more productive way to analyze images as argument is to return to neo-Aristotelian terms. Returning to Aristotle's (2006) initial classification of the means through which we come to be persuaded invokes the rhetorical proofs: ethos (credibility), pathos (emotion), and logos (logic). Notably, Aristotle never articulated a preference for one proof over the other. In fact, his only instructions on the potency of each rhetorical proof was to use the one "most appropri-ate" for the audience and occasion. Instead, the degradation of pathos in per-suasive decision-making arose in subsequent years, most notably during the Enlightenment, when scientific methodology relied on logos. While pathos may have fallen out of fashion during the Enlightenment period of Western knowledge-making, it has since gained back its momentum as theorists attempt to contend with our modern means of political rhetoric. While it may be true that discursive rhetoric is needed to track the flow of oppositional argument for posterity, this does not mean that visual argument, and thus pathos, is not hav-ing a strong impact on an image's audience in real time. It is precisely in the in-teraction with an image that one's ethos, logos, and pathos are forced to interact. We can further see the utility of visual rhetoric for argument studies by looking at Aristotle's classification of rhetorical devices.

The enthymeme is a rhetorical device wherein one premise of an argument is suppressed in a manner that allows the audience to contribute to argumenta-tion. Smith (2007) explains: "When the enthymeme is understood more broadly, visual communication can be classified as argumentation, thus enhancing the credibility of visual persuasion" (p. 114). It is a particularly potent tool of politi-cal rhetoric in that it allows a politician to say something—without really saying it. The enthymeme's rhetorical prowess is that it allows the audience to finish the argument for themselves.

Enthymematic potential is closely tied to ideology in that the emotional el-ement of the enthymeme assists in reflecting and shaping one's ideological per-spective. Ideology is loosely defined as a set of ideas about the world that become so potent, they shape a group's identity. Both discursive and visual rhetoric stud-ies aim to track ideology through the identification of ideographs, an abstract concept commonly used in the political sphere wherein an image has a unique potential to communicate ideology. The reliance on the ideograph in visual stud-ies speaks to the enthymematic nature of visual argument as well as the need to focus on the way images may speak to the collective. Condit and Lucaites (1993) put forth that "the ideological content or meaning of an ideograph can shift over time in response to historical exigencies and struggle among groups attempting to claim the ideograph" (p. 2).

The potential for theories related to rhetorical proofs, rhetorical devices like the enthymeme, and the function of the ideograph provides a potent framework for further situating visual rhetoric as a productive means to better understand political argument and the rhetorical presidency in our modern world. In 2012

Schill, advanced this avenue by offering a review of visual communication research in the field of political communication. His work organized a typology that examines the functions of visual rhetoric in the political sphere. Schill (2012) reasons that "the most important function of images in political communication is that they can have rhetorical impact and make persuasive arguments" (p. 122). Of his typology, he contends:

> Our current understanding of images suggests visual symbols have 10 important functions in politics: they serve as arguments, have an agenda setting function, dramatize policy, aid in emotional appeals, build the candidate's image, create identification, provide documentation, connect to societal symbols, transport the audience, and add ambiguity. (p. 122)

Schill's thesis advocates for a need to advance our understanding of these forms of argument. This study aims to do that by applying our current understanding of the role of visuals in political argument to a unique rhetorical exigence in presidential rhetoric: the second impeachment of President Donald J. Trump. This impeachment is rhetorically significant in a number of ways: the fact that it is the first time a president has been impeached a second time, the high level of media coverage following the spectacle of the January 6 insurrection, and the realities of engaging in rhetorical argument within the confines of legalized impeachment procedure. All of these factors have the potential to have a dramatic effect on our understanding of the rhetorical presidency as well as the means through which a president can be held accountable.

The Rhetorical Presidency, Accountability, and Public Opinion

Present scholarship demonstrates the importance of public opinion, rhetoric, and perception in impeachment hearings, as well as the larger impact they can have on the legacy of the president in question. Skowronek (1997) and Neustadt (1991) have long argued the importance of the president in shaping the public perception of his administration. Ceaser et al. (1981) noted the importance rhetoric and language played in how the president appealed to constituents, remarking that "popular or mass rhetoric, which Presidents once employed only rarely, now serves as one of their principal tools in attempting to govern a nation." In an era before social media, let alone the internet and 24/7 news cycle, the recognition of the president's ability to influence public opinion through rhetoric was a revolutionary concept and its essential argument remains as valid as ever (Crockett, 2003; Laracey, 2009; Lim, 2002; Stuckey, 2010).

More recent literature expands on this by examining the effect of Donald Trump's first impeachment on his public approval. The value of the president's public appeal can have a significant impact on his status within the party and in relationship to other leaders, determining whether he can pass his programs, set a legislative agenda, and promote a strong coattail effect for those within his party (Jacobson, 2020). Howell et al. (2017) found that using ritual and symbolism can help a president's appeal to the public. Significantly, they also note that the visual elements of these performances, rather than the content, were most the influential. During Trump's first impeachment trial, the use of symbolism played an essential role in the questions of constitutionality and the legitimacy in the questions of impeachment and removal (Goldstein, 2020).

Concurrent research in the field of rhetoric and communication builds upon a recognition of what Erickson (2000) calls the visual turn in presidential rhetoric. According to Erickson, "presidents stage photo-opportunities to influence, manipulate, entreat, entice, amaze, or otherwise assume power over witnesses" (p. 139). Crucial to this reality is an acceptance of the contention that witnesses tend to believe what they see rather than what they hear when presented with argument forms. In their study of the utilization of political imagery on television, Grabe and Bucy (2009) assert that "granting visuals their deserved status as reliable forms of political information requires somewhat of a paradigm shift in thinking about television news and democracy" (p. vii). Given the growing importance of visual imagery in the digital age, it is critical that we examine its usage in the impeachment trial of Donald J. Trump.

After reviewing the extant literature and experiencing the highly visual impeachment proceedings, we developed the following research questions.

RQ1: Into which categories of visual communication do the visual aids used in impeachment proceedings fall?

RQ2: What additional categories of visual political communication are present in impeachment proceedings?

RQ3: To what degree do visual aids align with the verbal arguments used in impeachment proceedings?

METHODS

In the present study, we analyzed the purpose of visual aids used in the second impeachment trial of Donald J. Trump. Speakers for both the House Judiciary Committee and the defense used visual aids to support their arguments. Examples of visual aids used include video of speeches, video of protestors using violence in the Capitol, images of tweets, photographs, images from the Constitution of the United States, a physical copy of *Quotations From Chairman Mao Tse-tung* by Mao Zedong, former chairman of the Chinese Communist Party, and images of testimony from various legal proceedings related to the case. All speakers relied heavily on the act of highlighting or circling relevant words or symbols within the images or video as a way of supporting their arguments.

Our process combined quantitative and qualitative elements. Quantitatively, we collected frequency counts of the types of visual symbols used and compared the frequencies of symbols used between parties. Qualitatively, we analyzed the relationships between the visual symbols used and the political and rhetorical strategies used. To support our qualitative analysis, we took notes on the verbal arguments used alongside each of the visual aids. We noted the content of the argument, significant quotes, and whether the verbal and visual arguments were congruent with one another. We followed Brown and Gershon's (2016) recommendations for using qualitative thematic analysis to "flesh out" the quantitative data described below. By analyzing the content of the arguments and symbolic purpose of the visual aids and relating the symbols to the relevant literature, we were able to capture important differences in frequency and the use of specific arguments, as well as new symbolic functions for the symbols.

Sample and Procedures

Our original sample consisted of 805 video clips from the impeachment proceedings stored in the C-SPAN Video Library. To obtain our sample, one author initially watched the entire impeachment proceedings and documented the timestamps when a visual aid was used. We developed a codebook of demographic data related to the speakers (party affiliation, date and time of speech) as well as descriptions for each of the 10 uses of visual symbols from Schill's (2012) typology. The codebook was then adapted into a Qualtrics survey.

Next we discussed and refined code descriptions. Then, to begin the coding process and ensure high intercoder agreement, we first coded 10% of the sample (randomly selected using a random number generator) independently and concurrently. After coding the initial 10%, our percent agreement was 79.8%. Percent agreement is an appropriate measure of agreement when dealing with nominal variables and when high agreement is expected. (Contrasted with Krippendorf's alpha or Cohen's kappa, which expect a certain level of disagreement). To strengthen our percent agreement, the authors discussed 15 instances of disagreement and came to a consensus based on examples from the literature. After this, our percent agreement was 92.4%. Per Nurjannah and Siwi (2017), percent agreement greater than 80% is acceptable, and over 90% is considered strong.

After achieving a strong percent agreement, we divided the remaining data into thirds and independently coded our assigned visual aids. Some visual aids were excluded from analysis. For example, a PowerPoint slide that contained only a table of contents or a statement about the schedule of events was not considered a symbolic visual aid used to support arguments. We also counted some video montages as a single unit of analysis, even though they were broken into smaller pieces. For example, a montage showing 12 different politicians using the word "fight" was counted as 1 unit, rather than 12, because the rhetorical aims for the videos were the same. After eliminating redundant or purely procedural data, we were left with a sample of 706 visual aids.

Frequency Results

In total, 11 individuals used visual aids during the impeachment proceedings. Table 5.1 lists their names, affiliations, and number of visual aids used. Nine of the individuals who used visual aids were House impeachment managers, while two were defense attorneys for President Trump.

Using Schill's (2012) typology of the symbolic uses of visual aids, we identified the primary uses of each visual aid used in the impeachment proceedings. Visual aids are used to make visual arguments, set the agenda, dramatize policy, produce an emotional response in the audience, construct the political image of the speaker, foster identification between the politician and the audience, document events, evoke societal symbols, transport the audience to a different setting, and increase the ambiguity of unpopular messages. Table 5.2 answers research question 1: *Into which categories of visual communication do the visual aids used in impeachment proceedings fall?* Our analysis revealed the frequency count shown in this table for each use of visual aids.

TABLE 5.1 *Number of Visual Aids Used per Speaker*

Speaker name	Affiliation	Number of visual aids used
Jamie Raskin	Democrat	46
Joe Neguse	Democrat	57
Madeleine Dean	Democrat	71
Ted Lieu	Democrat	36
Stacy Plaskett	Democrat	69
Eric Swalwell	Democrat	51
Joaquin Castro	Democrat	60
Diana DeGette	Democrat	48
David Cicilline	Democrat	62
Michael van der Veen	President's defense	77
David Schoen	President's defense	127

Prosecution number of visual aids = 500

Defense number of visual aids = 204

TABLE 5.2 *Frequency of Symbolic Functions of Visual Aids*

Symbolic function of visual aid	Frequency
To make visual arguments	324
To set the agenda	11
To dramatize policy	120
To produce an emotional response in the audience	39
To construct the political image of the speaker	1
To foster identification between the politician and the audience	0
To document events	181
To evoke societal symbols	13
To transport the audience to a different setting	10
To increase the ambiguity of unpopular messages	7

The most frequently used purpose among both the House impeachment managers and the former president's defense attorneys was the use of symbols to make a visual argument. We found 324 instances of this symbolic function total, with

96 coming from the defense and 228 coming from the House impeachment managers. According to Schill (2012), as well as Birdsell and Groarke (1996), a visual symbol's ability to persuade is one of its most powerful features.

Images are used as an enthymeme, and those watching are expected to make connections and fill in the gaps between the argument and the visual symbol using historical and social knowledge.

As shown in Table 5.2, the least used functions of visual aids include using them to construct the image of the speaker (one instance by David Schoen), and to increase the ambiguity of unpopular messages (six instances by Michael van der Veen and one by Ted Lieu). Because the focus of the trial was a single article of impeachment—inciting insurrection—this is an expected finding.

The top three utilized forms of symbolic argument (making visual argument, documentation, and dramatizing policy) compared to the bottom three utilized forms of symbolic argument (identification between politician and audience, construct political image of speaker, and increase ambiguity of messages) are not surprising as they reflect a highly polarized audience wherein most people had already solidified their opinion of the events of January 6 and the actors involved.

Our second research question was *What additional categories of visual political communication are present in impeachment proceedings?* To answer this question, we included a section in our Qualtrics survey to add notes about potential new argument functions. We identified one new function and one new sub-function; these visual aids also served additional functions from the original typology (e.g., to make visual arguments, but in ways not fully explored in the extant literature).

The preemption function

Primarily used by House impeachment managers, the preemption function served to disempower Republican ethos and arguments in favor of the president's acquittal by using tweets, video, audio, and written statements by other Republicans to support an argument by the House impeachment managers. For example, House impeachment managers used words from Marco Rubio, Pat Fallon, and other Republicans stating unequivocally that President Trump was responsible for the January 6 attack (Wideman, 2021b).

The compilation sub-function

Used by both sides, the compilation sub-function used the rhetorical device of repetition to support the primary function of the image. Rhetors compiled multiple instances of the same action in the form of audio, video, or image to give strength to their argument through sheer quantity. For example, David Schoen used a video compilation that was more than nine minutes long. In this compilation, he showed video of many Democrats using the word "fight" over and over, to make the argument that both sides used the same rhetoric and can't be blamed for its outcome. This finding was unique because it was used to support a variety of other functions, including documenting events, making visual arguments, and evoking emotional responses. Additionally, it highlights a strategic choice on the part of the defense to counter the breadth of visual evidence presented by the prosecution, with a depth of visual evidence in the form of image compilations (Wideman, 2021a).

Our final research question was *To what degree do visual aids align with the verbal arguments used in impeachment proceedings?* To answer this question, we noted and considered the verbal arguments accompanying the visual aids. In total, we found only 12 instances in which the verbal and visual arguments were not congruent. In 3 of these cases, it appeared to be an issue of timing the slides. In the remaining cases, speakers appeared to use video or images from unrelated cases to support their argument. For example, in David Schoen's "fight" montage, clips of Greta Thunberg and Nancy Rosen are used, but they are not talking about electoral fights in the way that others in the montage are.

While the numerical findings are important, our discussion extends these findings to examine the implications of new visual rhetoric strategies in the area of impeachment trials.

DISCUSSION

Rhetorical Implications

At the outset of this project, we expected to find overlap in Schill's (2012) typology. This is common to explorations of genre and form in rhetoric. However, what was revealing is the potential that emotion has in motivating Schill's topoi. It appears that emotion acts as a through line between each of the categories. This is prominently seen in the function of dramatization, but it can also be seen in the creation of a visual argument. The dominance of these two concurrent functions in the data suggest that one is motivating the other, or at least there is a correlation. At present, we hypothesize that the relationship could be reflective of the capacity of visuals to invoke emotion and audience interaction. This is demonstrated through the enthymematic function of visual images. As previously discussed, visual argument operates enthymematically by offering visual premises and inviting the audience to supply the suppressed claim or conclusion. This audience interaction is a prime sight for emotion to be activated and negotiated in civic discourse. Further exploration is needed, but the findings appear to support the inclusion of visual artifacts as elements of argumentation as well as the need for further exploration into the ubiquity of emotional political rhetoric.

Rhetorical Presidency Implications

When Ceaser et al. (1981) argued that the "new way" of presidential rhetoric emphasized communicating with the public rather than internally to members of Congress, they noted that visual symbols and imagery could enhance the president's argument and approach. What the authors could have likely never imagined is just how impactful visual aids and communicating directly to the people could be for a president. Ceaser et al. wrote at the beginning of the first term of the Reagan administration about the "new" approach presidents used to reach out directly to the people. As the idea of going public became more socially acceptable and effective for presidents, the leaders of the nation continued to pursue this strategy from the end of the 20th century and into the first three administrations of the 21st.

What remains less clear, however, is whether we have reached a limitation within this approach. The concept itself sounds inherently democratic—an elected leader is appealing directly to the people—and seems initially hard to critique. Following the Trump administration, and specifically the January 6 insurrection and the impeachment proceedings that followed, the potential harm of this approach is evident. Before instant and immediate access directly to the public through a social media platform, presidents were reliant on a passive approach in communication, using traditional news sources. They would transmit the narrative and strategize different times and angles with the hope that the public would be receptive. Barack Obama may have been the first social media president, but Donald Trump utilized the medium in a way unlike that of any politician of his time. He used it as a personal megaphone to directly and immediately connect with his supporters. It was "going public" (to generously borrow from the famed Tulis et al. phrase) in a way no one had or even really could before. This strategy gave the president access to followers in a unique way. This power is accompanied by tremendous responsibility, which essentially became the thesis argument of both the House impeachment managers and the defense in Trump's second impeachment trial of February 2021. Did the President cause or incite the violence? More aptly, to what extent is he responsible? By applying a massive arsenal of images, videos, headlines, legal documents, and social media artifacts, both sides of the argument on whether to convict President Donald J. Trump of removal through impeachment used every type of media at their disposal. Who was responsible, who was guilty, and of what were all central thematic questions posed, with widely different answers based on the perspectives of the side being argued.

Regardless of where one stands on the outcome, the centrality of the role visual imagery and communication played is clear. Going public can have great costs and benefits. To employ the method recklessly with interest only in the latter and forgoing the former lends to an unwieldy use of power. Democratic principles require tolerance of opposing perspectives, consensus on procedures and process, trust in the system and those who uphold it, and a general understanding or appreciation for the balance of pluralist government. It is ironic that, in utilizing this newer strategy and approach, the influence of the founding fathers and their ideas and aims were often interjected in the impeachment hearings accompanied by questions of their intent in procedure and principle. The risk of this outward communication strategy quite literally jeopardized American democracy at a moment in time when its future was not certain. The catalyst provoking such a volatile challenge involved the method and messages communicated by the president. The impeachment trial of February 2021 relied on an unprecedented breadth and depth in visual imagery to resonate with the audience (both the senators actually involved in the trial as jurors but also the public who followed attentively). Both sides made impassioned arguments through visual mediums and reinforced the power of such political communication. Though both the administration and trial have concluded, the message about the potential and foreseeable power, risk, and harm of utilizing an external, public approach in messaging has proven to be an important reminder in American history about the fragility of institutions and the power of those who occupy them.

REFERENCES

Aristotle. (2006). *On rhetoric: A theory of civic discourse* (G. A. Kennedy, Trans.; 2nd ed.). Oxford University Press.

Birdsell, D. S., & Groarke, L. (1996). Toward a theory of visual argument. *Argumentation and Advocacy*, *33*, 1–10.

Brown, N. E., & Gershon, S. A. (2016). Protecting (which?) women: A content analysis of the House floor debate on the 2012 reauthorization of the Violence Against Women Act. In Browning, R. X. (Ed.), *The year in C-SPAN archives research* (pp. 173–218). Purdue University Press. https://docs.lib.purdue.edu/ccse/vol3/iss1/1

Campbell, K. K., & Jamieson, K. H. (1990). *Deeds done in words: Presidential rhetoric and the genres of governance.* University of Chicago Press.

Ceaser, J. W., Thurow, G. E., Tulis, J., & Bessette, J. M. (1981). The rise of the rhetorical presidency. *Presidential Studies Quarterly, 11*(2), 158–171.

Charland, M. (1987). Constitutive rhetoric: The case of the *peuple québécois. Quarterly Journal of Speech, 78*(2), 133–150. https://doi.org/10.1080/00335638709383799

Condit, C. M., & Lucaites, J. L. (1993). *Crafting equality: America's Anglo-African word.* University of Chicago Press.

Crockett, D. A. (2003). George W. Bush and the unrhetorical rhetorical presidency. *Rhetoric & Public Affairs, 6*(3), 465–486.

Erickson, K. V. (2000). Presidential rhetoric's visual turn: Performance fragments and the politics of illusionism. *Communication Monographs, 67*(2), 138–157. https://doi.org/10.1080/03637750009376501

Fleming, D. (1996). Can pictures be arguments? *Argumentation & Advocacy, 33*(1), 11–22.

Foss, S. K. (1982). Rhetoric and the visual image: A resource unit. *Communication Education, 31*(1), 55–67. https://doi.org/10.1080/03634528209384659

Foss, S. K. (2004). Theory of visual rhetoric. In K. L. Smith, S. Moriarty, K. Kenney, & G. Barbatsis (Eds.), *Handbook of visual communication: Theory, methods, and media* (pp. 142–152). Routledge.

Goldstein, J. K. (2020). *The Senate, the Trump impeachment trial and constitutional morality.* Chicago-Kent Law Review, *95*, 475. https://scholarship.kentlaw.iit.edu/cklawreview/vol95/iss2/3

Grabe, M. E., & Bucy, E. P. (2009). *Image bite politics: News and the visual framing of elections.* Oxford University Press.

Hariman, R., & Lucaites, J. L. (2002). Performing civic identity: The iconic photograph of the flag raising on Iwo Jima. *Quarterly Journal of Speech, 88*(2), 363–392. https://doi.org/10.1080/00335630209384385

Higgins, M. (2019). The Donald: Media, celebrity, authenticity, and accountability. In C. Happer, A. Hoskins, & W. Merrin (Eds.). *Trump's media war.* Palgrave Macmillan, Cham. https://doi.org/10.1007/978-3-319-94069-4_9

Howell, W. G., Porter, E., & Wood, T. (2017). *Making a president: Performance, public opinion, and the (temporary) transmutation of Donald J. Trump.* SSRN. https://doi.org/10.2139/ssrn.3111903

Jacobs, S., & Schillemans, T. (2016). Media and public accountability: Typology and exploration. *Policy and Politics*, *44*(1), 23–40. https://doi.org/10.1332/030557315X14431855320366

Jacobson, G. C. (2020). Donald Trump and the parties: Impeachment, pandemic, protest, and electoral politics in 2020. *Presidential Studies Quarterly*, *50*(4), 762–795.

Kapur, S. (2021, February 10). *"Harsh reminder": Key takeaways from day two of Trump's second impeachment trial*. NBC News. https://www.nbcnews.com/politics/donald-trump/harsh-reminder-key-takeaways-day-two-trump-s-second-impeachment-n1257347

Laracey, M. (2009). *The Rhetorical Presidency* today: How does it stand up? *Presidential Studies Quarterly*, *39*(4), 908–931. https://doi.org/10.1111/j.1741-5705.2009.03714.x

Lim, E. T. (2002). Five trends in presidential rhetoric: An analysis of rhetoric from George Washington to Bill Clinton. *Presidential Studies Quarterly*, *32*(2), 328–348. https://doi.org/10.1111/j.0360-4918.2002.00223.x

McCormick, S., & Stuckey, M. (2013). Presidential disfluency: Literacy, legibility, and vocal political aesthetics in the rhetorical presidency. *Review of Communication*, *13*(1), 3–22. https://doi.org/10.1080/15358593.2012.760034

Mitchell, W. J. (2005). *What do pictures want?* University of Chicago Press.

Neustadt, R. E. (1991). *Presidential power and the modern presidents: The politics of leadership from Roosevelt to Reagan*. Simon and Schuster.

Nurjannah, I., & Siwi, S. M. (2017). Guidelines for analysis on measuring interrater reliability of nursing outcome classification. *International Journal of Research in Medical Sciences*, *5*(4), 1169. https://doi.org/10.18203/2320-6012.ijrms20171220

Olson, L. (2007). Intellectual and conceptual resources for visual rhetoric: A reexamination of scholarship since 1950. *Review of Communication*, *7*(1), 1–20. https://doi.org/10.1080/15358590701211035

Schill, D. (2012). The visual image and the political image: A review of visual communication research in the field of political communication. *Review of Communication*, *12*(2), 118–142. https://doi.org/10.1080/15358593.2011.653504

Sellnow, D. (2018). *The rhetoric of popular culture: Considering mediated texts*. Sage Publications.

Skowronek, S. (1997). *The politics presidents make: Leadership from John Adams to Bill Clinton*. Harvard University Press.

Smith, V. J. (2007). Aristotle's classical enthymeme and the visual argumentation of the twenty-first century. *Argumentation & Advocacy*, *43*(3/4), 114–123. https://doi.org/10.1080/00028533.2007.11821667

Stuckey, M. E. (2010). Rethinking the rhetorical presidency. *Review of Communication*, *10*(1), 38–52. https://doi.org/10.1080/15358590903248744

Tulis, J. K. (1987). *The rhetorical presidency*. Princeton University Press.

Wideman, S. L. (2017). *Pathetic politics: An analysis of emotion and embodiment in First Lady rhetoric* [Dissertation, Wayne State University]. https://digitalcommons.wayne.edu/oa_dissertations/1753

Wideman, S. L. [Widemans]. (2021a, October 17). *Clip of* Impeachment Trial, Day 4, Part 1 (February 12, 2021); *User clip: Fighting words from defense* [C-SPAN user video clip]. https://www.c-span.org/video/?c4982201/user-clip-fighting-words-defense

Wideman, S. L. [Widemans]. (2021b, October 17). *Clip of* Senate Impeachment Trial Day 2, Part 4 (February 10, 2021); *User clip: Pre-emptive function* [C-SPAN user video clip]. https://www.c-span.org/video/?c4982215/user-clip-pre-emptive-function

6

CONGRESSIONAL COMMITTEE HEARINGS AS PUBLIC SPECTACLE

Joshua Guitar, Sheri Bleam, Jenna Thomas, Madeline Studebaker, and Matthew George

INTRODUCTION

Whether Senator Bernie Sanders (I-VT) is calmly thanking C-SPAN for its presence (C-SPAN, 2014), or U.S. Supreme Court Justice nominee Brett Kavanaugh (now appointed) is emphatically lamenting the "media circus" surrounding his nomination (C-SPAN, 2018c), the rhetorical appeals within U.S. congressional hearings indicate constant media attention. Through the actions and utterances of those present, many congressional hearings transform from rudimentary deliberations to a mediated public spectacle. Our research here traces and evaluates the rhetorical patterns that inform this transformation.

As public hearings and testimonies within congressional committees have increasingly evolved into media spectacles, rhetorical performances manifest in a variety of identifiable forms. In some cases, like the Senate Judiciary Committee's confirmation hearing of Kavanaugh (C-SPAN, 2018c, 2018d), heated partisan posturing informs extensive public polemics. While the Kavanaugh hearings sparked fierce civic debates, the persuasive appeals proved to have a minor impact on the Senate's decision and only delayed the inevitability of Kavanaugh's confirmation by the Republican-led chamber. In other hearings, like media pundit Jon Stewart's 2019 plea alongside various September 11, 2001, first responders to the House of Representatives Judiciary Subcommittee on the Constitution, Civil

Rights, and Civil Liberties (C-SPAN, 2019d), mediated orations clearly influence legislation. In Stewart's case, the Never Forget the Heroes Act, which was set to expire at the end of 2020, was unanimously approved to extend through 2090.

Yet on other occasions, hearings function in an exploratory fashion, vaguely constructed as interrogative events centered upon contemporary public concerns. Recently, for example, media coverage has fixated on congressional hearings involving noteworthy public agents like Dr. Anthony Fauci, director of the National Institute of Allergy and Infectious Diseases, regarding the SARS-CoV-2 pandemic (e.g., C-SPAN, 2021e) and Mark Zuckerberg, cofounder and chief executive officer of Facebook (parent company now Meta Platforms), on internet censorship matters (e.g., C-SPAN, 2018a). Updates of committee hearings are often shared across social media platforms as they occur, demonstrating how invested the public becomes in these media spectacles (Vynck et al., 2021). In these iterations, members of Congress pose more as investigators than legislators.

Certainly it is difficult to identify the exact genesis of this phenomenon. Congressional hearings have always been engaged through the available media within their respective eras. Yet for as cringeworthy as the Army–McCarthy hearings were in the middle of the 20th century, the present bombardment of audio and video bites from congressional hearings saturating political discourse overwhelms the public forum in entirely new ways. Whether due to contemporary technological advancements or the progressively abrasive polemics of the current political climate, congressional hearings often transform into a media spectacle.

In recognizing that congressional hearings inform a significant portion of contemporary political discourse, we assume the task of theorizing the patterns of persuasive appeals within the confines of congressional hearings. Overall, while these committee hearings and testimonies are not new, their increasing media exposure obliges the attention of rhetoricians. Despite the regularity of congressional hearings attracting public attention, there remains a dearth of knowledge in this realm. Our research addresses this void and seeks to better understand how mediated congressional hearings influence public discourse.

In reviewing prominent congressional hearings that have captivated the public's attention in recent decades, we have formulated a genre of congressional hearing as public spectacle. Our essay first outlines academic literature informing our project. We then discuss our procedures for aggregating and evaluating our data. We employ genre critique, a method of rhetorical criticism, to identify and understand patterns of rhetorical behaviors within congressional hearings. Through our analysis, we identify and explain the generic components of rhetorical addresses that foster and respond to "the spectacular" within congressional hearings.

The essay concludes by discussing the implications of these findings. We theorize that these congressional hearing spectacles operate as a response to the continued elevation of the executive branch as an attempt to resituate and reaffirm legislative power. Also, we posit that despite the causticity of many of these present public spectacles, media coverage of these congressional hearings, especially through platforms like C-SPAN, serves vital democratic functions.

CONTEXT

Arguably, congressional hearings have always, to some extent, informed public spectacle, as can be seen from the historical documents of the First Continental Congress. In one instance, the Marine Committee's hearing in 1777 regarding complaints about Esek Hopkins, the first commodore of the Continental Navy, resulted in dramatic legal battles between Hopkins and some of his former sailors (Guitar, 2021). Despite the limitations of media at the time, the spectacle was still historicized.

With each development of recent technology, congressional hearings achieve greater salience in the mediated public forum. Although newspaper coverage of congressional hearings has been a staple throughout U.S. history, Congress was hesitant to welcome other forms of media into its proceedings. During the 20th century, Congress slowly accepted radio broadcasts of congressional events, waiting until 1970 to formally allow live radio broadcasts of congressional hearings. Similarly, Congress remained hesitant to accept television technology into its formal happenings (U.S. House of Representatives, n.d.). Today's media spectacle of congressional hearings was foreshadowed in the 1950s, as the political and public spheres intersected on television in the Army–McCarthy hearings. In allowing the public to view the previously inaccessible hearings, the media facilitated a surge in public investment in congressional hearings. Predicting that McCarthy would fail in front of the camera, Senator Lyndon Johnson (D-TX) and President Dwight Eisenhower encouraged its televised broadcast. For the first time on television, the public became privy to the political drama of Congress and largely concluded that McCarthy was a "vindictive bully" (Mansky, 2017; Troy, 2015). Thus, while mediated hearings can certainly humanize congresspersons and attendees, it also can facilitate their villainization.

Eventually, television media afforded access to congressional hearings, which became particularly prominent with the formation of C-SPAN in 1979. Certainly, as well, the development of cable news and the 24-hour news cycle, through networks like CNN, increased public access to congressional hearings. Most recently, the advent of new media and social media platforms has exponentially proliferated the capacity of the public to consume congressional hearings.

In addition to technological advancements, the growing interest in congressional hearings corresponds with the increasing regularity of spectacular events in these hearings. Major events like the Watergate hearings in 1973 and the House Judiciary Committee's 1974 impeachment inquiry of President Richard Nixon demanded the public's attention. Similar public attention centered on the Senate confirmation hearing of U.S. Supreme Court justice Clarence Thomas in 1991, allured by difficult and complex conversations regarding partisanship, race, sex, and gender. Later that decade, hearings informing the impeachment of President Bill Clinton captivated the public. Of course, as well, the events of September 11, 2001, directed media attention toward congressional hearings, like Attorney General John Ashcroft's plea to the Senate Judiciary Committee for stricter anti-terrorism laws (C-SPAN, 2001).

Over the past two decades, congressional hearings have become increasingly prominent in media given the broader accessibility to audiences, and the speakers' more calibrated on-air rhetorical appeals. For instance, the repeal of "Don't Ask, Don't Tell" in 2010 gained extensive media coverage (Condon, 2010). For the politicized Benghazi hearings, CNN published an hourly breakdown (Bradner et al., 2015). In this way, the separation between the political and the public has faded as media enhance the entertainment value of hearings like they did with the Flint, Michigan, Water Contamination Hearings in 2016 (Phillips, 2016). Hearings also include celebrity moments that garner significant public attention, like Ashton Kutcher's presentation during a 2017 hearing on Human Trafficking and Slavery (Klein, 2017).

Utilizing the C-SPAN Video Library, our research interrogates this phenomenon and advances knowledge in the fields of rhetoric and political communication, particularly as it relates to public address and democratic governance. Our research assembles and analyzes the corpus of congressional hearings and testimonies to determine the theoretical characteristics of the oratorical events themselves, and it specifically builds from the robust history of genre theory in the field of rhetoric.

ARTIFACTS

Scholars have long theorized and analyzed political speech genres, like the presidential inaugural address and the election concession address. However, few scholars have postulated the overarching generic and subgeneric components of congressional hearings. Akin to established literature on genres of political oratory, we build a similarly robust understanding of the genres and subgenres of congressional hearings. Our research examines the C-SPAN Video Library's collection of congressional hearings to better understand how rhetoric informs persuasive appeals within the hearings while also determining how the hearings function as spectacular rhetorical events.

We populated our list of artifacts by reviewing the C-SPAN Video Library for congressional hearings by view count, while also adding recent hearings that have captivated public attention. As a research team, we began by identifying recent congressional hearings that made news headlines. We then supplemented that list to ensure we included the most watched hearings in the C-SPAN Video Library. In this process, we identified the top twenty-five most viewed hearings for both the House of Representatives and Senate. We added these fifty hearings to our list and eliminated any duplicates. In sum, we populated 92 congressional hearings as artifacts pertinent to our research. The full list of artifacts exists as an appendix to this chapter. While we engaged the entirety of this list, our analysis focuses on the congressional hearings from the past two decades.

We concentrate on the hearings within recent years for two primary reasons. First, media spectacle requires media, and the proliferation of new media in the 21st century has made congressional hearings far more accessible to the public. Second, while spectacular congressional hearings exist across history, the increased media attention and subsequent public access augments congressional hearings as a genre of public oratory.

THEORY AND METHOD

Broadly, our scholarship advances knowledge of political rhetoric and communication by extrapolating the relationship between government officials, media agents, and members of a democratic public within the sites of congressional hearings. Certainly, we are not the first scholars to examine congressional hearings.

Lipari's (1994) analysis of the media coverage of Anita Hill's testimony during the confirmation hearings of Clarence Thomas operationalizes genre theory but demonstrates how media pundits, rather than the rhetors within the hearings, relied on overarching narratives outside of the hearings themselves. Regan's (1994) rhetorical analysis of the same hearing demonstrates the utility of rhetorical critique when studying congressional hearings but does not engage the situation from the perspective of genre. Gring-Pemble's (2001) examination of congressional discourse on welfare also gestures toward genre theory, but mostly utilizes narrative theory in analyzing broader public discourses rather than the specifics of congressional hearings.

Giglioni's (2020) recently published book most closely relates to our research as it responds to questions like ours regarding genre and congressional hearings. However, Giglioni (2020) approaches genre from a perspective rooted in linguistics and applies post-positivist methods central to discourse studies. While the findings assist us and astutely build scholarship on congressional hearings as spectacles of political communication, the ontological underpinnings of the study preclude substantive rhetorical analysis. Informed by contemporary reflections on classical theories of rhetoric, our analysis instead develops a theoretical perspective distinct to rhetoric scholarship within a humanistic tradition. Although numerous other scholars have interrogated congressional hearings, none have directly theorized the corpus of congressional hearings to rely upon and further develop genre theory from a rhetorical perspective. Like rhetoricians, discourse analysts (Bhatia, 1993; Giglioni, 2020; Swales, 1990) also engage in genre critique, oftentimes regarding the same texts, but do so from a social-scientific perspective grounded in linguistics and empiricism. Despite our humanistic ontological presuppositions, we in no way contest the empirical work of discourse analysts. Rather, we seek to complement it as rhetoricians concerned with the art of persuasion.

Within the Western tradition of rhetorical studies, the study of genre is as old as the field of rhetoric itself. In his original treatise on rhetoric, Aristotle (1991) theorizes three genres of public oratory: deliberative, forensic, and epideictic. Speeches within the deliberative genre are performed in legislative contexts where citizens discuss potential courses of action on a particular topic. Whereas deliberative rhetoric seeks to establish legislation, forensic rhetoric assesses and argues past events within established legalistic codes. Often referred to as judicial rhetoric, public addresses in the forensic category advocate for decisive action on the basis of past or contextual precedents. External to the legal realm, epideictic rhetoric encompasses orations that celebrate events. Often called ceremonial rhetoric, epideictic speeches occur when citizens and publics gather for celebratory events, like weddings, funerals, and presidential inaugurals.

With increased attention to rhetoric in the 20th century through scholars like Black (1965), Burke (1966), and Campbell and Jamieson (1978), these categories of rhetoric have evolved and progressed to include more nuance. Scholars have focused their attention on political rhetoric and genres of speeches and speech events. For instance, Campbell and Jamieson (1990), Sigelman (1996), and Guitar (2020), among others, have contributed to the understanding of inaugural presidential addresses. Scholars have also identified and evaluated presidential concession speeches as a genre of political speech (e.g., Corcoran, 1994; Neville-Shepard, 2014). Rhetorical critics have theorized a wide variety of genres of political speeches, including candidacy acceptance speeches (Neville-Shepard, 2016), victory speeches (Irimiea, 2010; Sheckels, 2010; Willyard & Ritter, 2005), and presidential apologia (Carcasson, 1998).

Genre critique maintains a robust history within the field of rhetorical studies. Genres help us historicize and understand cultural patterns, affording us lenses for understanding and evaluating rhetors and their exigencies (Miller, 1984). Oratorical genres often maintain public expectations within the realm of civic discourse (Corcoran, 1994). As rhetorical exigencies share similar situational elements, patterned rhetorical responses tend to develop (Bitzer, 1968) and groups of recurring speech acts construct oratorical themes (Campbell & Jamieson, 1978). Notably, genre analysis helps categorize and evaluate rhetorical events (Neville-Shepard, 2014). Although differences exist across the iterations of a particular exigency, elements of rhetorical situations nonetheless inform distinct rhetorical categories (Campbell & Jamieson, 1985).

Despite its important presence in rhetorical studies, genre analysis has received a fair amount of criticism. Most broadly, rhetorical scholars have noted that genres are not as formulaic as we originally assumed (Sheckels, 2010). Whereas formative theories on genre suggest that the constraints of a rhetorical situation will contain the abilities of the creator, thus creating patterns of oratory (Black, 1965), scholarly reflections have noted the severe limitations of such an approach, specifically in that it allows for minimal evaluative substance (Rowland, 1991). More traditional approaches to genre also limit the potential influence of the rhetorical agent (Benoit, 2000). Indeed, when employed haphazardly, genre analysis ignores the nuances of individual rhetors (Patton, 1976), removes important political context (Joslyn, 1986), and oversimplifies complex rhetorical events (Conley, 1986). Additionally, speech genres evolve with each iteration, thus blurring the prescribed boundaries (Sigelman, 1996).

Yet, when deployed appropriately, genre criticism can produce valuable analyses. Provided scholars account for contextual nuance (Willyard & Ritter, 2005), approach genre as informative rather than restrictive (Dudash, 2007), and refrain from assuming all similarly situated speeches automatically conform to a rhetorical theme (Miller, 1984), genre studies can help explain how subtleties operate to persuade across a category of speeches (Rowland, 1991). Indeed, productive approaches to genre foster the evolution of genre theory (Vigil, 2013). Genre critics should ensure that they avoid overemphasizing oratorical situations (Neville-Shepard, 2016) and remain attuned to situational characteristics (Rowland & Jerome, 2004). In this, genre critiques can illuminate and substantively explain rhetorical situations.

Thus, we assume the task of theorizing congressional hearings as a rhetorical genre with particular attention paid to the hearings that elevate to a public spectacle. Accommodating the nuance, we contend that congressional hearings as public spectacle function as a genre in that "they respond to the expectations and constraints of an occasion, make use of traditional topoi, and are linked in content" (Duffy, 1993, p. 284). Although we approach our research through a rhetorical lens, we arrive at this conclusion as we echo Giglioni (2019) in recognizing that congressional hearings have "a long history and specific procedural requirements and have other communicative purposes alongside their formal role as records of committees' activity" (p. 110), thereby justifying the usage of genre analysis.

In sum, our analysis advances the understanding of political rhetoric and its relationship to democracy on two primary fronts. First, our research develops scholarship through the theorization of the genres and subgenres of congressional hearings. In this, future research can more precisely evaluate specific iterations and the broader evolution of congressional hearings. Second, our research helps determine the most efficacious strategies for advancing persuasive appeals within the realm of congressional hearings. Not only can this research inform the orators involved in future congressional hearings, but it also builds critical awareness for the public audiences of congressional hearings. As congressional hearings achieve increased salience within the mediated forum, our scholarly reifications assist in the progression of democracy writ large by developing theoretical concepts that inform citizens as they engage in the deliberative processes of the political sphere.

ANALYSIS

Our present task first delineates between congressional hearings that elevate to media spectacle and those that do not. In doing so, we recognize that this distinction assumes an inherent fluidity and opacity. Our process of creating this demarcation refrains from theorizing, more broadly, a genre of congressional hearing address. We also do not concern ourselves here with the vast number of congressional hearings that fail to achieve the broad attention of the public. Whereas we support the continued theorization of the generic components of congressional hearings, our current project focuses intently on the unifying components of congressional hearings that create public spectacle and the persuasive appeals of the orators within those speech events.

Importantly, to categorize and evaluate the rhetorical appeals of the actors within congressional hearings, we must first recognize the various agencies that exist within the congressional hearing setting, noting the impracticality of accounting for all nuances within each hearing, from role to role. In our review, three distinct categories of actors emerge within congressional hearings. First, we note the members of the congressional committees as essential to the discourse. We will, at times, discuss certain subcategories of committee members, for instance across party lines or their existence as members of the majority or minority; however, our analysis remains focused on the committee members as a single unit of actors. Second, we note that committee hearings typically include guests who function as citizens within the democratic context more broadly but who do not hold legislative powers within Congress. We divide these citizen rhetors into two categories according to proposed rhetorical efficacy. We first identify citizen respondents who have been summoned to testify by a congressional committee. Second, we catalog citizen advocates who, while usually invited to appear before the congressional committee, seek to advance an objective. While both groups answer questions, the hearing proceedings show that the first is primarily there to be interrogated and the second is mostly concerned with advocating a cause. Although the desired efficacy and the implications of the rhetors within congressional hearings vary within these groupings, the overlap is strong enough within these contexts for us to substantively theorize the rhetorical situations of each.

Lastly, we do not distinguish between events that are preconstructed as media spectacle and those that elevate to media spectacle due to heated proceedings. In the end, given the trajectory of media coverage within congressional hearings, we argue again that establishing a firm genesis for this present phenomenon is imprudent. Planned and impromptu media spectacles are co-constitutive, and the end results remain inseparable. We focus intently on the rhetoric of congresspersons given spatial constraints. Our future research will extrapolate the rhetorical appeals of citizen respondents and citizen advocates within congressional hearings as public spectacle.

We contend that across these three oratorical roles, effective actors advance three overlapping persuasive themes and tend to advance two persuasive themes unique to their position within the hearing. These overlapping themes are fostering public spectacle, affirming cultural values, and empowering Congress. The definitions we assign to these themes will be discussed in turn. In addition, members of Congress also establish ethical primacy and advance their political values. Citizen respondents largely accommodate apologia and commit to cooperation. Citizen advocates broadly establish their exigency and demonstrate transcendence.

Establish Ethos

Establishing ethos is paramount within all public speaking contexts but is elevated in mediated congressional hearings. Thus, before advancing the appropriate genre appeals to create a public spectacle, congresspersons first demonstrate legitimacy within the congressional hearing. While ethos functions continuously throughout the hearings alongside its counterparts, pathos and logos, orators must ensure they present themselves as credible agents within the congressional hearing setting, which in turn establishes the platform for advancing the rhetoric of media spectacle.

Members of congressional committees establish themselves within the context of the congressional hearing and do so in three distinct ways. First, they labor to ensure that they speak within the established procedural confines of the hearing. Second, they actuate technological consciousness, particularly as it relates to microphones and cameras. Third, they posture as objective upholders of democratic ethics within the congressional hearing setting. Whereas these appeals of ethos precede our theorization of the genre, they performatively legitimize the hearing for media spectacle.

Even if formal congressional proceedings diverge from established parliamentary procedures, broadly defined, participants within congressional hearings admit and adhere to prescribed rules of order. Although not a requirement of congressional hearings, foremost of these formalities is the adherence to the oath by which attendees profess to speak truthfully. As performative rhetoric, the oath transitions the hearing from casual conversations to formal discourse within the congressional hearing setting. Oftentimes, but not always, oaths are administered at the beginning of congressional hearings. The chair of the committee generally decides whether the oath should be administered, but sometimes the committee votes on the matter. Oath requirements vary across committees as some committees use them regularly while others use them sparingly.

When ascending to public spectacle, the oath accentuates the formality. For instance, while the Senate Judiciary Committee does not require an oath for all participants within its hearings, the heavily politicized hearing regarding the sexual assault allegations of Brett Kavanaugh (C-SPAN, 2018c, 2018d), as an exigency, all but necessitated an oath as a matter of ethos. In this hearing, the oath served as a prominent public checkpoint for both Kavanaugh and witness Christine Blasey Ford. In many ways, the swearing process itself functioned as spectacle and confirmed to the onlooking public that the subsequent statements would be truthful under penalty of perjury.

In other instances, the oath is administered more as a formality to highlight the gravity of the hearing, but not command absolute attention on one orator or one moment. For instance, in the September 25, 2019, House Judiciary Committee hearing regarding mass shootings and gun policy (C-SPAN, 2019h), committee chair Jerrold Nadler (D-NY) administered an oath to all seven citizen advocates at once. This portion of the hearing demanded much less attention than it did for Blasey Ford and Kavanaugh (C-SPAN, 2018c, 2018d). Nevertheless, as the camera panned the entire panel while they took the oath collectively, an aura of authenticity was established.

The formal oath of congressional hearing participants is innately positioned as public spectacle. Given that Section 1001 within Title 18 of the U.S. legal code forbids citizens from knowingly and willfully making false statements before any branches of the U.S. federal government, oath proceedings within congressional hearings mean little beyond public spectacle. Regularly, members of congressional committees attempt to use the enduring oath to their rhetorical advantage. For example, Senator Joshua Hawley (R-MO) made the following request of Mark Zuckerberg: "Why don't you commit, while I've got you here under oath—it's so much better to do this under oath—will you commit now to providing a list from the TASKS platform of every mention of Google or Twitter?" (C-SPAN, 2020c). In another instance of political spectacle, Senator Rand Paul (R-KY) addressed Dr. Fauci directly with an interrogative monologue that began, "Dr. Fauci, as you are aware it is a crime to lie to Congress" and ended with "Knowing that it is a crime to lie Congress, do you wish to retract your statement of May eleventh where you claimed that the NIH [National Institutes of Health] never funded gain of function research in Wuhan?" (C-SPAN, 2021f).

Beyond the affirmations of honesty, situational ethos saturates congressional hearing discourses. Participants regularly reference and honor, or violate and get reprimanded, allotments of time for their speeches, evidenced by Senator John Kennedy's (R-LA) statement, "I'm over [on time] Mr. Chairman, I'm sorry" (C-SPAN, 2017d). As well, orators ensure that they recognize the members of the hearing by their formal, situational titles like "ranking member" and "chair." Congressional hearing participants also employ more casual utterances to identify other participants to establish their ethos. For instance, members of Congress often refer to their fellow congresspersons as "friends" or "colleagues" to show that their position in the hearing is not innately combative. These processes of establishing ethos afford hearing participants with a sturdy platform for achieving public spectacle while honoring the aura of the legislature.

Genre: Congressional Hearings as Public Spectacle

Through our investigation of congressional hearings that have captivated the public, we identify five general themes within each of the three established categories of speakers. Three of the themes exist across categories. First, orators foster the spectacle. While this appears tautological, it is evident from our review that acknowledging and participating in media spectacle is central to the elevation of congressional hearings and the ongoing justification of the legislature. Second, congressional hearing actors tend to affirm cultural values. This generic component uniquely connects the broader ethos of the orator to the specific discourse within the congressional event. Third, rhetors labor to empower Congress. Regardless of the polemics that evolve at times in the hearings, particularly concerning media spectacle, the participants nonetheless reaffirm congressional power. Congresspersons, also attempt to (fourth) establish ethical primacy and (fifth) affirm their political values.

APPEALS BY CONGRESSPERSONS

Assuredly, congressional hearings require members of Congress to engage each other and the public in a smaller capacity than the regular chamber, and within the context of the committee itself. In developing the generic components of persuasive oratory within the congressional hearings for the committee members, it is important to recall that the genre is defined by more than the situational context. In other words, while the presence of congresspersons within a committee room establishes the basis for rhetorical exigency, the platform itself does fully encapsulate the rhetorical appeals. This is especially evident as we identify and evaluate congressional appeals that elevate to public spectacle. This section identifies and explains the components of the rhetorical appeals made by members of Congress who sit on the respective committees. Our research provides a broad analysis regardless of the various positions of power within the hearings. For instance, we have not fully accounted for the extensive variances that might exist due to political party, relationship to the majority, or experience on the committee. We recognize the importance of these descriptors and urge future scholarship to interrogate the generic elements of them.

Foster Spectacle

First, to productively engage in the situation of congressional hearings as public spectacle, congresspersons must foster the public spectacle. This component of the rhetorical situation public establishes that congresspersons recognize the potential for media spectacle and that they are actors within it. Congresspersons achieve this element through three primary means: acknowledging media, creating audio/video bites, and communicating the imprudence of media presence.

Acknowledge media
Although Congress has resisted media presence in committees throughout history, media regularly now attend congressional hearings. Oftentimes, members of the committee extend gratitude for the media coverage. For instance, Representative Eliot Engel (D-NY) included a welcome in his opening statement: "Let me also welcome all our members, the public, and the press, and we're glad to have our friends from C-SPAN here this morning to cover our hearing" (C-SPAN, 2019a). Sen. Sanders (I-VT) has stated similarly, "We want to thank C-SPAN for

covering this important hearing" (C-SPAN, 2014). At other times, media are recognized indirectly, but still celebrated, like when Senator John Thune (R-SD) reminded his audience, and in particular the witnesses, "We are listening. America is listening, and quite possibly, the world is listening, too" (C-SPAN, April 10, 2018). Similarly, Representative Elijah Cummings (D-MD) commended the witnesses in a House Oversight and Reform Committee hearing, noting, "It is not easy to on national TV . . . talk about your pain, and you're talking about some of the things that are so very, very personal" (C-SPAN, 2019g). At times as well, congresspersons express a desire for more spectacle, like when Senator Marie Cantwell (D-WA) stated:

> I'm a little concerned today not seeing a press table. I know we have press in the room. . . . I would feel more comfortable if we asked Senator Blunt where the press table is supposed to be in the room so that we can accommodate both the press having a place to write and feel comfortable here and having some audience participation. (C-SPAN, 2020a)

As we know, however, exchanges between Congress and the press are not always pleasant.

While members of Congress often express gratitude for the media presence, they also regularly reproach media for the existence of spectacle, despite the realization that they themselves assist in fostering it. For example, consider Representative Bill Huizenga's (R-MI) comment "I was going to ask each one of you why you think you are here today . . . but I will dispense with that and give you the answer: political theatre. That is what this hearing is today" (C-SPAN, 2021a). Representative Devin Nunes (R-CA) made similar accusations within the Robert Mueller hearings on Russian interference in the 2016 election, stating they were just a "television moment" and "political theater" (C-SPAN, 2019f). Yet members of Congress also scold the media for not creating enough spectacle, like when Representative Jamie Raskin (D-MD) admonished the lack of media attention on prescription drug prices, albeit still to recognize and foster the spectacle, by stating:

> I wish that all of the media which swarm over this Congress when we conduct oversight into government corruption and criminality were here today because this is a crime too. (C-SPAN, 2019g)

He further advocated that people should share the testimonies of the day widely across social media (C-SPAN, 2019g).

In recognizing that the spectacle extends beyond the committee rooms, congresspersons also foster media spectacle by advancing snide critiques of media institutions. Angry that some media had received reports vital to the testimony of Michael Cohen, former attorney to Donald Trump, before the House Oversight Committee, Representative Jim Jordan (R-OH) exclaimed, "You know who had this before we had it? CNN had it!" (C-SPAN, 2019b). In the same hearing, Representative Mark Meadows (R-NC) critiqued the media coverage of the situation, admonishing CNN and demanding that a *Vanity Fair* article about the story be formally entered into the record (C-SPAN, 2019b). When the tension in this hearing became palpable, Rep. Cummings (D-MD) reminded all media present of the need to be credentialed and demanded the respectful presence of spectators (C-SPAN, 2019b). Although less direct, Senator Bill Cassidy (R-LA) underhandedly critiqued the spectacle surrounding the nomination of Betsy DeVos for education secretary: "I am really struck by the kind of reaction your nomination has elicited" (C-SPAN, 2017a). As well, although it was a specific critique of foreign media, Senator Dan Sullivan (R-AK) complained that there are always "journalists sticking a microphone in your face" (C-SPAN, 2020a). Despite the complaints, congresspersons know the political benefits of having a media platform.

Create audio/video bites

As is a regular occurrence in contemporary politics, congresspersons engage in combative rhetoric primed for media consumption. For instance, Representative Rashida Tlaib (D-MI) interrogated Secretary of Homeland Security Kevin McAleenan by consistently stressing that McAleenan just wanted to "keep the kids longer" in cages at the U.S.–Mexico border (C-SPAN, 2019e). Applicable here, as well, are Sen. Paul's (R-KY) attempts to combat Dr. Fauci over the NIH funding "gain of function" research in Wuhan, China (C-SPAN, 2021e), and Representative Glenn Grothman's (R-WI) heated exchanges with Fauci (C-SPAN, 2020b). When Rice University professor Doug Brinkley challenged Representative Don Young (R-AK) regarding oil drilling in Alaska, Young contested Brinkley, calling his words "garbage" and reprimanding Brinkley, saying, "You be quiet. You be quiet. You sit in that chair. You sit in that chair!" (C-SPAN, 2011). Also noteworthy are Representative Ilhan Omar's (D-MN) exchanges with Elliott Abrams, Special Envoy for Venezuela, who refused to answer Omar's questions (C-SPAN,

2019a) and the tense moments over accusations of racism between Tlaib (R-MI), and peripherally Representative Alexandria Ocasio-Cortez (D-NY) and Representative Ayanna Pressley (D-MA), who expressed nonverbal cues to repudiate Representative Mark Meadows (R-NC) and Representative Jim Jordan (R-OH) (C-SPAN, 2019b). When Tlaib accused Meadows of using an African American woman as a prop, Meadows interrupted, "Mr. Chairman, please strike her words from the record." Jordan interjected, "I want the words read back! I want to know exactly what she said about a colleague." Rep. Cummings (D-MD) then hit the gavel multiple times in response to Jordan: "Excuse me, excuse me, no!" Whether these exchanges occur across parties in a hearing room or through the screen of a virtual hearing, like when Representative Patrick McHenry (R-NC) accosted GameStop CEO and cofounder Vlad Tenev for the hypocrisy of his private company trying to "democratize finance" (C-SPAN, 2021a), these regularly occurring combative moments are primed for media consumption.

Audio and video bites supply news media with rhetorical snippets. Sometimes the snippets maintain a respectful tone, like when Senator Richard Burr (R-NC) directed the cameras to shift to recently deceased Senator John McCain's (R-AZ) customary chair to honor his recent passing (C-SPAN, 2018b). Senator Mark Warner (D-VA) employed similar directing tactics when noting that Google "chose not to" send a representative to the Senate Intelligence Committee's hearing on foreign influence and social media. The camera then included the empty chair and nameplate where the representative would have sat (C-SPAN, 2018b).

At other times, the spectacle erupts when meetings are abruptly called to recess, like when Representative Carolyn Maloney (D-NY) adjourned the House Oversight and Reform Committee's March 11, 2020, emergency SARS-CoV-2 hearing:

> Let me intervene here. I have been told that our witnesses need to leave now. I don't know what is going on at the White House. The White House is telling reporters that this meeting is not an emergency. … There seems to be a great deal of confusion and lack of coordination at the White House. I hope this does not reflect the broader response to this crisis. (C-SPAN, 2020b)

Rep. Maloney's (D-NY) statement resulted in a chaotic sequence within the hearing, primed for media consumption, where panelists and committee members buzzed with confusion in an era of already palpable political tension.

In many instances, the video and sound bites epitomize political tension. Regularly, committee chairs are tasked with maintaining order, which often results in chaotic snippets, like when Representative Maxine Waters (D-CA) rebuked Representative Patrick McHenry (R-NC), exclaiming, "You are not recognized!" as she banged her gavel (C-SPAN, 2021a). Other outbursts conducive to media spectacles include Representative Brian Mast's (R-FL) accusations that Secretary of State Antony Blinken lies to the public: "He lies in front of the camera. . . . We don't need to hear lies!" (C-SPAN, 2021h).

The video and sound bite moments also manifest when members of Congress employ terms that have substantial political weight. For instance, Representative Bennie Thompson (D-MS) accused Trump of pulling "children from their parents" (C-SPAN, 2021c). Representative Joe Wilson (R-SC) accused President Joe Biden's administration of allowing "terrorists to enter American neighborhoods and suicide bombers to murder as many Americans as possible" (C-SPAN, 2021h). Representative Ralph Norman (R-SC) both critiqued and augmented the charged rhetoric surrounding the detention center crisis at the U.S.–Mexico border, stating, "I really take issue with the rhetoric that we've had over the last couple of weeks, with drinking out of toilets, children in cages" (C-SPAN, 2019e).

Representative Raja Krishnamoorthi (D-IL) similarly accosted Joe Ferreira, chief executive officer of the Nevada Donor Network:

 What you are spending on the LA Raiders, the Golden Knights, Napa Valley, and Sonoma have one thing in common: they have nothing to do with recovering organs for . . . dying patients on the organ donor list. (C-SPAN, 2021d)

These types of rhetorical snippets saturate congressional hearings and often attract media attention around the verbiage used, like when Rep. Omar (D-MN) tied Abrams to a 1982 rape and massacre in El Salvador (C-SPAN, 2019a), when Rep. Ocasio-Cortez (D-NY) highlighted a report that identified "about 10,000 potential current and former CBP [Customs and Border Protection] officers in a violently racist and sexist Facebook group" (C-SPAN, 2019e), and when Sen. Sanders (I-VT) postulated that Betsy DeVos only garnered her nomination because she is "a multi-billionaire who has donated millions to the Republican Party" (C-SPAN, 2017a). Within the hearings, the snippets exist within a particular context and have rhetorical value; however, they also cater to the rapid consumption of political discourse as it has been reduced to snippets of audio and video.

Communicate imprudence

In addition, congresspersons also foster public spectacle by admitting the imprudence of hearings, effectively communicating that the hearings do little beyond creating public spectacles. At times, this occurs through references to meetings that occurred with the witnesses before the hearings. Sen. Cassidy (R-LA) told Betsy DeVos, "Good to see you again; I enjoyed our meeting in anticipation of this" (C-SPAN, 2017a). Similarly, Senator John Thune (R-SD) began his address to Mark Zuckerberg by stating, "As we discussed in my office yesterday" (C-SPAN, April 10, 2018). Senator Mike Enzi (R-WY) effectively relayed to Betsy DeVos that her nomination would get approved as he stated, "I enjoyed our meeting last month and I look forward to working with you as we consider your nomination and then after that. You're going to be dealing with a great variety of states . . ." (C-SPAN, 2017a).

At other times, congresspersons are far more abrasive with their rhetoric in communicating imprudence. Rep. Young (R-AK) once exclaimed in a hearing, "If you ever want to see an exercise in futility, this is it. That side has already made up its mind, this side has already made up its mind" (C-SPAN, 2011). Representative Lee Zeldin (R-NY) accosted Secretary of State Antony Blinken for not giving answers consistent with their previously held briefing and told him he "should resign" (C-SPAN, 2021h). In making a similar observation regarding the futility of some congressional hearings, Senator Sheldon Whitehouse (D-RI) minced few words, stating:

> It doesn't make sense. And the protocol that has developed for answering questions in this committee makes the committee look preposterous, it makes the witnesses, the nominees look preposterous. We have got to get beyond this if we are going to have meaningful hearings and not just verbal jousting and gamesmanship. (C-SPAN, 2017d)

In the end, whether members of Congress bemoan the public spectacle, they nonetheless help foster it to their advantage.

Affirm Cultural Values

Despite partisan polemics, certain cultural values exist across party lines. Especially as they recognize the broad mediated reach of their hearings, congressional rhetors labor to entrench themselves into the cultural fabric of the country they represent. While these cultural affirmations are not apolitical, they nonetheless advance an ethic of unification. In particular, the commentary enshrines American democracy through an emphasis on its core tenets.

Expectedly, the concept of freedom, as a core component of American culture, saturates congressional hearing discourse. For example, Senator Marco Rubio (R-FL) asked Jack Dorsey how Twitter upholds freedom of expression (C-SPAN, 2018b). In grappling with WikiLeaks and the exposure of classified information, Representative John Conyers (D-MI) opined that freedom of speech should be upheld, and that banning bad speech was not the appropriate response to the situation (C-SPAN, 2010). Senator Dianne Feinstein (D-CA) has advanced similar ethics, contending that Congress concerned itself with "protecting individual privacy" (C-SPAN, March 13, 2018).

Discussions of freedom and liberty tend to arise when congresspersons unite against common antagonists. It has been particularly commonplace to reproach Russia in these deliberations (Senator Lindsey Graham [R-SC; see C-SPAN, 2019c]; Sen. Burr [R-NC; see C-SPAN, 2017c]). Senator Mark Warner (D-VA) once contended that "Russian disinformation has revealed a dark underbelly of the entire online ecosystem. And this threatens to cheapen American discourse . . . erode truth and undermine our democracy on a previously unimagined scale" (C-SPAN, 2018b).

Akin to Russia, congresspersons reference other foreign and domestic adversaries regularly as well. Joe Biden, as a senator (D-DE), compared the Iraq War to the Vietnam War to demonstrate the futility of ongoing war efforts (C-SPAN, 2007). Representative Michael McCaul (R-TX) disparaged different foreign actors as he argued, "I think we have an historic opportunity to . . . transform Venezuela into a democracy . . . and for the first time in decades have an influence on Cuba" (C-SPAN, 2019a). In a later hearing, Rep. McCaul (R-TX) accused Secretary of State Antony Blinken of violating these cultural values as U.S. troops were withdrawn from Afghanistan in 2021, stating, "We abandoned Americans behind enemy lines. We left behind interpreters who you, Mr. Secretary, and the president promised to protect" (C-SPAN, 2021h). The American heroism rhetoric has sustained throughout recent decades, as indicated by Representative Louie Gohmert's (R-TX) criticism of WikiLeaks that embarrassed the country and "endangered American troops" (C-SPAN, 2010) and Liz Cheney's (R-WY) gratitude toward Capitol police after the January 6, 2021, attempted coup: "It is because of you. You held the line. You defended all of us. You defended the Capitol, and you defended the Constitution and our republic" (C-SPAN, 2021g). Yet in other utterances, the highlighted cultural values are less overtly political.

Congresspersons regularly recognize the importance of family. Rep. Cummings (D-MD) employed heavy pathos when discussing children in two different hearings near the end of his career. He first commented regarding child detention centers at the U.S.–Mexico border, "When dealing with children it is not the deed, but the memory that will haunt them until the day they die" (C-SPAN, 2019e), and then invited the public to consider the grave situation of having to "choose between having a roof over your head and saving your child's life" as Congress grappled with rising drug prices (C-SPAN, 2019g). Despite their differences, Sen. Feinstein (D-CA) applauded Justice Amy Coney Barrett's family values, a deeply rooted American ethic, stating, "On a personal level, you're amazing to have seven children and do what you do" (C-SPAN, 2017d).

Additionally, congresspersons affirm a variety of other cultural values, many of which position the U.S. as a beacon of moral and economic superiority. Rep. Omar (D-MN) iterated strongly that the "American people want to know that we are not committing genocide and that our values are being upheld abroad" (C-SPAN, 2019a). Rep. Krishnamoorthi (D-IL) argued that Americans "want our taxpayer money to be spent on collecting organs, not on extravagance" (C-SPAN, 2021d), while Senator Roger Wicker (R-MS) desired to position "the United States to win the global race to 5G" (C-SPAN, 2020a). Although these utterances often correspond with palpable politicization, the cultural values they depict nonetheless coalesce the congressional body and the rhetorical appeals within it.

Empower Congress

In addition to working to foster public spectacle and affirm cultural values, members of Congress also advance a collective rhetoric that defends and empowers the legislature. This is especially interesting given the recent trajectory of American politics that trends toward the executive branch (Peterson, 2019). While congresspersons may not agree on much across the aisle, they certainly agree that Congress should be appropriately respected in the governing process.

Congressional hearings often include a noticeable disdain for the executive branch of government. Sometimes the rhetoric is subtle, like when Rep. Cummings (D-MD) discussed information that Congress "forced the Trump administration to produce" (C-SPAN, 2019e). Representative William Delahunt

(D-MA) emphasized that Congress is the "*first* branch of government" as he chided the executive branch for bureaucratic overclassification of information (C-SPAN, 2010), commanding the next Congress to assert its power on this front. Rep. Cummings (D-MD) appealed similarly on February 27, 2019, as he noted, "Everyone in this room has a duty to be a check on the executive branch" (C-SPAN, 2019b). Likewise, Sen. Biden (D-DE) questioned Secretary of State Condoleeza Rice about executive power and constitutional authority as it pertained to the Iraq War (C-SPAN, 2007). When the interrogation of Brett Kavanaugh began supporting the investigative power of the executive branch too strongly, Senator Chuck Grassley (R-IA) firmly interjected (which coincidentally also helped Kavanaugh out of a predicament), "Stop the clock! This committee is running this hearing, not the White House, not Don McGahn, not even you as a nominee!" (C-SPAN, 2018c). When the Trump administration attempted to halt the House Oversight and Reform Committee's March 11, 2020, emergency SARS-CoV-2 hearing, Representative Chip Roy (R-TX) and Rep. Maloney (D-NY) united to repudiate the attempt by the White House to stop the hearing. Rep. Roy (R-TX) stated:

> We want you to do your work but it's important you come back. We have urgent questions. . . . I sent a letter, Dr. Fauci, to the Department of Defense two and a half weeks ago and have not received a response. I am troubled by the lack of response. . . . I want answers to those questions when we come back, and I hope that is this afternoon. (C-SPAN, 2020b)

Rep. Maloney (D-NY) augmented Rep. Roy's (R-TX) comments and complained that they keep getting misinformation from the White House. Rep. Maloney (D-NY) stated emphatically, "They're not going to adjourn this hearing. I am going to recess it" in a clear rebuke of the executive branch. It is clear by the rhetoric that congresspersons show no favor to those who trivialize the legislature, as evidenced by the reiteration that it is a felony to lie to Congress. (See, for instance, Sen. Grassley [R-IA; C-SPAN, 2018c] and Rep. Meadows's [R-NC] rebuke of Michael Cohen for showing "disdain for this body" [C-SPAN, 2019b].) Rep. Young (R-AK) epitomized this defensive posture as he reminded Doug Brinkley, "When we are here, we are the ones who ask the questions. You answer the questions" (C-SPAN, 2011).

Congresspersons also affirm their power by making demands of the witnesses and panelists. Sen. Hawley (R-MO) reminded Mark Zuckerberg that if he would not commit to providing the requested materials, Congress "could of course subpoena this information" (C-SPAN, 2020c). Representative Ami Bera (D-CA) spoke candidly to Antony Blinken, "What I will ask is that we use every resource we can in a difficult situation—in a challenging situation—to get every American citizen, visa holder, SIV [special immigrant visa], and vulnerable Afghan citizen out. Can I get that promise?" (C-SPAN, 2021h). Sen. Whitehouse (D-RI) similarly commanded social media executives to establish their corrective measures before Congress had to legislate on the matter: "Can you come to us and say you've accomplished X; you as a Congress don't have to worry about legislating in this space. Can you do that for me?" (C-SPAN, 2017e). Rep. Krishnamoorthi (D-IL) firmly informed Joe Ferreira that Congress would be directing "you as the president of the OPO [organ procurement organization] to provide us with five years of itemized records and the ministry of your expenses" (C-SPAN, 2021d). These affirmations of congressional power operate to coalesce the legislature across party lines.

———

Of the five generic components of congressional hearings as public spectacle, these first three (foster spectacle, affirm cultural values, and empower congress) help unite the legislature on screen for the American public. The remaining two components, establish ethical primacy and affirming political values, are where congresspersons fight for power within the legislature and attempt to advantage themselves and their parties.

Establish Ethical Primacy

Appeals to ethical primacy are central to the rhetoric congresspersons within congressional hearings. Given the power dynamics within the hearings, legislators are constantly grasping for authority. As appeals to resituate power within the legislature, congresspersons regularly posture as ethically superior to their counterparts.

Even though partisan polemics often overpower deliberative discourse within the legislature, congresspersons regularly position themselves as cooperative and bipartisan to denigrate their political opponents. For instance, Representative Ted Poe (R-TX) commended retiring Rep. Delahunt (D-MA), stating, "I hate to see him go, even though we disagree on just about everything" (C-SPAN, 2010). Representative Katie Hill (D-CA) advanced ethical primacy in the February 27, 2019, interrogation of Michael Cohen, saying:

I represent a purple district; I did not come here for partisan bickering. I actively wanted to avoid it. . . . I come from a family of service members who swore to follow the orders of the president, and we all swore an oath to protect the Constitution. I do not have a vendetta against the president. (C-SPAN, 2019b)

During the Brett Kavanaugh testimony, Sen. Graham (R-SC), exhausted by the deliberations, accused the Democrats of propagating a "disgraceful" "unethical sham" and said, "I hate to say this because these have been my friends" but if "you're looking for a fair process, you came to the wrong town at the wrong time" (C-SPAN, 2018c).

Partisan posturing like Sen. Graham's (R-SC) is typical within congressional hearings. Rep. Jordan (R-OH) admonished his Democratic counterparts, contending, "We are better than this. . . . This is all so the Democrat operatives can start the impeachment process" (C-SPAN, 2019b). Sen. Grassley (R-IA) similarly scolded the actions of "the minority" (Democrats) in the Kavanaugh hearing, whereas the Democrats returned fire in the Blinken hearing on the withdrawal from Afghanistan. In that September 13, 2021, hearing, Rep. Bera (D-CA) rebuked the previous Republican administration under President Trump: "Thank you, Mr. Secretary, for appearing before the committee and answering every question. That is not something your predecessor did." Representative Karen Bass (D-CA) followed: "Thank you, Mr. Secretary, for attending this meeting, and thank you for your patience with the theatrics of my colleagues on the other side of the aisle" (C-SPAN, 2021h).

Establishing ethical primacy influences the negotiation of partisan tensions. Sometimes congresspersons express disappointment with their political opposition, like when Rep. Tlaib (D-MI) defended her Democratic cohort against Republican rebukes: "There's been a lot of discussion in this committee about rhetoric and kind of dismissing and discrediting many of my colleagues, including Congresswoman Escobar" (C-SPAN, 2019e). Other times, committee members attempt to establish ethical primacy by demanding order according to the established procedural rules of the committee, like when Rep. Meadows (R-NC) pleaded for order: "I appeal the ruling of the chair! Do the rules matter?" (C-SPAN, 2019b). Yet as well, congresspersons may labor to establish ethical primacy when in a contentious position within their own party, as can be seen by Rep. Cheney's (R-WY) rebuke of her fellow Republicans for resisting the formation of a commission to investigate the January 6, 2021, insurrection, insisting that the events should "be investigated by a bipartisan commission, selected by each party and modeled on the 9/11 commission. Though such a commission was opposed, it passed with the support of 35 Republican members" (C-SPAN, 2021g).

Appeals to ethical primacy are advanced through a variety of other means as well. In considering WikiLeaks in 2010, Representative Sheila Jackson Lee (D-TX) outwardly recognized the ethical quandary between freedom of expression and national security, thus abstaining from partisan banter. As a member of the House Homeland Security Committee, Rep. Lee (D-TX) positioned herself as reflective, rather than reactive, which advanced an ethical aura (C-SPAN, 2010). Senator Christopher Dodd (D-CT) attempted to establish ethical primacy as he argued Iraq War policy by reminding the committee that "those of us who have been to Iraq recently have seen it with our own eyes, heard it with our own ears" (C-SPAN, 2007). In a hearing on modern-day human trafficking, Senator Todd Young (R-IN) opened his remarks by referencing his newly proposed legislation on the matter and thus insinuated that he and his Republican colleagues had already been working to address the matter in question (C-SPAN, 2017b). In other instances, congresspersons position their political opponents as antithetical to the will of the American people. Rep. Cummings (D-MD) reproached his Republican colleagues for not wanting Michael Cohen to speak to Congress: "You've made it clear that you do not want the American people to hear what this man has to say. But the American people have a right to hear" (C-SPAN, 2019b). Senator Richard Blumenthal (D-CT) similarly criticized President Trump and the Republican party for trying to "overturn the will of the voters" (C-SPAN, 2020c).

The posturing for ethical primacy was palpably evident during the testimony of Christine Blasey Ford amid the allegations of sexual assault by Brett Kavanaugh (C-SPAN, 2018d). In the hearing, Republican senators, led by Sen. Grassley (R-IA), labored to create an objective, welcoming environment for Blasey Ford, despite the clear indication that Kavanaugh would be confirmed regardless. Sen. Grassley (R-IA) opened with an apology to Blasey Ford and assured her that her voice would be heard. As a matter of optics, the Republicans on the Senate Judiciary Committee, saturated with white men and posturing as self-aware, albeit in cringeworthy fashion, hired a woman to interrogate Blasey Ford on their behalf. The employment of a woman representative was a clear attempt to establish ethical primacy by the Republicans on the committee (C-SPAN, 2018d).

Affirm Political Values

Lastly, in congressional hearings, congresspersons work to affirm their political values. Like the establishment of ethical primacy, this component of the genre functions as a means for individual politicians to advance their interests and the interests of their party. Whereas these rhetorical appeals are common within congressional hearings, they do not operate to coalesce the legislature.

Oftentimes, congresspersons in committee hearings find ways to advance the political ideas that are most important to them. In a March 11, 2014, hearing on health care, Sen. Sanders (I-VT) opened his questioning by asking, "Should citizens have the basic right to health care?" (C-SPAN, 2014). Sen. Sanders (I-VT) asked a similar question of Betsy DeVos on January 17, 2017, but this time regarding free public education, another important agenda item for Sanders: "Will you work with me to make public universities free?" (C-SPAN, 2017a). In a hearing on organ donors, Representative Hank Johnson (D-GA) worked the conversation toward African American rights and equitable health care across racial lines, a primary talking point within the political context:

 Black Americans are three times more likely than white Americans to have a kidney failure. Despite this . . . Black kidney patients are less likely to be identified as transplant candidates and less likely to receive a transplant. (C-SPAN, 2021d)

In discussing the withdrawal from Afghanistan, Representative David Cicilline (D-RI) requested that the Biden administration ensure the protection of LGBTQIA refugees (C-SPAN, 2021h), which echoed some of Cicilline's most strongly held political convictions.

When not advancing more personal politics, congresspersons often attempt to advance the political values of their parties. To counter Sen. Sanders (I-VT) in the March 11, 2014, health care hearing, Sen. Burr (R-NC) repeated popular Republican talking points, like "Repeal Obamacare." Sen. Feinstein (D-CA) and Sen. Cantwell (D-WA) positioned statements in another hearing to question the legitimacy of the 2016 election given Russian interference, a major political agenda item for Democrats during the Trump presidency (C-SPAN, April 13, 2018). While interrogating Betsy DeVos, Sen. Cassidy (R-LA) and Senator Orrin Hatch (R-UT) both advanced the "school of choice" narrative: "Do you support the rights of all children regardless of income or race . . . to have the option to choose the school that meets their child's needs?" (Cassidy) and requested that DeVos assist in "restoring local autonomy over schools" (Hatch) (C-SPAN, 2017a).

Oftentimes, these partisan utterances repeat the common contextual talking points of their party leaders. Regarding reports of post-election violence, Senator Mike Lee (R-UT) reiterated a primary Trump sound bite: "The only violence I'm aware of has occurred in connection with ANTIFA" (C-SPAN, 2020c). Perpetuating hyper-conservative fears, Rep. McCaul (R-TX) criticized the Biden administration's withdrawal from Afghanistan by exclaiming, "We are now at the mercy of the Taliban's reign of terror, all while a dark veil of Sharia law covers Afghanistan" (C-SPAN, 2021h). In her interrogation of U.S. Supreme Court Justice nominee Amy Coney Barrett, Sen. Feinstein (D-CA) advocated for the reproductive rights of women, a primary political stance of contemporary Democrats: "You are controversial because many of us who have lived our lives as women recognize the value of finally being able to control our reproductive rights" (C-SPAN, 2017d). When discussing 5G technology and cybersecurity, Senators Dan Sullivan (R-AK) and Ron Johnson (R-WI) both advanced anti-China rhetoric, a common theme of contemporary Republicans (C-SPAN, 2020a).

————

Although we recognize that divisions within parties exist, in fact starkly at times, a partisan cohesion nevertheless permeates the general rhetoric of the congressional hearing. This is particularly salient given that most congresspersons campaign for reelection during their term.

DISCUSSION

The push to create public spectacle within congressional hearings aligns with a variety of contemporary phenomena, most notably the increasing extension of power by the executive branch (Peterson, 2019). Broadly, these events of public spectacle urge the public to respect the legislature's existence. Yet, paradoxically, congressional hearings as public spectacle work to re-center the legislative branch in public discourse while also delegitimizing the legislature by perpetuating a palpable, lingering disdain for "Washington" among the public. Although congressional hearings are often investigative or interrogative as it pertains to the consideration of legislation or executive branch appointees, rather than legislative assemblies proper, they nonetheless labor to augment the legislature as a viable body of American governance.

Notwithstanding the polemics endemic to contemporary hearings, legislators of all political inclinations coalesce on three main fronts, most notably to defend their branch of government. Interesting as well, it is evident that the legislature, despite its volatile relationship with the media, recognizes the benefits of media presence. Although congresspersons regularly grumble about reporters and their coverage, successful deliberating now includes effective usage of microphone and camera technologies.

As new media continue to develop and congresspersons indulge in an unending reelection campaign cycle, our research here can inform future scholarship, particularly relating to rhetorical performances within congressional hearings. While our categorization of the rhetorical themes remains fluid enough to ensure situational flexibility for the rhetorical critic, we emphasize that the generic components of congressional hearings as public spectacle offer scholars a substantive lens through which they can extend this important analysis. In the end, this work not only advances our understanding of contemporary political processes, but it also produces knowledge in an area where it is lacking—at the intersection of media, congressional discourse, and public perception. Thus, our research not only supplements research in the field of political communication, it also informs citizen investiture in the democratic process, however abrasive that may be.

ACKNOWLEDGMENTS

We sincerely thank Dr. Robert X. Browning, Andrea Langrish, and the staff at the Center for C-SPAN Scholarship & Engagement for the commendable management of this volume and the 2021 CCSE conference. We appreciate the constructive feedback provided to us by the reviewers of our manuscript and attendees of our 2021 CCSE conference presentation. As well, we are grateful for the support provided to us by our Young Harris College community, most notably Dr. Jennifer Hallett, Dr. Eloise Whisenhunt, and Dr. Jason Pierce. Funding for this project was provided by the C-SPAN Education Foundation.

REFERENCES

Aristotle. (1991). *On rhetoric: A theory of civic discourse* (G. A. Kennedy, Trans.). Oxford University Press.

Benoit, W. L. (2000). Beyond genre theory: The genesis of rhetorical action. *Commu-

nication Monographs, 67(2), 178–192. https://doi.org/10.1080/03637750009376503

Bhatia, V. K. (1993). *Analysing genre: Language use in professional settings.* Longman. https://doi.org/10.1017/S0272263100013668

Bradner, E., Kopan, T., Zeleny, J., & Collinson, S. (2015, October). *11 Benghazi takeaways: One for each hour.* CNN. https://www.cnn.com/2015/10/22/politics/hillary-clinton -benghazi-hearing-takeaways/index.html

Bitzer, L. F. (1968). The rhetorical situation. *Philosophy and Rhetoric, 1*(1), 1–14. http:// www.jstor.org/stable/40237697

Black, E. (1965). *Rhetorical criticism: A study in method.* Macmillan.

Burke, K. (1966). *Language as symbolic action: Essays on life, literature, and method.* University of California Press.

Campbell, K. K., & Jamieson, K. H. (1978). Form and genre in rhetorical criticism: An introduction. In K. K. Campbell & K. H. Jamieson (Eds.), *Form and genre: Shaping rhetorical action* (pp. 9–32). Speech Communication Association.

Campbell, K. K., & Jamieson, K. H. (1985). Inaugurating the presidency. *Presidential Studies Quarterly, 15*(2), 394–411. https://www.jstor.org/stable/27550215

Campbell, K. K., & Jamieson, K. H. (1990). *Deeds done in words: Presidential rhetoric and the genres of governance.* University of Chicago Press.

Carcasson, M. (1998). Herbert Hoover and the presidential campaign of 1932: The fail-ure of apologia. *Presidential Studies Quarterly, 28*(2), 349–365. https://www.jstor .org/stable/27551864

Condon, S. (2010, December). *Congress passes "Don't Ask, Don't Tell" repeal.* CBS News. https://www.cbsnews.com/news/congress-passes-dont-ask-dont-tell-repeal/

Conley, T. (1986). The Linnaean blues: Thoughts on the genre approach. In H. W. Si-mons & A. A. Aghazarian (Eds.), *Form, genre, and the study of political discourse* (pp. 59–78). University of South Carolina Press.

Corcoran, P. E. (1994). Presidential concession speeches: The rhetoric of defeat. *Polit-ical Communication, 11*(2), 109–131. https://doi.org/10.1080/10584609.1994.9963019

C-SPAN (Producer). (2001, September 25). *Homeland defense and anti-terrorism leg-islation* [Video]. https://www.c-span.org/video/?166281-1/homeland-defense-anti -terrorism-legislation

C-SPAN (Producer). (2007, January 11). *U.S. policy toward Iraq* [Video]. https://www .c-span.org/video/?196140-1/us-policy-iraq

C-SPAN (Producer). (2010, December 16). *Wikileaks, the Espionage Act, and the Con-stitution* [Video]. https://www.c-span.org/video/?297115-1/wikileaksthe-espionage -act-constitution

C-SPAN (Producer). (2011, November 18). *Jobs and drilling in Arctic National Wild-*

life Refuge [Video]. https://www.c-span.org/video/?302781-1/jobs-drilling-arctic
-national-wildlife-refuge

C-SPAN (Producer). (2014, March 11). *International health care models* [Video]. https://
www.c-span.org/video/?318225-1/hearing-health-care-access-costs

C-SPAN (Producer). (2017a, January 17). *Education secretary confirmation hearing*
[Video]. https://www.c-span.org/video/?421224-1/education-secretary-nominee
-betsy-devos-testifies-confirmation-hearing

C-SPAN (Producer). (2017b, February 15). *Human trafficking and slavery* [Video]. https://
www.c-span.org/video/?424036-1/ashton-kutcher-testifies-modern-slavery
-human-trafficking

C-SPAN (Producer). (2017c, June 8). *Campaign 2018—Russian interference in 2016 election* [Video]. https://www.c-span.org/video/?429381-1/fbi-director-comey-testifies
-dismissal

C-SPAN (Producer). (2017d, September 6). *Judicial and Justice Department pending
nominations* [Video]. https://www.c-span.org/video/?433501-1/amy-coney-barrett
-testifies-seventh-circuit-confirmation-hearing-2017

C-SPAN (Producer). (2017e, October 31). *Facebook, Google and Twitter executives on
Russian disinformation* [Video]. https://www.c-span.org/video/?436454-1/facebook
-google-twitter-executives-testify-russia-election-ads

C-SPAN (Producer). (2018a, April 10). *Facebook CEO Mark Zuckerberg hearing on data
privacy and protection* [Video]. https://www.c-span.org/video/?443543-1/facebook
-ceo-mark-zuckerberg-testifies-data-protection

C-SPAN (Producer). (2018b, September 5). *Foreign influence and social media* [Video].
https://www.c-span.org/video/?450990-1/foreign-influence-social-media

C-SPAN (Producer). (2018c, September 27). *Supreme Court nominee Brett Kavanaugh
sexual assault hearing, Judge Kavanaugh testimony* [Video]. https://www.c-span
.org/video/?451895-2/supreme-court-nominee-brett-kavanaugh-sexual-assault
-hearing-judge-kavanaugh-testimony

C-SPAN (Producer). (2018d, September 27). *Supreme Court nominee Brett Kavanaugh
sexual assault hearing, Professor Blasey Ford testimony* [Video]. https://www.c-span
.org/video/?451895-1/professor-blasey-ford-testifies-sexual-assault-allegations-part-1

C-SPAN (Producer). (2019a, February 13). *Political situation in Venezuela* [Video].
https://www.c-span.org/video/?457781-1/venezuela-envoy-elliott-abrams-testifies
-political-crisis

C-SPAN (Producer). (2019b, February 27). *Michael Cohen testimony before House Oversight Committee* [Video]. https://www.c-span.org/video/?458125-1/michael-cohen
-president-trump-he-racist-con-man-cheat

C-SPAN (Producer). (2019c, May 1). *William Barr testimony on Mueller report before Senate Judiciary Committee* [Video]. https://www.c-span.org/video/?459922-1/william -barr-testimony-mueller-report-senate-judiciary-committee

C-SPAN (Producer). (2019d, June 11). *September 11 Victim Compensation Fund reauthorization* [Video]. https://www.c-span.org/video/?461603-1/jon-stewart-advocates -testify-911-victims-compensation-fund-hearing

C-SPAN (Producer). (2019e, July 18). *Migrant children and border security* [Video]. https://www.c-span.org/video/?462642-1/migrant-children-border-security

C-SPAN (Producer). (2019f, July 24). *Robert Mueller testifies before House Intelligence Committee* [Video]. https://www.c-span.org/video/?462629-1/robert-mueller -testifies-house-intelligence-committee

C-SPAN (Producer). (2019g, July 26). *House Oversight and Reform Committee hearing on prescription drug prices* [Video]. https://www.c-span.org/video/?463028-1/house -oversight-reform-committee-hearing-prescription-drug-prices

C-SPAN (Producer). (2019h, September 25). *House Judiciary Committee hearing on assault weapons* [Video]. https://www.c-span.org/video/?464471-1/house-judiciary -committee-hearing-assault-weapons

C-SPAN (Producer). (2020a, March 4). *Hearing on 5G technology and cybersecurity* [Video]. https://www.c-span.org/video/?469983-1/hearing-5g-technology-cyber security

C-SPAN (Producer). (2020b, March 11). *House Oversight and Reform Committee hearing on coronavirus response, Day 1* [Video]. https://www.c-span.org/video/?470224-1 /dr-fauci-warns-congress-coronavirus-outbreak-worse

C-SPAN (Producer). (2020c, November 17). *Facebook and Twitter CEOs testify on regulating social media content* [Video]. https://www.c-span.org/video/?478048-1 /facebook-twitter-ceos-testify-regulating-social-media-content

C-SPAN (Producer). (2021a, February 18). *GameStop hearing, Part 1* [Video]. https:// www.c-span.org/video/?508545-1/gamestop-hearing-part-1

C-SPAN (Producer). (2021b, February 18). *GameStop hearing, Part 2* [Video]. https:// www.c-span.org/video/?508545-2/gamestop-hearing-part-2

C-SPAN (Producer). (2021c, April 27). *House hearing on unaccompanied migrant children* [Video]. https://www.c-span.org/video/?511225-1/house-hearing-unac companied-migrant-children

C-SPAN (Producer). (2021d, May 4). *House hearing on organ transplant system* [Video]. https://www.c-span.org/video/?511457-1/house-hearing-organ-transplant-system

C-SPAN (Producer). (2021e, May 11). *Dr. Fauci and CDC director Walensky testify*

on efforts to combat COVID-19 [Video]. https://www.c-span.org/video/?511511-1/dr
-fauci-cdc-director-walensky-testify-efforts-combat-covid-19

C-SPAN (Producer). (2021f, July 20). *Senate hearing on COVID-19 response* [Video].
https://www.c-span.org/video/?513400-1/senate-hearing-covid-19-response&live

C-SPAN (Producer). (2021g, July 27). *Capitol and D.C. police testify on January 6 attack*
[Video]. https://www.c-span.org/video/?513434-1/capitol-dc-police-testify-january
-6-attack

C-SPAN (Producer). (2021h, September 13). *House Foreign Affairs hearing on U.S.
withdrawal from Afghanistan* [Video]. https://www.c-span.org/video/?514505-1
/secretary-blinken-afghanistan-withdrawal-inherited-deadline-inherit-plan

Dudash, E. (2007). International appeal in the presidential inaugural: An update on
genre and an expansion of argument. *Contemporary Argumentation and Debate,
28*(1), 47–64.

Duffy, B. K. (1993). President George Bush's inaugural address, 1989. In H. R. Ryan
(Ed.), *The inaugural addresses of twentieth-century American presidents*. Praeger.

Giglioni, C. (2019). Discursive construction of ethos-based framework for public identity: Investigative congressional hearings. *Lingue e Linguaggi, 33*, 109–124. https://
doi.org/10.1285/i22390359v33p109

Giglioni, C. (2020). *Linguistic and rhetorical perspectives on congressional hearings.*
Frank & Timme GmbH.

Gring-Pemble, L. M. (2001). "Are we going to now govern by anecdote?": Rhetorical
constructions of welfare recipients in congressional hearings, debates, and legislation, 1992–1996. *Quarterly Journal of Speech, 87*(4), 341–365. https://doi.org/10.1080
/00335630109384345

Guitar, J. (2020). Reclaiming white spaces: Reading Trump's inaugural address as a eu-
logy for the <American dream>. *Western Journal of Communication, 85*(3), 299–
318. https://doi.org/10.1080/10570314.2020.1789728

Guitar, J. (2021). *Dissent, discourse, and democracy: Whistleblowers as sites of political
contestation.* Lexington Books.

Irimiea, S. (2010). A rhetorical and comparative study of the victory speeches of Barack Obama and Mircea Geoana. *Journal of Linguistic and Intercultural Education,
3*(1), 41–53.

Joslyn, R. A. (1986). Keeping politics in the study of political discourse. In H. W. Si-
mons & A. A. Aghazarian (Eds.), *Form, genre, and the study of political discourse*
(pp. 301–338). University of South Carolina Press.

Klein, B. (2017, February). *Kutcher passionately testifies on his anti-sex trafficking ef-*

forts. CNN. https://edition.cnn.com/2017/02/15/politics/ashton-kutcher-testifies
-before-the-senate-on-sex-trafficking/index.html

Lipari, L. (1994). As the word turns: Drama, rhetoric, and press coverage of the Hill-
Thomas hearings. *Political Communication, 11*(3), 299–308. https://doi.org/10.1080
/10584609.1994.9963034

Mansky, J. (2017, June). How watching congressional hearings became an American
pastime: Decades before Watergate, mobsters helped turn hearings into must-see
television. *Smithsonian Magazine.* https://www.smithsonianmag.com/history/how
-watching-congressional-hearings-became-american-pastime-180963614/

Miller, C. R. (1984). Genre as social action. *Quarterly Journal of Speech, 70*(2), 151–167.
https://doi.org/10.1080/00335638409383686

Neville-Shepard, R. (2014). Triumph in defeat: The genre of third party presidential
concessions. *Communication Quarterly, 62*(2), 214–232. https://doi.org/10.1080/01
463373.2014.890119

Neville-Shepard, R. (2016). Unconventional: The variant of third-party nomination
acceptance addresses. *Western Journal of Communication, 80*(2), 121–139. https://
doi.org/10.1080/10570314.2015.1128560

Patton, J. (1976). Generic criticism: Typology at an inflated price. *Rhetoric Society
Quarterly, 6*(1), 4–8. https://www.jstor.org/stable/3885340

Peterson, E. (2019, Summer). Presidential power surges. *Harvard Law Bulletin.* https://
today.law.harvard.edu/feature/presidential-power-surges/

Phillips, A. (2016, March 17). The 9 most heated moments from Rick Snyder's
congressional hearing on the Flint water crisis. *Washington Post.* https://www
.washingtonpost.com/news/the-fix/wp/2016/03/17/the-9-most-heated-moments
-from-rick-snyders-congressional-hearing-on-the-flint-water-crisis/

Regan, A. (1994) Rhetoric and political process in the Hill-Thomas hearings, *Political
Communication, 11*(3), 277–285. https://doi.org/10.1080/10584609.1994.9963032

Rowland, R. C. (1991). On generic categorization. *Communication Theory, 1*(2), 128–
144. https://doi.org/10.1111/j.1468-2885.1991.tb00009.x

Rowland, R. C., & Jerome, A. M. (2004). On Organizational Apologia: A Reconceptu-
alization, *Communication Theory, 14*(3) 191–211. https://doi.org/10.1111/j.1468-2885
.2004.tb00311.x

Sheckels, T. F. (2010). Place, genre, and polyphony in Barack Obama's election night address. *American Behavioral Scientist, 54*(4), 394–405. https://doi.org/10.1177/00027
64210381715

Sigelman, L. (1996). Presidential inaugurals: The modernization of a genre. *Political
Communication, 13*(1), 81–92. https://doi.org/10.1080/10584609.1996.9963096

Swales, J. M. (1990). *Genre analysis: English in academic and research settings.* Cambridge University Press.

Troy, T. (2015, October). Congressional hearings aren't what they used to be. Here's how to make them better. *Washington Post.* http://www.washingtonpost.com /posteverything/wp/2015/10/21/congressional-hearings-arent-what-they-used-to -be-heres-how-to-make-them-better/

U.S. House of Representatives. (n.d.). *Electronic technology in the House of Representatives.* https://history.house.gov/Exhibitions-and-Publications/Electronic-Tech nology/House-Technology/

Vigil, T. R. (2013). George W. Bush's first three inaugural addresses: Testing the utility of the inaugural genre. *Southern Communication Journal, 78*(5), 427–446. https:// doi.org/10.1080/1041794X.2013.847479

Vynck, G. D., Zakrzewski, C., Dwoskin, E., & Lerman, R. (2021, March). Big tech CEOs face lawmakers in House hearing on social media's role in extremism, misinformation. *Washington Post.* https://www.washingtonpost.com/technology/2021/03/25 /facebook-google-twitter-house-hearing-live-updates/

Willyard, J., & Ritter, K. (2005). Election 2004 concession and victory speeches: The influence of genre, context, and speaker on addresses by presidential and vice presidential candidates. *American Behavioral Scientist, 49*(3), 488–509. https://doi .org/10.1177/0002764205279439

APPENDIX: ARTIFACTS

C-SPAN Watergate hearing video clips (Senate Select Presidential Campaign Activities Committee) [Videos]. https://www.c-span.org/search/?searchtype=Videos&s ort=Newest&sponsorid[]=22790

C-SPAN (Producer). (1975, September 16). *William Colby Church committee hearing* [Video]. https://www.c-span.org/video/?409091-1/william-colby-church-com mittee-hearing

C-SPAN (Producer). (1991, October 11). *Thomas second hearing day 1, Part 2* [Video]. https://www.c-span.org/video/?22097-1/clarence-thomas-confirmation-hearing

C-SPAN (Producer). (1998, November 19). *Impeachment inquiry pt. 2* [Video]. https:// www.c-span.org/video/?115500-1/impeachment-inquiry-pt-2

C-SPAN (Producer). (2001, September 25). *Homeland defense and anti-terrorism legislation* [Video]. https://www.c-span.org/video/?166281-1/homeland-defense-anti -terrorism-legislation

C-SPAN (Producer). (2002, March 13). *Budget resolution markup* [Video]. https://www.c-span.org/video/?169114-1/budget-resolution-markup-opening-statements

C-SPAN (Producer). (2005, March 17). *Steroid use in baseball players* [Video]. https://www.c-span.org/video/?185904-2/players-testify-steroid-baseball

C-SPAN (Producer). (2006, February 15). *Internet in China* [Video]. https://www.c-span.org/video/?191220-1/internet-china

C-SPAN (Producer). (2007, January 11). *U.S. policy toward Iraq* [Video]. https://www.c-span.org/video/?196140-1/us-policy-iraq

C-SPAN (Producer). (2007, November 6). *Internet privacy in China* [Video]. https://www.c-span.org/video/?202134-1/internet-privacy-china

C-SPAN (Producer). (2008, April 8). *Report on Iraq* [Video]. https://www.c-span.org/video/?204754-1/report-iraq

C-SPAN (Producer). (2008, July 23). *Gays and lesbians in the military* [Video]. https://www.c-span.org/video/?206528-1/gays-lesbians-military

C-SPAN (Producer). (2009, March 4). *Senate committee fiscal year 2010 budget overview* [Video]. https://www.c-span.org/video/?284419-1/senate-committee-fiscal-year-2010-budget-overview

C-SPAN (Producer). (2009, March 24). *Geithner and Bernanke testimony on AIG bonuses* [Video]. https://www.c-span.org/video/?284797-1/geithner-bernanke-testimony-aig-bonuses

C-SPAN (Producer). (2009, March 26). *Senate fiscal year 2010 budget markup, Part 1* [Video]. https://www.c-span.org/video/?284890-1/senate-fiscal-year-2010-budget-markup-part-1

C-SPAN (Producer). (2009, July 15). *Sotomayor confirmation hearing, Day 3, Part 1* [Video]. https://www.c-span.org/video/?287723-1/sotomayor-confirmation-hearing-day-3-part-1

C-SPAN (Producer). (2010, February 4). *Comcast and NBC Universal merger, Part 2* [Video]. https://www.c-span.org/video/?291928-2/comcast-nbc-universal-merger-part-2

C-SPAN (Producer). (2010, March 3). *Gays and lesbians in the military* [Video]. https://www.c-span.org/video/?292350-1/gays-lesbians-military

C-SPAN (Producer). (2010, April 27). *Investment banks and the financial crisis, Goldman Sachs chair and CEO* [Video]. https://www.c-span.org/video/?293196-3/goldman-sachs-ceo-testifies-financial-crisis

C-SPAN (Producer). (2010, April 27). *Marine mammal education* [Video]. https://www.c-span.org/video/?293204-1/marine-mammal-education

C-SPAN (Producer). (2010, September 24). *Immigrant farm workers* [Video]. https://www.c-span.org/video/?295639-1/immigrant-farm-workers

C-SPAN (Producer). (2010, December 16). *Wikileaks, the Espionage Act, and the Constitution* [Video]. https://www.c-span.org/video/?297115-1/wikileaksthe-espionage-act-constitution

C-SPAN (Producer). (2011, June 28). *Senior military commander nominees* [Video]. https://www.c-span.org/video/?300255-1/senior-military-commander-nominees

C-SPAN (Producer). (2011, November 18). *Jobs and drilling in Arctic National Wildlife Refuge* [Video]. https://www.c-span.org/video/?302781-1/jobs-drilling-arctic-national-wildlife-refuge

C-SPAN (Producer). (2013, March 7). *Gun control legislation markup* [Video]. https://www.c-span.org/video/?311364-1/gun-control-legislation-markup

C-SPAN (Producer). (2013, October 1). *EPA investigation of John Beale* [Video]. https://www.c-span.org/video/?315368-1/epa-investigation-john-beale

C-SPAN (Producer). (2014, March 11). *International health care models* [Video]. https://www.c-span.org/video/?318225-1/hearing-health-care-access-costs

C-SPAN (Producer). (2014, May 21). *Extraterrestrial life* [Video]. https://www.c-span.org/video/?319504-1/hearing-astrobiology-extraterrestrial-life

C-SPAN (Producer). (2015, March 24). *Deputy attorney general confirmation hearing* [Video]. https://www.c-span.org/video/?324983-1/confirmation-hearing-deputy-attorney-general-nominee-sally-quillian-yates

C-SPAN (Producer). (2015, March 26). *Diplomacy and foreign aid fiscal year 2016 budget* [Video]. https://www.c-span.org/video/?325026-1/ben-affleck-bill-gates-testimony-diplomacy-national-security

C-SPAN (Producer). (2015, October 22). *Hillary Clinton testimony at House Select Committee on Benghazi, Part 1* [Video]. https://www.c-span.org/video/?328699-1/hillary-clinton-testimony-house-select-committee-benghazi-part-1

C-SPAN (Producer). (2016, February 3). *Contaminated drinking water in Flint, Michigan* [Video]. https://www.c-span.org/video/?404078-1/hearing-contaminated-drinking-water-flint-michigan

C-SPAN (Producer). (2016, March 15). *Flint, Michigan water contamination* [Video]. https://www.c-span.org/video/?406539-1/hearing-flint-michigan-water-contamination

C-SPAN (Producer). (2016, July 7). *Hillary Clinton email investigation, Part 1* [Video]. https://www.c-span.org/video/?412315-1/fbi-director-james-comey-testifies-hillary-clinton-email-probe

C-SPAN (Producer). (2017, January 17). *Education secretary confirmation hearing* [Video]. https://www.c-span.org/video/?421224-1/education-secretary-nominee-betsy-devos-testifies-confirmation-hearing

C-SPAN (Producer). (2017, February 15). *Human trafficking and slavery* [Video]. https://

www.c-span.org/video/?424036-1/ashton-kutcher-testifies-modern-slavery
-human-trafficking

C-SPAN (Producer). (2017, March 20). *Campaign 2018—Russian election interference* [Video]. https://www.c-span.org/video/?425087-1/fbi-director-investigating-links -trump-campaign-russia

C-SPAN (Producer). (2017, May 8). *Campaign 2018—Russian interference in 2016 election* [Video]. https://www.c-span.org/video/?427577-1/white-house-warned -general-flynn-compromised

C-SPAN (Producer). (2017, June 8). *Campaign 2018—Russian interference in 2016 election* [Video]. https://www.c-span.org/video/?429381-1/fbi-director-comey-testifies- dismissal

C-SPAN (Producer). (2017, July 27). *Foreign Agents Registration Act* [Video]. https:// www.c-span.org/video/?431852-1/william-browder-overturning-magnitsky-act -putins-top-priority

C-SPAN (Producer). (2017, September 6). *Judicial and Justice Department pending nominations* [Video]. https://www.c-span.org/video/?433501-1/amy-coney-barrett -testifies-seventh-circuit-confirmation-hearing-2017

C-SPAN (Producer). (2017, October 11). *Opioid crisis* [Video]. https://www.c-span .org/video/?435560-1/house-members-testify-opioid-crisis-response

C-SPAN (Producer). (2017, October 31). *Facebook, Google and Twitter executives on Russian disinformation* [Video]. https://www.c-span.org/video/?436454-1/facebook -google-twitter-executives-testify-russia-election-ads

C-SPAN (Producer). (2017, December 7). *Environmental Protection Agency mission* [Video]. https://www.c-span.org/video/?438060-1/epa-administrator-testifies -house-energy-panel

C-SPAN (Producer). (2018, April 10). *Facebook CEO Mark Zuckerberg hearing on data privacy and protection* [Video]. https://www.c-span.org/video/?443543-1/facebook -ceo-mark-zuckerberg-testifies-data-protection

C-SPAN (Producer). (2018, July 12). *FBI deputy assistant director Peter Strzok on 2016 investigations* [Video]. https://www.c-span.org/video/?447953-1/fbi-deputy-assistant -director-peter-strzok-testifies-2016-investigations

C-SPAN (Producer). (2018, September 5). *Foreign influence and social media* [Video]. https://www.c-span.org/video/?450990-1/foreign-influence-social-media

C-SPAN (Producer). (2018, September 27). *Supreme Court nominee Brett Kavanaugh sexual assault hearing, Judge Kavanaugh testimony* [Video]. https://www.c-span .org/video/?451895-2/supreme-court-nominee-brett-kavanaugh-sexual-assault -hearing-judge-kavanaugh-testimony

C-SPAN (Producer). (2018, September 27). *Supreme Court nominee Brett Kavanaugh sexual assault hearing, Professor Blasey Ford testimony* [Video]. https://www.c-span.org/video/?451895-1/professor-blasey-ford-testifies-sexual-assault-allegations-part-1

C-SPAN (Producer). (2019, February 13). *Political situation in Venezuela* [Video]. https://www.c-span.org/video/?457781-1/venezuela-envoy-elliott-abrams-testifies-political-crisis

C-SPAN (Producer). (2019, February 27). *Michael Cohen testimony before House Oversight Committee* [Video]. https://www.c-span.org/video/?458125-1/michael-cohen-president-trump-he-racist-con-man-cheat

C-SPAN (Producer). (2019, May 1). *William Barr testimony on Mueller report before Senate Judiciary Committee* [Video]. https://www.c-span.org/video/?459922-1/william-barr-testimony-mueller-report-senate-judiciary-committee

C-SPAN (Producer). (2019, June 11). *September 11 Victim Compensation Fund reauthorization* [Video]. https://www.c-span.org/video/?461603-1/jon-stewart-advocates-testify-911-victims-compensation-fund-hearing

C-SPAN (Producer). (2019, July 16). *Online platforms and entrepreneurship* [Video]. https://www.c-span.org/video/?462660-1/online-platforms-entrepreneurship

C-SPAN (Producer). (2019, July 17). *Facebook digital currency* [Video]. https://www.c-span.org/video/?462708-4/facebook-digital-currency

C-SPAN (Producer). (2019, July 18). *Migrant children and border security* [Video]. https://www.c-span.org/video/?462642-1/migrant-children-border-security

C-SPAN (Producer). (2019, July 24). *Robert Mueller testifies before House Intelligence Committee* [Video]. https://www.c-span.org/video/?462629-1/robert-mueller-testifies-house-intelligence-committee

C-SPAN (Producer). (2019, July 26). *House Oversight and Reform Committee hearing on prescription drug prices* [Video]. https://www.c-span.org/video/?463028-1/house-oversight-reform-committee-hearing-prescription-drug-prices

C-SPAN (Producer). (2019, September 18). *House hearing on climate change* [Video]. https://www.c-span.org/video/?464405-1/youth-activists-urge-lawmakers-action-climate-change

C-SPAN (Producer). (2019, September 25). *House Judiciary Committee hearing on assault weapons* [Video]. https://www.c-span.org/video/?464471-1/house-judiciary-committee-hearing-assault-weapons

C-SPAN (Producer). (2019, October 23). *Facebook CEO testimony before House Financial Services Committee* [Video]. https://www.c-span.org/video/?465293-1/facebook-ceo-testimony-house-financial-services-committee

C-SPAN (Producer). (2019, November 19). *Impeachment hearing with Lieutenant Colo-*

nel Vindman and Jennifer Williams [Video]. https://www.c-span.org/video/?466376
-1/impeachment-hearing-lt-col-vindman-jennifer-williams

C-SPAN (Producer). (2020, March 4). *Hearing on 5G technology and cybersecurity* [Video].
https://www.c-span.org/video/?469983-1/hearing-5g-technology-cybersecurity

C-SPAN (Producer). (2020, March 11). *House Oversight and Reform Committee hearing
on coronavirus response, Day 1* [Video]. https://www.c-span.org/video/?470224-1
/dr-fauci-warns-congress-coronavirus-outbreak-worse

C-SPAN (Producer). (2020, March 12). *House Oversight and Reform Committee hearing
on coronavirus response, Day 2* [Video]. https://www.c-span.org/video/?470277-1
/federal-health-officials-testify-coronavirus-outbreak-response

C-SPAN (Producer). (2020, May 12). *White House Coronavirus Task Force members
testify on coronavirus response and reopening phases* [Video]. https://www.c-span
.org/video/?471837-1/white-house-coronavirus-task-force-members-testify
-coronavirus-response-reopening-phases

C-SPAN (Producer). (2020, June 3). *Former deputy attorney testimony on the FBI's Russia
investigation* [Video]. https://www.c-span.org/video/?472540-1/deputy-attorney
-testimony-fbis-russia-investigation

C-SPAN (Producer). (2020, June 10). *House Judiciary Committee hearing on police reform*
[Video]. https://www.c-span.org/video/?472839-1/house-judiciary-committee
-hearing-police-reform

C-SPAN (Producer). (2020, June 30). *Senate hearing on COVID-19 and the IRS*
[Video]. https://www.c-span.org/video/?473495-1/senate-hearing-covid-19-irs

C-SPAN (Producer). (2020, July 28). *Attorney General Barr testifies on Justice Department
mission and programs* [Video]. https://www.c-span.org/video/?473384-1/attorney
-general-barr-testifies-justice-department-mission-programs

C-SPAN (Producer). (2020, July 29). *Heads of Facebook, Amazon, Apple & Google testify
on antitrust law* [Video]. https://www.c-span.org/video/?474236-1/heads-facebook
-amazon-apple-google-testify-antitrust-law

C-SPAN (Producer). (2020, October 12). *Barrett confirmation hearing, Day 1, Part 1*
[Video]. https://www.c-span.org/video/?476315-1/barrett-confirmation-hearing
-day-1-part-1

C-SPAN (Producer). (2020, October 13). *Barrett confirmation hearing, Day 2 Part 1*
[Video]. https://www.c-span.org/video/?476316-1/barrett-confirmation-hearing
-day-2-part-1

C-SPAN (Producer). (2020, October 14). *Barrett confirmation hearing, Day 3 Part 2*
[Video]. https://www.c-span.org/video/?476317-2/barrett-confirmation-hearing
-day-3-part-2

C-SPAN (Producer). (2020, November 17). *Facebook and Twitter CEOs testify on regulating social media content* [Video]. https://www.c-span.org/video/?478048-1/facebook-twitter-ceos-testify-regulating-social-media-content

C-SPAN (Producer). (2020, December 16). *Senate hearing on U.S–China economic policy* [Video]. https://www.c-span.org/video/?507327-1/senate-hearing-us-china-economic-policy

C-SPAN (Producer). (2021, January 19). *Secretary of state confirmation hearing* [Video]. https://www.c-span.org/video/?507953-1/secretary-state-nominee-antony-blinken-testifies-confirmation-hearing

C-SPAN (Producer). (2021, February 18). *GameStop hearing, Part 1* [Video]. https://www.c-span.org/video/?508545-1/gamestop-hearing-part-1

C-SPAN (Producer). (2021, February 18). *GameStop hearing, Part 2* [Video]. https://www.c-span.org/video/?508545-2/gamestop-hearing-part-2

C-SPAN (Producer). (2021, March 10). *House Foreign Affairs Committee hearing on Biden administration foreign policy priorities* [Video]. https://www.c-span.org/video/?509633-1/house-foreign-affairs-committee-hearing-biden-administration-foreign-policy-priorities

C-SPAN (Producer). (2021, March 17). *Senate Judiciary Committee holds hearing on LGBTQ rights legislation* [Video]. https://www.c-span.org/video/?509953-1/senate-judiciary-committee-holds-hearing-lgbtq-rights-legislation

C-SPAN (Producer). (2021, April 27). *House hearing on unaccompanied migrant children* [Video]. https://www.c-span.org/video/?511225-1/house-hearing-unaccompanied-migrant-children

C-SPAN (Producer). (2021, May 4). *House hearing on organ transplant system* [Video]. https://www.c-span.org/video/?511457-1/house-hearing-organ-transplant-system

C-SPAN (Producer). (2021, May 10). *Threat assessment of January 6 attack on U.S. Capitol* [Video]. https://www.c-span.org/video/?511542-1/house-hearing-january-6-us-capitol-attack

C-SPAN (Producer). (2021, May 11). *Dr. Fauci and CDC director Walensky testify on efforts to combat COVID-19* [Video]. https://www.c-span.org/video/?511511-1/dr-fauci-cdc-director-walensky-testify-efforts-combat-covid-19

C-SPAN (Producer). (2021, June 9). *Office of Management and Budget fiscal year 2022 budget request* [Video]. https://www.c-span.org/video/?512435-1/white-house-budget-director-young-testifies-presidents-fy-2022-reques

C-SPAN (Producer). (2021, June 15). *FBI director Christopher Wray testifies on U.S. Capitol attack* [Video]. https://www.c-span.org/video/?512552-1/fbi-director-christopher-wray-testifies-us-capitol-attack

C-SPAN (Producer). (2021, June 15). *House hearing on January 6 U.S. Capitol attack* [Video]. https://www.c-span.org/video/?512551-1/us-capitol-police-inspector-general -testifies-january-6-attack

C-SPAN (Producer). (2021, June 24). *House hearing on Department of Education priorities* [Video]. https://www.c-span.org/video/?512743-1/house-hearing-department -education-priorities

C-SPAN (Producer). (2021, July 20). *Senate hearing on COVID-19 response* [Video]. https://www.c-span.org/video/?513400-1/senate-hearing-covid-19-response&live

C-SPAN (Producer). (2021, July 27). *Capitol and D.C. police testify on January 6 attack* [Video]. https://www.c-span.org/video/?513434-1/capitol-dc-police-testify-january -6-attack

C-SPAN (Producer). (2021, September 13). *House Foreign Affairs hearing on U.S. withdrawal from Afghanistan* [Video]. https://www.c-span.org/video/?514505-1/secretary -blinken-afghanistan-withdrawal-inherited-deadline-inherit-plan

7

STRONG MEN, CARING WOMEN?
How Gender Shapes Emotional Political Rhetoric

Jared McDonald and Zachary Scott

INTRODUCTION

Despite record numbers of women running for and winning elected office (CAWP, 2020), research on politics and gender consistently shows that women face a unique set of barriers to public service (e.g., Bauer, 2020; Dolan et al., 2019). Such barriers stem from the historical fact that political leadership has been dominated by men, and thus classical conceptions of leadership are imbued with a masculine set of qualities. Scholarship drawing on theories in social cognition, gender stereotyping, and candidate character find that women and men face different incentives in terms of the traits they can convey to the general public (McDonald & Piatak, in press). Because "agentic" traits (i.e., those conveying an individual's independence from others) such as strong, decisive leadership are perceived as "owned" by men while "communal" traits (i.e., those conveying an individual's ability to work well with others) such as caring or compassion are "owned" by women (Hayes, 2011) due to gender stereotyping (Alexander & Andersen, 1993), politicians who go against gendered stereotypes may be viewed less favorably.

At the same time, other scholarship has suggested that partisanship is the overwhelming factor that shapes citizens' attitudes toward political leaders (e.g., Mason, 2018). Drawing on Petrocik's (1996) theory of issue ownership, Hayes (2005) shows that voters perceive each party as enjoying advantages on distinctive characteristics or traits. Republicans are perceived to "own" the trait of strong leadership while Democrats are perceived to "own" the trait of compassion or empathy due to the policies and issue positions they champion. Recognizing that voters are likely to infer the traits of candidates based on both partisanship and gender, Hayes (2011) shows that partisanship is often the primary driver of trait perceptions in Senate elections, though gender still plays an important role in citizens' inferences about various candidates. What is less clear, however, is whether politicians act in ways that suggest they are aware of the incentives they face and the assumptions made about them. In other words, are men and women politicians aware of the gendered and partisan expectations in their public messaging strategies and do they respond accordingly? Do Republicans and Democrats follow suit as well? If politicians do, in fact, play to type, there is the additional question of whether those politicians are responding to incentives or if achieving political success is simply predicated on a tendency to hew to type. With this research, we examine these questions as they relate to rhetorical displays of traits and gender and partisan stereotyping. Specifically, we investigate the use of rhetoric invoking the conventionally masculine and Republican trait of authority and the conventionally feminine and Democratic trait of caring by men and women, Republican and Democratic politicians. Furthermore, we conduct this investigation across an array of political contexts. This allows us to explore whether the political circumstances—like the issue content, whether the political figure is engaged in campaigning or in governing, or whether they are messaging during particularly emotionally turbulent times—affect concordance between politician gender, partisanship, and rhetorical style. Doing so allows us to gain purchase on the mechanism underpinning any gendered or partisan differences in the use of trait appeals. If there is a great deal of consistency across contexts, then this would suggest that effects are driven by the types of people who successfully navigate politics. If the effects vary, however, then this would suggest that the primary culprit is politicians actively appealing to the preferences of audiences.

This research relies on data from the C-SPAN Video Library, which provides robust access to rhetoric from many political figures in varied contexts. We utilized the C-SPAN Video Library in three ways. First, by retrieving remarks made by presidential primary candidates at campaign events broadcast and archived by C-SPAN. This provides a corpus of nearly 3,400 speeches by more than 100 distinct campaigns, including 12 by women candidates. These events clearly involve politicians acting primarily in their role as campaigners and are highly emotional and public. Second, by retrieving floor speeches made by members of the House of Representatives during the second impeachment of Donald Trump (January

11–13, 2021). While still highly public, this context involves politicians acting primarily as governing agents. The overarching circumstances are also highly emotional. Third, by retrieving floor speeches made by members of the House of Representatives between March 17 and March 19, 2021. This also involves the politician acting as a governing agent but represents a less publicly salient circumstance, and a time period dealing directly with gendered issues (including the renewal of the Violence Against Women Act and revoking the lapsed deadline for the Equal Rights Amendment).[1] As a final test to make sure that any observed results are not purely a function of politicians responding to the cameras, we replicate the results using the DCinbox archive of emails from members of Congress from 2010 to 2020. These emails are sent to a list of supporters and so are best characterized as capturing the politicians as campaigners in a less public communicative venue.

We apply the Moral Foundations Dictionary (Graham et al., 2009) to these four text corpora, paying special attention to the volume of language related to the traditionally masculine "authority" dimension and the more feminine "caring" dimension. The findings are most consistent with the notion of party-owned traits—Republicans are far more likely to use authority-oriented language and Democrats are more likely to use caring-oriented language. Yet, to a lesser degree, we find important shifts in trait-based rhetoric depending on the gender of the politician. Women, especially Republican women, are more likely to employ caring language in the context of governing and emails to supporters, but in only one case (House floor speeches on gendered issues) do we find them using less authority language. Among Democrats, gendered differences are scant, with women using more caring language only in the context of emails sent to lists of supporters. In light of this, we posit that partisanship often overwhelms the effect of gender in trait-based rhetoric, but that Republican women may be responsive.

Because political leadership remains a largely male-dominated profession, we further suggest that women are far more restricted in the type of language they can use without fear of penalty and, by extension, the types of policies they can champion. This research deepens our understanding of the types of gendered communications we may see in the future and provides important context for the pressures men and women face when seeking to connect with an electorate that has different expectations for men and women politicians.

We proceed in four parts. First, we lay out the ways in which political science has approached questions of candidate character. We draw on the social psychological framework of agency and communion as two meta-traits that comprise multiple subtypes and discuss the various ways political scientists have conceptualized candidate character. Second, we draw on evidence in studies of leadership that suggest that men are pressured to emphasize agentic skills while women face incentives to emphasize communion. This research informs our expectations of the types of language we should expect from men and women, and from Republicans and Democrats. Third, we describe the data and present findings consistent with the hypotheses that individuals in political leadership most often employ character-based rhetoric that is in line with their partisanship and gender. Fourth, we discuss the implications of the findings in the context of gender bias and the barriers women face when seeking public office.

CANDIDATE CHARACTER AND GENDER STEREOTYPES

The Dimensions of Candidate Character

The literature on candidate character is highly contested. Scholars have debated the exact dimensions of candidate character (Aaldering & Vliegenthart, 2016), though Kinder's (1986) work on presidential character is widely credited with conceptualizing the original framework for categorizing traits, including competence, leadership, integrity, and empathy. In the decades since Kinder's conceptualization, scholars working in the American and European contexts have struggled to identify the precise dimensions of political character. Some have argued for as few as two dimensions with others arguing for as many as six (see e.g., Aaldering & Vliegenthart, 2016; Greene, 2001).

Psychologists working on perceptions of traits have focused on two distinct dimensions, which can be thought of as "meta-traits" in that they encompass many of the more specific traits identified by Kinder (1986) and others. These include dimensions related to agency (i.e., competence) and communion (i.e., warmth) (Cuddy et al., 2008; Fiske et al., 2007; Fiske et al., 2002). Traits associated with both agency and communion are viewed as influencing perceptions of overall candidate favorability (Barker et al., 2006; Funk, 1999), though some (e.g., Miller et al., 1986) suggest that perceptions of agentic traits are far more consequential since the warmth of a leader offers no instrumental benefit (Fiorina, 1981).

Clifford (2018), drawing on research in psychology, notes that warmth may comprise both sociability and morality, though only the latter is considered valuable in a leader (Goodwin, 2015), which ultimately drives positive feelings toward the leader (Brambilla et al., 2013; Leach et al., 2007). Drawing on this framework,

Clifford (2018) suggests that candidate characteristics can be best viewed through the lens of moral foundations theory (MFT), which offers a structure for moral judgment (Davies et al., 2014; Federico et al., 2013; Graham et al., 2009; Haidt & Joseph, 2004). The dimensions of moral character are thought to comprise authority (e.g., strong leadership, toughness), sanctity (e.g., purity, modesty), fairness (e.g., honest, unbiased), care (e.g., empathy, sympathy), and loyalty (e.g., patriotism), to which Clifford (2018) adds competence (e.g., intelligence, knowledge). For the purposes of the present research, it is important to note that, regardless of the precise framework or number of dimensions, scholars consistently find that perceptions of leadership/authority and caring/empathy are strongly related to overall evaluations of candidates and vote choice (Campbell, 1983; Greene, 2001; Holian & Prysby, 2015; McDonald, 2020; Miller et al., 1986).[2]

Although it may be entirely rational for citizens to use evaluations of candidate character to inform their voting decisions (Holian & Prysby, 2015), the processes by which individuals come to view politicians as strong or caring leaders may be biased. Constituents rarely get to know their elected officials intimately as people and are thus left to make judgments based on a limited number of characteristics. Drawing from the literature on trait ownership, we focus on two key characteristics: gender and partisanship.

Gender Penalties for Going "Against Type"

Using the paradigm of agency and communion as meta-traits, scholars have shown that men are perceived as excelling on agentic traits while women are perceived as stronger on communion traits (Abele et al., 2008 Alexander & Andersen, 1993; Banwart, 2010; Banwart & McKinney, 2005). Agency comprises qualities like assertiveness, decision-making, and intelligence, while communion comprises compassion, friendliness, and fair-mindedness.

Women, however, face a dilemma when seeking positions of leadership. Masculine qualities related to agency are generally viewed as preferable for those positions (Huddy & Terkildsen, 1993). Further complicating matters, women face a backlash for going "against type" and evoking qualities traditionally viewed as masculine (Eagly & Karau, 2002; McDonald & Piatak, in press; Rudman, 1998). Jamieson (1995) famously argued that women in leadership face a double bind, meaning a successful woman seeking a leadership role is pressured to convey historically masculine qualities such as competence and confidence, but in turn is penalized for appearing less feminine. It is not surprising then that, although women have been running for and winning elected office at high rates, research finds that women who win are more qualified than the men with whom they serve (Bauer, 2020; Holman et al., 2017), as those able to overcome these barriers must be truly talented politicians.

Scholarship in psychology, sociology, and public administration suggests competing, though somewhat complimentary, theories for why women seeking leadership positions often face a backlash. For example, expectancy violation theory (e.g., Burgoon, 1993) argues that the public is more reactive to information that runs counter to expectations—expectations often informed by gender stereotypes of women as maternal, nurturing individuals rather than strong leaders. A woman who conveys her qualifications as a strong leader thus violates the expectations of the observer. Role incongruity theory (e.g., Eagly, 1987; Rudman et al., 2012) similarly suggests that some may view women as compassionate and therefore a poor fit for certain types of leadership roles. It is not that women are penalized for making claims about their leadership skills per se, but that individuals apply sexist stereotypes to women regardless of their individual qualifications and therefore view them as not meeting the criteria for a leadership role. Finally, implicit leadership theory (e.g., Lord et al., 2020) posits that people mentally generate a prototype of a leader that is based in part on real-world examples of leaders, where men are overrepresented. Taken together, we note that individual biases regarding gender and gender roles in society shape perceptions of who is a leader and who is not.

Do the same limitations apply to men? In some ways, the answer may be yes. After all, men who emphasize characteristics related to caring are subverting gendered stereotypes in the same way as a woman who conveys strong leadership or authority. Yet men are likely still advantaged for two reasons. First, as previously noted, some research finds that qualities owned by men, such as leadership and authority, are considered more crucial for holding leadership positions (Fiorina, 1981; Huddy & Terkildsen, 1993). Second, it is not just that traditionally masculine qualities are considered more relevant for political leadership but that the presence of a woman in leadership (regardless of the qualities she possesses) may be considered incongruent. Men have traditionally occupied leadership positions, so there are fewer messages that would appear incongruent. Whether it is Bill Clinton claiming to "feel your pain" or George W. Bush portraying himself as a "compassionate conservative," there are numerous examples of men in American political history evoking the trait of compassion. Women's participation in politics lacks this history. Instead, women have been more welcome when their participation comes from the background of advocating on a narrowly defined set of women's issues and when the women are seen as advocating on the basis of their roles as mothers, teachers, or some other "caring" position. This explains why women are more successful seeking office in collaborative environments such as legislatures than when seeking executive positions (Fox & Oxley, 2003).

These literatures paint a compelling picture: Citizens reward leaders with particular qualities, but this reward may be conditional. If a voter perceives a candidate to be making a claim about their leadership skills or capacity for compassion and it conflicts with a gendered stereotype, the message may backfire. These dynamics create an incentive for men and women in politics to play to type, leading us to our first hypothesis.

Gender constraints hypothesis: *Women politicians will use more caring language and less authority language than men in similar positions.*

Partisan Penalties for Going "Against Type"

Gender is not the only factor influencing perceptions of candidate character. Voters make inferences about politicians' issue positions, ideologies, and connections to social groups on the basis of partisanship (Feldman & Conover, 1983; Lau & Redlawsk, 2001; Rahn, 1993). Hayes (2005) argues that partisan stereotypes even extend to the character traits of the politicians. Republicans are routinely rated as stronger leaders than Democrats, while Democrats are routinely rated more positively on the trait of empathy (Holian & Prysby, 2015). Even in the 2004 presidential campaign, when the popular narrative was that Democrat John Kerry was a wealthy, windsurfing New England elitist compared to the folksy, "compassionate conservative" incumbent president, Kerry was still rated on public opinion surveys as being the more caring of the two.[3]

Given these lines of research, partisanship may influence the types of character-based appeals in two ways. First, the Democratic Party's ownership of compassion and the Republican Party's ownership of strong leadership may lead to a similar mechanism that exists for gender, whereby voters generate expectations about the types of personal appeals politicians *should* make on the basis of partisanship and punish politicians who go against type. Conversely, Republicans and Democrats may themselves be appealing to different electorates that value different characteristics in public officials. Because the Democratic Party owns compassion, Democratic-leaning voters may prefer candidates who employ messages in line with this trait, whereas Republicans may respond more positively to politicians who convey strong, decisive leadership. In the case of partisan primaries, politicians are literally making their case to separate groups of voters, though even in general elections there are reasons to suspect that politicians may only try to appeal to the subset of voters they believe are necessary to win office.

Both partisanship and gender may be considered heuristics by which individuals make assessments about the characteristics of candidates, which in turn put pressures on those candidates to conform to expectations. Which of these factors should be most important? Hayes (2011) examines the 2006 U.S. Senate elections, concluding that, although both party and gender influence the assumptions people make about the candidates, party is ultimately the dominant factor. This leaves open the possibility that politicians will not adopt different rhetorical strategies on the basis of their gender once we account for the influence of partisanship. This leads us to a second hypothesis for the types of messages we may expect to see from politicians.

Partisan constraints hypothesis: *Democratic politicians will use more caring language and less authority language than Republicans in similar positions.*

Though the primary goal of the present research is to investigate these two hypotheses, we hope to go one step further by looking at different contexts to see when gender and partisanship may appear to be a more dominant influence on the rhetorical choices of candidates. By doing so, we think it is possible to gain suggestive insight into the mechanism driving any partisan or gendered difference in trait appeals. If, for example, a difference is largely consistent across varied contexts, then this would suggest that the difference is driven primarily by the people making the trait appeals. Alternatively, if there is a great deal of variation across contexts with divergent audiences, then this would suggest that rhetorical choices are an attempt to appease audiences with differing preferences. Such suggestive evidence would be invaluable to scholars of gender and politics as it would point toward root causes. We do this in two ways.

First, we look at data sources ranging from presidential primary speeches, to floor speeches made in the U.S. Congress, to emails sent by members of the U.S. Congress to those on their fundraising lists. These types of communication vary greatly in terms of their public visibility. If differences are most apparent in contexts with the highest visibility (primary campaign speeches), it suggests that politicians are making active decisions to alter the language of their communications to avoid any electoral punishment for not conforming to gendered norms. If differences appear across all data sources, however, regardless of the visibility, it suggests that perhaps these choices are not made intentionally. Instead, it may be that successful politicians are those who instinctively use language that conforms to gender stereotypes.

Second, we examine floor speeches in very distinct contexts. In certain contexts, the public's demand for authority language may be relatively high (e.g., after a violent attack from an adversarial group). In other contexts, the demand for caring language may be relatively high (e.g., when the agenda is focused on helping those who have suffered some trauma). If we find that women/men or Democrats/Republicans are responsive to these contexts, it suggests that they are aware of their party's distinct advantage on matters of compassion and leadership and are making strategic decisions about the use of trait-based rhetoric.

DATA AND METHODS

Testing these hypotheses inherently requires a diverse set of corpora that include politicians facing myriad incentive structures. Fortunately, C-SPAN has been recording politicians and transmitting their messages largely unfiltered for decades, with the results of these efforts being helpfully archived with the C-SPAN Video Library. We turn to this resource as the primary means of assembling a collection of data sources capable of providing insight into critical questions about the intersection of politician gender, partisanship, and political context.

We began by identifying corpora that document politicians in the act of governing. We furthermore attempted to differentiate between highly salient governing contexts, where politicians are reasonably sure that their remarks will be closely scrutinized, and less salient governing contexts, where politicians can rest assured that only the most devoted political junkie is tuning in. For the former, we used floor speeches made by members of the House of Representatives during the second impeachment of Donald Trump (January 11–13, 2021).

Members of Congress were acting on their constitutionally charged responsibility and were about as temporally removed from an election incentive as is possible, making it a governing context, but the event itself was historic in nature and highly emotionally charged, making it an unusually salient one. For a less salient governing act, we choose a three-day window in March (17–19) to mirror the impeachment corpus. Floor debates covered several topics on the House agenda, but none commanded anywhere near as much attention as the second impeachment. As such, politicians remain acting as governing agents but can rest assured that they likely face weaker audience pressures since fewer people are tuning in to their every word. We retrieved the closed caption transcript from the House session for each day and separated excerpts by speaker.

Next, we looked for corpora that capture politicians as campaigners, speaking not of the merits and demerits of policy but in advocacy of themselves and opposition to those who would diminish their self-interest. First, we used the Presidential Primary Communication Corpus (PPCC) (Scott, 2021a, 2021b), which contains the transcripts of nearly 3,400 speeches by major presidential primary candidates from 2000 through 2020. These transcripts were collected from the C-SPAN Video Library. These are declared candidates on the trail actively speaking on why they deserve their party's nomination and so are highly salient campaign events. Finally, we use DCinbox (https://www.dcinbox.com/), which includes emails from members of Congress to their lists of supporters. We retrieved the complete corpus, more than 120,000 emails, from January 2010 to December 2020. This corpus also gives insight into politicians as self-advocates, capturing their work as dutiful campaigners. But it also documents their behavior away from the glare of C-SPAN cameras. As such, we can observe how members of Congress deploy rhetoric when they think very few, and only those already inclined to support them, are paying attention. These therefore are a low salience form of politician's campaign communication.

The diversity and scope of these corpora are essential for testing our hypotheses but present a notable challenge: identifying a means of reliably and validly measuring the key concepts of interest that works equally well across all of these corpora. We settled on the Moral Foundations Dictionaries (Graham et al., 2009), specifically the measures of Authority/Respect and Harm/Care. These dictionaries measure the amounts of moral appeals to the need to respect social order and to the need for compassion for the suffering of others, respectively. As Clifford (2018) argues, moral foundations serve as the guiding principle behind candidate trait evaluations, making them an apt basis of comparison for our stated hypotheses. They have been carefully validated in a range of corpora. As such, we are confident in their ability to measure our core concepts of interest in all four corpora. We applied each dictionary to each of our corpora and used the percentage of words identified in concordance with the moral dimensions of authority and care as our dependent variables.[4]

Our two main independent variables are the politician's gender, measured with an indicator variable coded 1 if the politician is a woman, and the politician's partisanship, measured with an indicator variable coded 1 if the politician is a Republican. We expect the politician's gender to have largely positive relationships with the measure of caring rhetoric and largely negative relationships with the measure of authority rhetoric. We also expect Republicans will be more likely to use authority language and less caring language, as the theory of trait ownership would suggest (Hayes, 2011). Scholars of rhetoric and political parties further suggest that Democrats and Republicans deploy different rhetorical styles (Gitlin, 2007; Hart et al., 2013; Weaver, 1953) and that there are more women in office in the Democratic party. As such, we need to ensure that any observed relationships can really be attributed to politician gender rather than partisanship, which we accomplish by controlling for the latter.

We include several control variables to account for other candidate and contextual attributes that may influence caring or authority rhetoric. First is seniority, or the politician's amount of political experience. Those with more political experience naturally accumulate more authority and occupy positions of privilege in the political hierarchy. As such, we might expect that senior politicians use more authority language. If women are less likely to stay in politics, this could also create a spurious relationship. Thus, we control for the number of Congresses a member has served (in the second impeachment, March 17–19, and DCinbox corpora) or the total number of years of political office (in the primary speeches corpus). For this same reason, we also control for majority status within the chamber, majority leadership, and minority leadership in the DCinbox corpus. To the extent that these are conflated with gender or partisanship, they could hinder our ability to document true relationships.[5] Finally, we control for whether an email was sent in an election year or not in models using the DCinbox corpus. We might expect that politicians use more caring language when they must face their electorate sooner rather than later.

Our dependent variables are continuous measures warranting ordinary least squares (OLS). A key assumption of linear regression is the independence of observations. In our two governing corpora, we think there is good reason to believe this assumption holds. Each member talks only a few times at most and remarks are largely prepared so that the order is of little consequence. But this assumption is tenuous in the presidential primary speech and DCinbox corpora. The times may incentivize the use of caring or authority appeals. For example, authority rhetoric may be more useful when war is the main issue of the day, as in the 2004 Democratic primary, while caring rhetoric may be the best strategy when in the throes of an economic recession, as in the later stages of the 2008 Democratic primary. Observations that are temporally proximate are therefore not independent. We account for this by including campaign fixed effects in the models of primary speeches and Congress fixed effects in the models of the DCinbox.[6] Second, individual politicians may have idiosyncratic speaking styles that are more or less caring or authoritative.

Observations attributable to the same speaker are therefore not independent. We account for this by using robust standard errors clustered on the politician in models of both corpora.[7]

RESULTS

Table 7.1 presents the models regressing the total amount of caring language on politician gender, partisanship, and the aforementioned control variables from each of the four corpora datasets. Table 7.2 does the same for the total amount of authority language. To reiterate, our first hypothesis is that women politicians will use more caring language than their men counterparts, while men will use more authority language than women politicians. As such, we expect the coefficient of politician gender to be consistently positive in Table 7.1 and consistently negative in Table 7.2. The results are somewhat supportive of these hypotheses. The coefficients are indeed positive across all four models in Table 7.1, but only statistically significant in half. Furthermore, only half of the coefficients in Table 7.2 are in the expected direction and none are statistically significant. In general, this suggests that women politicians embrace a more caring rhetorical style—as expectancy violation, role incongruity, and implicit leadership theories suggest—but there is no clear evidence that this comes at the expense of their ability to invoke authority relative to men in the same political situations. This may be attributable, as Jamieson (1995) suggests, to the need for women to convey *both* masculine and feminine traits to be perceived as qualified to hold public office, whereas men are more likely to receive the benefit of the doubt.

Partisanship exerts a stronger and more consistent effect in the hypothesized direction. Across all four models in Table 7.1, Republican politicians consistently use less caring language than Democrats. The coefficients are all statistically significant and the most substantively powerful in each model. While Democrats

TABLE 7.1 *Effect of Politician Gender on Care Rhetoric*

	Impeachment floor debate (1)	March 17–19 floor debates (2)	Primary speeches (3)	DCinbox (4)
Woman	0.143	0.389*	0.124	0.142*
	(0.181)	(0.221)	(0.076)	(0.039)
Republican	−0.661*	−0.618*	−0.277*	−0.147*
	(0.184)	(0.236)	(0.067)	(0.030)
Seniority	−0.061*	−0.048*	0.003	0.010*
	(0.018)	(0.020)	(0.002)	(0.003)
Senate				0.133*
				(0.035)
Chamber majority				0.022
				(0.019)
Majority leadership				−0.066
				(0.097)
Minority leadership				0.002
				(0.074)
Election year				0.039*
				(0.008)
Constant	2.069*	2.059*	1.015*	1.101*
	(0.181)	(0.263)	(0.075)	(0.033)
Observations	215	285	3,395	120,120
R²	0.091	0.062	0.095	0.031
Fixed effects	None	None	Campaign	Congress
Clustered standard errors	None	None	Candidate	MC

Note: Dependent variables sum of Moral Foundations Dictionaries of Caring–Virtue and Caring–Vice. All models OLS regression. MC = member of Congress.
*$p < .05$, one-tailed.

were much more likely to use authority language during the second impeachment trial of President Trump, which is almost assuredly due to the specific political circumstances, Republicans used more authority language in the other three corpora. The coefficient is statistically significant in two and nears statistical significance ($p = .115$) in the remaining one. Again, the coefficients are substantively important in that they show partisanship strongly predicts authority language in comparison to the other variables.

TABLE 7.2 *Effect of Politician Gender on Authority Rhetoric*

	Impeachment floor debate (1)	March 17–19 floor debates (2)	Primary speeches (3)	DCinbox (4)
Woman	0.177	−0.011	0.015	−0.014
	(0.217)	(0.122)	(0.057)	(0.015)
Republican	−0.652*	0.267*	0.090	0.157*
	(0.221)	(0.130)	(0.054)	(0.016)
Seniority	−0.009	0.008	0.003	0.005*
	(0.022)	(0.011)	(0.002)	(0.001)
Senate				0.016
				(0.019)
Chamber majority				−0.018*
				(0.008)
Majority leadership				0.171*
				(0.071)
Minority leadership				0.080*
				(0.034)
Election year				−0.007
				(0.004)
Constant	2.499*	0.757*	0.808*	0.383*
	(0.217)	(0.146)	(0.059)	(0.017)
Observations	215	285	3395	120,120
R^2	0.050	0.018	0.066	0.038
Fixed effects	None	None	Campaign	Congress
Clustered standard errors	None	None	Candidate	MC

Note: Dependent variables sum of Moral Foundations Dictionaries of Authority–Virtue and Authority–Vice. All models OLS regression. MC = member of Congress.
*$p < .05$, one-tailed.

While this is certainly illuminating, we are also interested in the contextual nature of gendered differences in rhetorical style. Are there situations where women politicians do not use more caring language than men? Where women politicians avoid authority rhetoric? As we suggested above, understanding the role of context can shed light on the role of audience expectations in imposing gendered rhetorical requirements.

To aid in assessing the answers to these and related questions, we plot the co-efficients of the effect on politician gender on caring and authority language from each of these eight models in Figure 7.1. In Figure 7.1(a), which presents the coefficients from the models of caring language, we can see that context appears to play a very small role influencing gendered differences in this one rhetorical regard. The coefficients from the models of caring language in the second impeachment trial of President Trump, the PPCC collection of presidential primary candidate speeches, and the DCinbox are all indistinguishable from either a substantive or a statistical perspective. The confidence intervals vary predictably according to the number of observations in each corpus, but the consistency in magnitude is remarkable. The coefficient from the March 17–19 House floor debates is noticeably larger, however. Substantively, the coefficient more than doubles the size of the others, yet it is not statistically distinguishable from them. It is worth noting that these floor speeches are the least public facing of the four corpora and the corpus that most neatly captures politicians in the act of governing. Furthermore, some of what they were governing on were explicit gendered issues, which may introduce a more nuanced evaluation of audience preferences and context, an issue that we take up below. It is possible that these contexts specifically amplify gendered differences in caring rhetoric, although the small sample size and overlapping confidence intervals suggest that caution against overinterpreting is prudent.

Figure 7.1(b) presents the same coefficient plot for the authority rhetoric models. Again, we see largely muted contextual differences. The coefficients for the presidential primary speeches, March 17–19 House floor debates, and DCinbox all hover almost precisely at zero. The only coefficient that is notably distanced from the others is that from the model of the second impeachment trial corpus, although it is in the opposite of the hypothesized direction. While it is possible that highly salient governing contexts lead women politicians to specifically embrace highly authoritative rhetorical styles, given the overlapping confidence intervals it is more likely that there is simply no gendered difference in the use of authority language regardless of political context.

We next turn to our partisan constraints hypothesis, which predicted that Democrats would use more caring rhetoric and less authority rhetoric than their Republican colleagues. This hypothesis is also tested in Tables 7.1 and 7.2 as well as in Figure 7.2, which plots the coefficients for partisanship from the eight models. The results are strongly supportive of our expectations.

Across all four corpora, Republicans consistently use less caring language than Democrats. Republicans use more authority language than Democrats in three

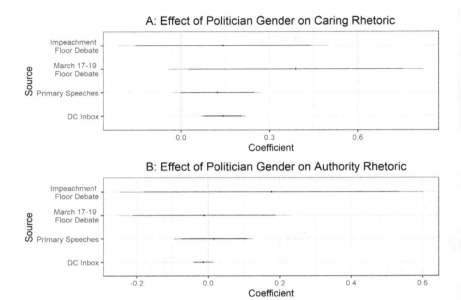

FIGURE 7.1. Effect of politician gender on caring rhetoric (a) and authority rhetoric (b). The gender variable in each was coded such that women politicians received a value of 1 and men politicians received a value of 0.

of the four corpora. Two of those three coefficients are statistically significant at conventional levels, while the remaining one nears the threshold ($p = .115$). In the remaining model, Republicans use *less* authority language than their Democratic counterparts. This itself is informative about the role of context in shaping partisan rhetorical differences as it occurs during the second impeachment trial of Donald Trump, a time when Republicans would reasonably be on the defensive. Still, that contextual factors could lead to a complete inversion in rhetorical patterns is striking. Otherwise, the most noticeable pattern that emerges regarding the effect of partisanship on trait mentions across contexts is of remarkable consistency.

The control variables are themselves informative. More senior members of Congress used less caring language than their more junior colleagues in both House floor speeches corpora retrieved via the C-SPAN Video Library, although seniority is positively related to the use of caring language in emails. More senior members of Congress also employed more authority rhetoric in their emails, as expected given the literal authority that seniority conveys in both chambers. Those in party leadership positions used more authority language than others, which also is consistent with the relationship between actual, positional authority

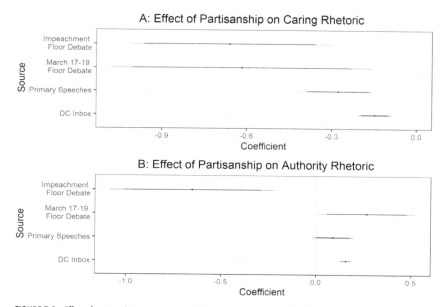

FIGURE 7.2. Effect of partisanship on caring rhetoric (a) and authority rhetoric (b). The partisanship variable in each was coded such that Republican politicians received a value of 1 and Democratic politicians received a value of 0.

and projected, rhetorical authority. Furthermore, majority leaders use more than twice as much authority language as minority leaders. Interestingly, majority status within the chamber itself is negatively related to the use of authority language. Perhaps this is because individual members want to downplay their ability to actually legislate to avoid responsibility for unmet expectations (Weaver, 1986). And members of Congress use more caring language in election years, which is in accordance with our suspicion that politicians will attempt to signal compassion to develop bonds with constituents as elections near (McDonald, 2020).

Given the powerful relationships between partisanship and rhetoric and given the simple fact that there is and has long been a large gap between the two parties in terms of gender representation (Elder, 2021), we next replicated the models from Tables 7.1 and 7.2 separately for Democrats and Republicans. Table 7.3 has the eight models regressing caring language on the established covariates while Table 7.4 has the eight models using authority language as the dependent variable. The odd-numbered models include only Republicans while the even-numbered models include only Democratic politicians. Figures 7.3 (caring) and 7.4 (authority) present side-by-side comparisons of the politician gender coefficients by partisanship for each of the four contexts.

TABLE 7.3 *Effect of Politician Gender on Care Rhetoric by Party*

	Impeachment floor debate (GOP) (1)	Impeachment floor debate (Dem) (2)	March 17–19 floor debates (GOP) (3)	March 17–19 floor debates (Dem) (4)
Woman	0.626*	−0.027	0.917*	0.235
	(0.293)	(0.234)	(0.316)	(0.305)
Seniority	−0.059	−0.055*	0.042	−0.068*
	(0.037)	(0.022)	(0.037)	(0.026)
Senate				
Chamber majority				
Majority leadership				
Minority leadership				
Election year				
Constant	1.315*	2.099*	0.940*	2.317*
	(0.210)	(0.210)	(0.227)	(0.324)
Observations	77	138	126	159
R²	0.136	0.046	0.064	0.049
Fixed effects	None	None	None	None
Clustered standard errors	None	None	None	None

Continued

In short, it appears that the hypothesized expectation that women politicians use more caring and less authority language than their men colleagues is an apt descriptor of Republican women politicians in the act of governing. In both the second impeachment trial and March 17–19 House floor debate corpora, Republican women use more caring language than Republican men. Both of these differences are substantively large and statistically significant. No such difference between Democratic women and Democratic men emerges. Republican women also use less authority rhetoric than Republican men in both of these corpora, with the difference being statistically significant in the March 17–19 House floor debate data. Again, the substantive magnitudes are impressive. Democratic women tend to use more authority rhetoric than Democratic men, although the

TABLE 7.3 *Continued*

	Primary speeches (GOP) (5)	Primary speeches (Dem) (6)	DCinbox (GOP) (7)	DCinbox (Dem) (8)
Woman	0.058	0.145	0.146˙	0.145˙
	(0.068)	(0.097)	(0.052)	(0.055)
Seniority	0.005	0.002	0.007˙	0.012˙
	(0.003)	(0.003)	(0.003)	(0.004)
Senate			0.074˙	0.258˙
			(0.043)	(0.056)
Chamber majority			0.004	−0.169˙
			(0.036)	(0.048)
Majority leadership			−0.101	0.086
			(0.112)	(0.098)
Minority leadership			−0.134	0.023
			(0.138)	(0.071)
Election year			0.053˙	0.009
			(0.009)	(0.014)
Constant	0.682˙	1.139˙	0.955˙	1.282˙
	(0.049)	(0.061)	(0.040)	(0.062)
Observations	1,504	1,891	77,721	42,399
R^2	0.039	0.027	0.015	0.028
Fixed effects	Campaign	Campaign	Congress	Congress
Clustered standard errors	Candidate	Candidate	MC	MC

Note: Dependent variables sum of Moral Foundations Dictionaries of Caring–Virtue and Caring–Vice. All models OLS regression. MC = member of Congress.
*$p < .05$, one-tailed.

differences are slightly smaller and neither is statistically significant. Altogether, then, our hypotheses appear met for this specific cohort.

These relationships do not persist when we turn to the two corpora more attuned to politician rhetoric in the act of campaigning, whether that be speeches given in the pursuit of executive office or emails to supporters. Both Republican and Democratic women use more caring language in their emails than their partisan men peers, although the substantive effects are much smaller than in the House floor speeches corpora. The same is generally true when looking at the presidential primary speech corpus, although neither coefficient meets the

TABLE 7.4 *Effect of Politician Gender on Authority Rhetoric by Party*

	Impeachment floor debate (GOP) (1)	Impeachment floor debate (Dem) (2)	March 17–19 floor debates (GOP) (3)	March 17–19 floor debates (Dem) (4)
Woman	−0.382	0.314	−0.470*	0.137
	(0.336)	(0.284)	(0.245)	(0.130)
Seniority	−0.060	−0.006	−0.060*	0.022*
	(0.042)	(0.026)	(0.028)	(0.011)
Senate				
Chamber majority				
Majority leadership				
Minority leadership				
Election year				
Constant	2.159*	2.420*	1.414*	0.549*
	(0.241)	(0.254)	(0.176)	(0.138)
Observations	77	138	126	159
R^2	0.031	0.009	0.047	0.032
Fixed effects	None	None	None	None
Clustered standard errors	None	None	None	None

Continued

traditional threshold of statistical significance and only the difference between Democratic women and Democratic men comes even remotely close ($p = .167$). No gender differences in the use of authority rhetoric emerge by partisanship in either corpus.

Altogether, this suggests that in the domain of governance, Republican women utilize a rhetorical style with more caring and fewer authority appeals than their co-partisan men counterparts while Democratic women and men largely use similar styles. But when politicians shift to campaign mode, all women appear to elevate their caring rhetoric relative to co-partisan men, although no gendered difference in the amount of authority language is apparent.

TABLE 7.4 *Continued*

	Primary speeches (GOP) (5)	Primary speeches (Dem) (6)	DCinbox (GOP) (7)	DCinbox (Dem) (8)
Woman	0.051	0.034	0.002	−0.023
	(0.112)	(0.057)	(0.023)	(0.020)
Seniority	0.001	0.005˙	0.004	0.008*
	(0.006)	(0.003)	(0.002)	(0.002)
Senate			0.010	0.021
			(0.027)	(0.024)
Chamber majority			−0.061˙	−0.020
			(0.021)	(0.023)
Majority leadership			0.209˙	0.004
			(0.077)	(0.054)
Minority leadership			0.196˙	0.031
			(0.051)	(0.039)
Election year			−0.011˙	0.001
			(0.006)	(0.006)
Constant	0.938˙	0.674˙	0.523˙	0.397˙
	(0.066)	(0.054)	(0.019)	(0.028)
Observations	1,504	1,891	77,721	42,399
R^2	0.022	0.077	0.020	0.021
Fixed effects	Campaign	Campaign	Congress	Congress
Clustered standard errors	Candidate	Candidate	MC	MC

Note: Dependent variables sum of Moral Foundations Dictionaries of Authority–Virtue and Authority–Vice. All models OLS regression. MC = member of Congress.

*$p < .05$, one-tailed.

A number of plausible explanations exist for this variation. In the context of governance, where only GOP women use more care language, it does not appear to be the case that GOP women use more care language than Democratic women, but rather that Democratic men use especially high volumes of care rhetoric in a collaborative, legislative setting. It may be that, in the legislative context, Democrats are at the upper end of care language usage, so the gender of the politician matters relatively less. Similarly, Republican men exhibit a particular proclivity for authority language, though here differences are inconsistent due to the overwhelming influence of partisanship.

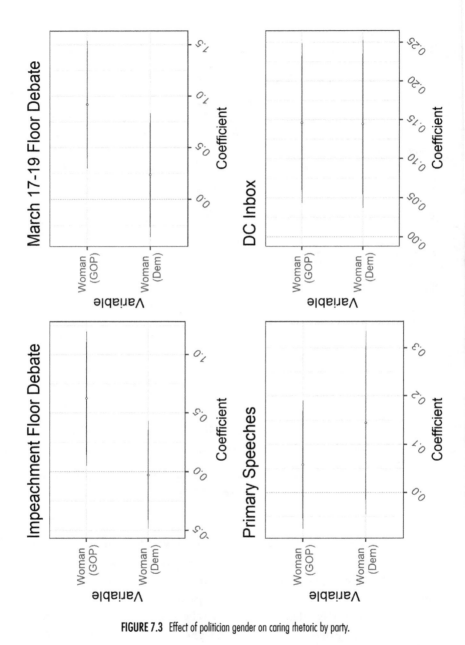

FIGURE 7.3 Effect of politician gender on caring rhetoric by party.

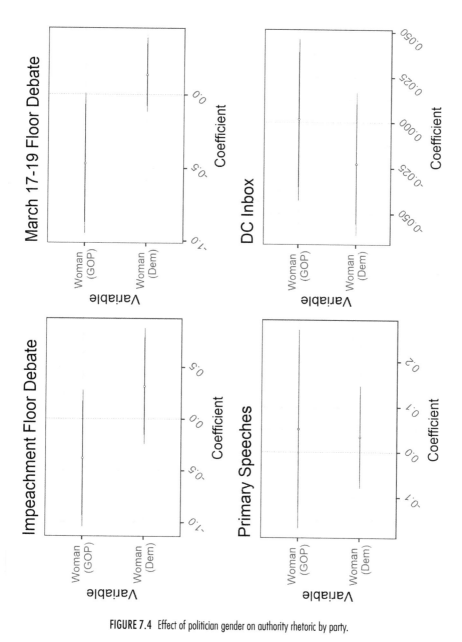

FIGURE 7.4 Effect of politician gender on authority rhetoric by party.

As a final consideration, we look at whether the topic of rhetoric affects gender differences in caring and authority language. The House debated several issues over the course of the three days included in the March corpus. Some of these were explicitly gender-related issues. H.J. Resolution 17 proposed removing the expiration deadline on the Equal Rights Amendment, H.R. 1620 would reauthorize the Violence Against Women Act of 1994, and H.R. 243 would amend the Public Health Service Act to prevent abortion providers from qualifying for family planning grants. Additionally, there were a series of speeches on March 17 in celebration of Women's History Month. Other addressed issues do not have as clear a gendered lens, including a resolution condemning the coup in Burma and a bill dealing with the immigration status of alien farmworkers.

We reran the analysis on the March 17–19 corpus separately for explicitly gendered and non-gendered topics. The results are presented in Table 7.5 and Figures 7.5 and 7.6. Notably, we begin to deal with a very small number of observations, especially with regard to the gendered topic models, so caution is warranted. But the results can still be suggestive.

TABLE 7.5. *Effect of Politician Gender on Caring and Authority Rhetoric by Topic*

	Caring		Authority	
	Gendered topic (1)	Non-gendered topic (2)	Gendered topic (3)	Non-gendered topic (4)
Woman	0.061	0.101	0.025	0.151
	(0.472)	(0.269)	(0.206)	(0.164)
Republican	−0.481	−0.555*	−0.236	0.444*
	(0.482)	(0.268)	(0.211)	(0.164)
Seniority	−0.068*	−0.040*	0.005	0.011
	(0.040)	(0.023)	(0.017)	(0.014)
Constant	2.938*	1.853*	0.751*	0.650*
	(0.573)	(0.296)	(0.250)	(0.181)
Observations	80	205	80	205
R^2	0.046	0.034	0.022	0.036

Note: Dependent variables for Models 1 and 2 are sum of Moral Foundations Dictionaries of Caring–Virtue and Caring–Vice. Dependent variables for Models 3 and 4 are sum of Moral Foundations Dictionaries of Authority– Virtue and Authority–Vice. All models OLS regression. All models use March 17–19 House floor speeches corpus.

*$p < .05$, one-tailed.

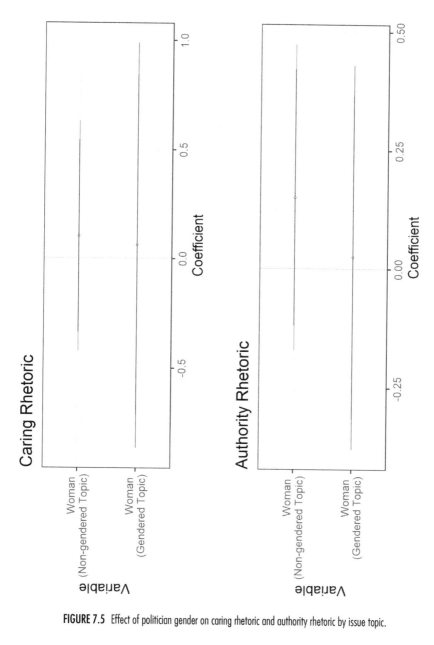

FIGURE 7.5 Effect of politician gender on caring rhetoric and authority rhetoric by issue topic.

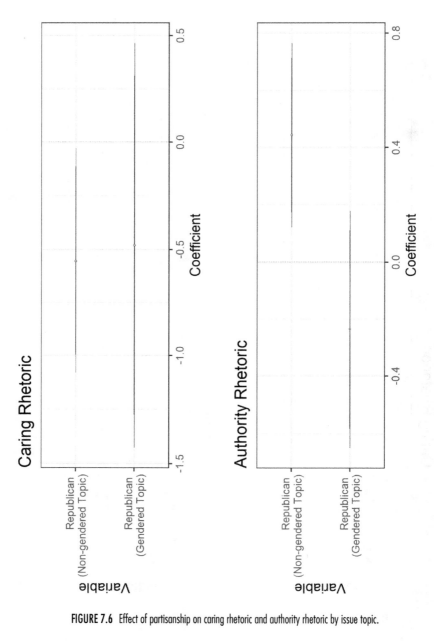

FIGURE 7.6 Effect of partisanship on caring rhetoric and authority rhetoric by issue topic.

We find no clear effect of politician gender on the use of caring or authority rhetoric by the topic of debate. There is no evidence that women or men changed their rhetorical style relative to the other depending on the topic. We do, however, find some interesting partisan differences. Republicans use less caring language than Democrats on both gendered and non-gendered topics, although only the latter is statistically distinguishable from zero. This is likely due to the small number of observations of speeches on gendered topics. Inversely, Republicans use more authority language than Democrats when discussing non-gendered topics but less authority language than Democrats when the topic is explicitly gendered. Again, this second result is not statistically significant as the n is small, but it is suggestive that Republicans are more on the defensive on gendered topics, a finding that is sensible given the parties' different electoral coalitions and histories and again points toward a contextually driven interest in appealing to audiences as a primary motivator of politician trait appeals.

CONCLUSION

Walter Lippmann (1922) noted that politics is simply too abstract for most to truly understand, which creates a tendency to personalize as a means of simplification. Weighing the pros and cons of policy proposals is difficult. Identifying who is a good or bad person, competent or incompetent is an activity with which even the least judgmental among us is intimately acquainted. And so it should hardly be surprising that cognitive miserliness (Downs, 1957) is easily and efficiently offset by a reliance on trait evaluations (Campbell, 1983; Greene, 2001; Holian & Prysby, 2011, 2014, 2015; McDonald, 2020; Miller et al., 1986).

But robust literatures suggest that these trait evaluations are significantly tied to the gender (Abele et al., 2008; Alexander & Andersen, 1993; Banwart, 2010; Banwart & McKinney, 2005; Meeks, 2013) and partisanship (Hayes, 2005; Holian & Prysby, 2015) of the elite being evaluated. People stereotype. Implicitly or explicitly, they assume that women are caring and nurturing while men are strict leaders. They expect Republicans to be assertive and decisive while Democrats should be empathetic. It is reasonable to think that these expectations create a self-fulfilling prophecy. If an audience expects you to be a certain way, then it might be in your best interest to give them what they want. Or maybe *being* what they want is the only real way to succeed.

We've brought an impressive array of data to the proverbial table to test whether this is indeed the case. Employing all of these data allows us to speak with heretofore unattainable precision as to the contextual consistency (or lack thereof) of gender and partisan differences in trait appeals. But in marshalling this much data—2 dependent variables across 4 distinct corpora with 28 total statistical models—it can be easy to lose sight of the topline conclusions. We therefore take some time to delineate what we see as the most significant sources of consistency and divergence (both of which are interesting in their own ways).

The most consistent finding is the close adherence of Democrats and Republicans to their owned traits. There is a clear pattern of Democrats using care-related appeals while Republicans employ authority rhetoric. But what is also striking are the few instances in which that pattern breaks down. When speaking during the second impeachment trial of Donald Trump, Democrats adopted a much more authority-based rhetorical style relative to their Republican peers. And Republicans eschewed authority language relative to Democrats when speaking on gendered topics in the March 17–19 floor debates, although the difference is not quite statistically significant. It is certainly possible to speculate as to why. But beyond this speculation is the underlying point that stylistic differences are subject to influence from contextual factors. When all you have is a hammer, everything looks like a nail. And yet here are two instances in which partisans thought another tool more appropriate. This suggests a flexibility that is more consistent with a story of rhetoric as a response to context rather than to the ingrained personality of the speaker. If only caring Democrats could get elected to high office while being a naturally assertive leader were a prerequisite for electoral success in Republican political circles, it is unlikely we would find them so readily abandoning those styles, let alone completely reversing their tendencies as in the impeachment case.

It is the inconsistency that is most notable regarding the effect of gender on trait appeals. Women appear to utilize somewhat more caring language than men, although the differences are substantively much weaker than for partisanship. Women also don't appear to use less authority language than men, which runs counter to expectations. Decomposing the results by party provides some purchase as to why. Republican women do seem to use less caring and more authority rhetoric than their co-partisan men colleagues, although these effects are largely cloistered to the corpora from the House floor. This leads us to conclude that gender differences in the use of trait appeals, as motivated by gendered perceptions of trait ownership, appear largely conditional on other, contextual factors. Of course, this does not say anything about the significance of such differences, which we return to shortly.

This study is not without limitations. The relationship between gender and partisanship is certainly endogenous. We can say nothing about why certain politicians choose certain parties, parties which themselves have long-lasting reputations regarding the sorts of traits its members possess. Inherently, all of our models treat this issue as a two-dimensional image, which undoubtedly collapses into irrelevance a great deal of important dynamism undergirding the relationships. Using multiple and diverse data should circumvent this problem somewhat by allowing us to view a complex, three-dimensional construct from two-dimensional images taken at different angles. But other approaches are certainly possible and would complement this study. One possibility is to look at instances in which individuals change their partisanship. When Jeff van Drew left the Democratic party in December of 2019, did he also leave behind a caring rhetorical style for one of authority? Using this and other instances to examine cases in which the dynamic process of identity and rhetoric play out (even if the occurrences are themselves not random or necessarily representative) would provide a useful foil.

Finally, we close with a missive on normative implications. That our results display only inconsistent and weak gender differences in the use of caring and authority appeals does not directly imply anything about the literature on voter perceptions of traits or imply that women no longer face backlashes for going against type. There are multiple potential explanations as to why. Perhaps women politicians are unaware of the penalties they would face. Perhaps women politicians are aware but are willing to pay the cost. Or perhaps women have concluded that the price to pay will be minimal when partisanship is so strong as to overwhelmingly determine vote choice. Furthermore, we do find results consistent with expectations under certain conditions.

And some women politicians do operate under those conditions every day. Those are very real restrictions that we should carefully monitor and seek to remove if possible.

NOTES

1.   H.R. 1620—117th Congress. Passed by the House of Representatives on 3/17/2021. https://www.congress.gov/bill/117th-congress/house-bill/1620

2. Clifford (2018) notes that the dimensions of leadership and empathy in Kinder's (1986) conceptualization fit primarily with the MFT dimensions of authority and care, respectively.

3. This is based on data provided by the American National Election Studies. Although the gap on perceptions of compassion between the Democratic and Republican presidential candidates was narrower in 2004 than it was in any election from 1992 to 2020, Kerry was still rated as more compassionate.

4. The Moral Foundation Dictionaries include two measures for each of the five dimensions: one for "virtue" and one for "vice." We are fundamentally interested in a proclivity to engage in certain types of trait or morality appeals and so the virtue/vice distinction is largely irrelevant to our purposes. As such, we simply sum both the virtue and vice variables for a composite "authority" and "caring" measure.

5. Given the small number of observations in both the January 11–13 and March 17–19 corpora, we do not include equivalent controls. In several cases, such variables would operate as near perfect predictors.

6. Fixed effects are appropriate because the number of observations is largely evenly dispersed across this hierarchical level.

7. Robust standard errors are the preferable solution over fixed effects as the number of observations is not evenly dispersed across this hierarchical level. We have more speeches by prominent primary candidates and some members of Congress serve longer than others, for example.

REFERENCES

Aaldering, L., & Vliegenthart, R. (2016). Political leaders and the media. Can we measure political leadership images in newspapers using computer-assisted content analysis? *Quality and Quantity, 50*, 1871–1905. https://doi.org/10.1007/s11135-015-0242-9

Abele, A. E., Cuddy, A. J. C., Judd, C. M., & Yzerbyt, V. (2008). Fundamental dimensions of social judgment. *European Journal of Social Psychology, 38*(7), 1063–1065. https://doi.org/10.1002/ejsp.574

Alexander, D., & Andersen, K. (1993). Gender as a factor in the attribution of leadership traits. *Political Research Quarterly, 46*(3), 527–545. https://doi.org/10.1177/106591299304600305

Banwart, M. C. (2010). Gender and candidate communication: Effects of stereotypes in the 2008 election. *American Behavioral Scientist, 54*(3), 265–283. https://doi.org/10.1177/0002764210381702

Banwart, M. C., & McKinney, M. S. (2005). A gendered influence in campaign debates? Analysis of mixed-gender United States Senate and gubernatorial debates. *Communication Studies, 56*(4), 353–373. https://doi.org/10.1080/10510970500319443

Barker, D. C., Lawrence, A. B., & Tavits, M. (2006). Partisanship and the dynamics of "candidate centered politics" in American presidential nominations. *Electoral Studies, 25*(3), 599–610. https://doi.org/10.1016/j.electstud.2005.09.001

Bauer, N. M. (2020). Shifting standards: how voters evaluate the qualifications of female and male candidates. *Journal of Politics, 82*(1), 1–12. https://doi.org/10.1086/705817

Brambilla, M., Sacchi, S., Pagliaro, S., & Ellemers, N. (2013). Morality and intergroup relations: Threats to safety and group image predict the desire to interact with outgroup and ingroup members. *Journal of Experimental Social Psychology, 49*(5), 811–821. https://doi.org/10.1016/j.jesp.2013.04.005

Burgoon, J. K. (1993). Interpersonal expectations, expectancy violations, and emotional communication. *Journal of Language and Social Psychology, 12*(1–2), 30–48. https://doi.org/10.1177/0261927X93121003

Campbell, J. E. (1983). Candidate image evaluations: Influence and rationalization in presidential primaries. *American Politics Quarterly, 11*(3), 293–313. https://doi.org/10.1177/004478083011003002

Center for American Women and Politics (CAWP). (2020). *Women in elective office 2020.* Rutgers University. Retrieved September 15, 2020. https://cawp.rutgers.edu/facts/current-numbers/women-elective-office-2020

Clifford, S. (2018). Reassessing the structure of presidential character. *Electoral Studies, 54*, 240–247. https://doi.org/10.1016/j.electstud.2018.04.006

Cuddy, A. J. C., Fiske, S. T., & Glick, P. (2008). Warmth and competence as universal dimensions of social perception: The stereotype content model and the BIAS Map. *Advances in Experimental Social Psychology, 40*, 61–149. https://doi.org/10.1016/S0065-2601(07)00002-0

Davies, C. L., Sibley, C. G., & Liu, J. H. (2014). Confirmatory factor analysis of the Moral Foundations questionnaire: Independent scale validation in a New Zealand sample. *Social Psychology, 45*(6), 431–436. https://doi.org/10.1027/1864-9335/a000201

Dolan, J., Deckman, M. M., & Swers, M. L. (2019). *Women and politics: Paths to power and political influence.* Rowman & Littlefield.

Downs, A. (1957). *An economic theory of democracy.* HarperCollins.

Eagly, A. H. (1987). *Sex differences in social behavior: A social-role interpretation.* Erlbaum.

Eagly, A. H., & Karau, S. J. (2002). Role congruity theory of prejudice toward female leaders. *Psychological Review, 109*(3), 573–598. https://doi.org/10.1037/0033-295X.109.3.573

Elder, L. (2021). *The partisan gap: Why Democratic women get elected but Republican women don't.* NYU Press.

Federico, C. M., Weber, C. R., Ergun, D., & Hunt, C. (2013). Mapping the connections between politics and morality: The multiple sociopolitical orientations involved in moral intuition. *Political Psychology, 34*(4), 589–610. https://doi.org/10.1111/pops.12006

Feldman, S., & Conover, P. J. (1983). Candidates, issues, and voters: The role of inference in political perception. *Journal of Politics, 45*(4), 810–839.

Fiorina, M. (1981). *Retrospective voting in American elections.* Yale University Press.

Fiske, S. T., Cuddy, A. J. C., & Glick, P. (2007). Universal dimensions of social cognition: Warmth and competence. *Trends in Cognitive Sciences, 11*(2), 77–83. https://doi.org/10.1016/j.tics.2006.11.005

Fiske, S. T., Cuddy, A. J. C., Glick, P., & Xu, J. (2002). A model of (often mixed) stereotype content: Competence and warmth respectively follow from perceived status and competition. *Journal of Personality and Social Psychology, 82*(6), 878–902. https://doi.org/10.1037/0022-3514.82.6.878

Fox, R. L., & Oxley, Z. (2003). Gender stereotyping in state executive elections. *Journal of Politics, 65*(3), 833–850. https://doi.org/10.1111/1468-2508.00214

Funk, C. L. (1999). Bringing the candidate into models of candidate evaluation. *Journal of Politics, 61*(3), 700–720. https://doi.org/10.2307/2647824

Gitlin, T. (2007). *The bulldozer and the big tent: Blind Republicans, lame Democrats, and the recovery of the American ideals.* John Wiley & Sons.

Goodwin, G. P. (2015). Moral character in person perception. *Current Directions in Psychological Science, 24*(1), 38–44. https://doi.org/10.1177/0963721414550709

Graham, J., Haidt, J., & Nosek, B. A. (2009). Liberals and conservatives rely on different sets of moral foundations. *Journal of Personality and Social Psychology, 9*(5), 1029–1046. https://doi.org/10.1037/a0015141

Greene, S. (2001). The role of character assessments in presidential approval. *American Politics Research, 29*(2), 196–210. https://doi.org/10.1177/1532673X01029002004

Haidt, J., & Joseph, C. (2004). Intuitive ethics: How innately prepared intuitions generate culturally variable virtues. *Daedalus: Special Issue on Human Nature, 133*(4), 55–66. https://doi.org/10.1162/0011526042365555

Hart, R. P., Childers, J. P., & Lind, C. J. (2013). *Political tone: How leaders talk and why.* University of Chicago Press.

Hayes, D. (2005). Candidate qualities through a partisan lens: A theory of trait ownership. *American Journal of Political Science, 49*(3), 908–923. https://doi.org/10.1111/j.1540-5907.2005.00163.x

Hayes, D. (2011). When gender and party collide: Stereotyping in candidate trait attribution. *Politics & Gender*, 7(2), 133–165. https://doi.org/10.1017/S1743923X11000055

Holian, D. B., & Prysby, C. (2015). *Candidate character traits in presidential elections.* Routledge.

Holman, M. R., Merolla, J. L., & Zechmeister, E. J. (2017). Can experience overcome stereotypes in times of terror threat? *Research & Politics*, 4(1). https://doi.org/10.1177/2053168016688121

Huddy, L., & Terkildsen, N. (1993). Gender stereotypes and the perception of male and female candidates. *American Journal of Political Science*, 37(1), 119–147. https://doi.org/10.2307/2111526

Jamieson, K. H. (1995). *Beyond the double bind: Women and leadership.* Oxford University Press.

Kinder, D. R. (1986). Presidential character revisited. In R. R. Lau & D. O. Sears (Eds.), *Political cognition* (pp. 233–255). Erlbaum.

Lau, R. R., & Redlawsk, D. P. (2001). Advantages and disadvantages of cognitive heuristics in political decision making. *American Journal of Political Science*, 45(4), 951–971. https://doi.org/10.2307/2669334

Leach, C. W., Ellemers, N., & Barreto, M. (2007). Group virtue: The importance of morality (vs. competence and sociability) in the positive evaluation of in-groups. *Journal of Personality and Social Psychology*, 93(2), 234–249. https://doi.org/10.1037/0022-3514.93.2.234

Lippmann, W. (1922). *Public opinion.* Harcourt, Brace and Company.

Lord, R. G., Epitropaki, O., Foti, R. J., & Keller Hansbrough, T. (2020). Implicit leadership theories, implicit followership theories, and dynamic processing of leadership information. *Annual Review of Organizational Psychology and Organizational Behavior*, 7, 49–74. https://doi.org/10.1146/annurev-orgpsych-012119-045434

Mason, L. (2018). *Uncivil agreement: How politics became our identity.* University of Chicago Press.

McDonald, J. (2020). Who cares? Explaining perceptions of compassion in candidates for office. *Political Behavior*, 43, 1371–1394. https://doi.org/10.1007/s11109-020-09592-8

McDonald, J., & Piatak, J. (in press). Penalties for going against type: How candidate gender shapes leadership perceptions. *Behavioral Science and Policy*.

Meeks, L. (2013). He wrote, she wrote: Journalist gender, political office, and campaign news. *Journalism & Mass Communication Quarterly*, 90(1), 58–74. https://doi.org/10.1177/1077699012468695

Miller, A. H., Wattenberg, M. P., & Malanchuk, O. (1986). Schematic assessments of presidential candidates. *American Political Science Review, 80*(2), 521–540. https://doi.org/10.2307/1958272

Petrocik, J. R. (1996). Issue ownership in presidential elections, with a 1980 case study. *American Journal of Political Science, 40*(3), 825–850. https://doi.org/10.2307/2111797

Rahn, W. (1993). The role of partisan stereotypes in information processing about political candidates. *American Journal of Political Science, 37*(2), 472–496. https://doi.org/10.2307/2111381

Rudman, L. A. (1998). Self-promotion as a risk factor for women: The costs and benefits of counterstereotypical impression management. *Journal of Personality and Social Psychology, 74*(3), 629–645. https://doi.org/10.1037/0022-3514.74.3.629

Rudman, L. A., Moss-Racusin, C. A., Phelan, J. E., & Nauts, S. (2012). Status incongruity and backlash effects: Defending the gender hierarchy motivates prejudice against female leaders. *Journal of Experimental Social Psychology, 48*(1), 165–179. https://doi.org/10.1016/j.jesp.2011.10.008

Scott, Z. (2021a). Lost in the crowd: The effect of volatile fields on presidential primaries. *American Politics Research, 49*(2), 221–232. https://doi.org/10.1177/1532673X20959618

Scott, Z. (2021b). Read the room: The effect of campaign event format on the use of emotional language. In R. X. Browning (Ed.), *The Year in C-SPAN Research* (7th ed., pp. 29–55). Purdue University Press.

Weaver, R. K. (1986). The politics of blame avoidance. *Journal of Public Policy, 6*(4), 371–398. https://doi.org/10.1017/S0143814X00004219

Weaver, R. M. (1953). *The ethics of rhetoric.* Henry Regnery.

8

CRACKING THE GLASS CEILING IN THE NEWSROOM

A Historical Examination of Women Journalists' Perspectives on Gender in the Media

Newly Paul

Journalism is a gendered institution. Gendered perceptions shape the practices, norms, routines, and structures of journalism (Iiris & Sinikka, 2018). A vast body of scholarly work has demonstrated how gender perceptions affect the dynamics within and outside the newsroom. Within the newsroom, gender affects story assignments (Byline Blog, 2012; Harp, 2007), newsroom hiring and promotion practices (Engstrom & Ferri, 1998), newsroom management styles (Everbach, 2006), and journalists' overall satisfaction with the profession (Barnes, 2016). Outside the newsroom, gendered perceptions affect source selection (Craft & Wanta, 2004; Freedman & Fico, 2005), news framing (Correa & Harp, 2011; Meeks, 2013), and audience perceptions of a journalist's credibility (Armstrong & McAdams, 2009; Brann & Himes, 2010). Given the continued importance of gender in journalism, it is essential to explore "the historical and institutional intertwining of journalism and gender" (Ruoho & Torkkola, 2018, p. 67), with special reference to how women journalists' conceptions of gender influence their journalistic practices.

Scholars of journalism history have used various resources such as personal papers, autobiographies, news articles, oral histories, and interviews to document the contribution of women journalists. Historical journalism has explored the development of women journalist associations (Jenkins et al., 2018); gendered practices in newsrooms (Lumsden, 1995); and the contributions of individual women journalists in various contexts such as war (Edy, 2019), civil rights (Broussard, 2003), and the suffragist movement (John, 2003).

The C-SPAN Video Library offers a unique way to extend this work by conducting comparative analyses of women journalists' experiences through the ages and across various types of media specializations. The Video Library contains oral histories featuring women journalists specializing in various topics such as politics, sports, and photojournalism, where they discuss how gender shaped their identities as journalists. These first-person experiences are important because when we exclude women's perspectives from journalism history, we create a distorted account of what journalism is and how it has evolved (Nicholson et al., 2009). Drawing connections between the gendered experiences of women and the journalism they produce will help us understand better how journalists' identities shape their views of the world, and consequently, news coverage.

In this essay I draw from oral history interviews of six women journalists in the C-SPAN Video Library to explore the role of gender in the newsroom. In particular, I examine the following questions: How did women's lived experiences in the newsroom color their reporting practices? What strategies did the women use to counter gender-based discrimination? How did women adapt to the changing norms of journalism? How did gender norms shape their identities as journalists? How did their perceptions vary depending on the type of journalism they practiced and the era in which they lived?

The six oral histories analyzed in this paper are filled with rich details from the lives of these women. They include information about their childhood; their introduction to journalism; their interactions with hostile editors, sources, and colleagues; descriptions of the kinds of stories they covered; incidents of sexual harassment at the workplace; and their attempts to balance family life with the demands of the workplace. Together, these oral histories present a composite picture of what it meant to be a woman journalist in the 20th century. In the sections below, I begin by describing the data and methods used in this study. I then briefly discuss the history of women in journalism in the early and mid-20th century, followed by a discussion of gender role socialization theory as a framework to explore my research questions. My findings indicate that broader social norms related to gender had a deep impact on women's professional identities.

DATA AND METHODOLOGY

This study uses the C-SPAN Video Library to examine how six women journalists described the impact of gender on their reporting practices and their identities as journalists. Table 8.1 lists the journalists whose histories were included in this study. Five out of the six interviews used in this study were conducted for the Washington Press Club Foundation as part of its oral history project "Women in Journalism." Mary Garber, Dorothy Gilliam, Ruth Cowan Nash, Betsy Wade, and Eileen Shanahan were part of the Washington Press Club project. Diana Walker's interview was conducted by the Briscoe Center for American History at the University of Texas at Austin to mark the occasion of adding her photographs to its archive of photos taken by nationally acclaimed photojournalists.

The Washington Press Club Foundation's "Women in Journalism" project started in 1986. It includes 57 transcripts and audio- and videotapes of interviews with 60 women journalists whose careers spanned three eras: from 1920 to World War II, from the end of World War II to the passage of the Civil Rights Act of 1964, and after 1964 when discrimination on the basis of gender and race became illegal. The press club project aimed to "show not only how journalism evolved as more women entered but also how American society evolved—technologically as well as in attitude—and how women adapted to the changes around them" (Fuchs, 2003, p. 192).

Oral histories include personal stories as well as stories that are handed down through generations. Thus, they "reveal a group's collective memory and indicate values embedded in the culture" (Yow, 2015, p. 15) The stories are per-

TABLE 8.1 *Women Journalists Interviewed in C-SPAN Oral History Archives*

Journalist	Specialization	Media organization	Years active	Date interview recorded
Ruth Cowan Nash	Reporter	Associated Press	1929–1956	03/29/1990
Mary Garber	Sports journalist	Winston-Salem Journal	1940–1992	11/04/1990
Betsy Wade	Copy editor	New York Times	1956–2001	05/21/1994
Dorothy Gilliam	Reporter	Washington Post	1961–2003	12/13/1993
Eileen Shanahan	Reporter	New York Times	1962–1977	05/21/1994
Diana Walker	Photojournalist	Time magazine	1979–2004	03/08/2013

sonal narratives of the journalists, but they reflect larger patterns and signify the experiences of women journalists as a group. As Yow explains, "Oral history aims at discovering testimony for understanding a historical time or a present era and for understanding individual lives in society" (p. 16). Thus, the stories of the journalists are invaluable in understanding cultural norms of the times and their effect on newsrooms.

The oral history approach has a number of merits. The interactive nature of the interviews allows the journalists to reflect and comment on the subjects under discussion. It also allows them to recount facts, which helps interpret their experiences in the context of a life review. As Yow (2015) explains, oral histories tend to be authentic as "people tend, with the passage of time, to be more, rather than less, candid" (p. 22). When people are in the midst of an active career, they might think twice about speaking candidly for fear of repercussions, but near the end of one's professional life, "there is a need to look at things as honestly as possible to make sense of experiences over a lifetime" (p. 22), which grants oral histories a sense of authenticity.

In order to address the research questions, I listened to each interview and took notes, paying special attention to the parts where the interviewees addressed gender and its impact on their career. Out of the six women in this sample, only one was African American; the rest were white. As shown in Table 8.1, the journalists were active in the late 1920s to the mid-2000s. The interviews were conducted in 1990, 1993, and 1994, with the exception of Diana Walker, who was interviewed in 2013. The interviews are of varying length, with the longest being the interview of Mary Garber, which lasted about 2 hours and 10 minutes, and the shortest being the interview of Ruth Cowan Nash, which lasted about 50 minutes. In the next section, I briefly outline how sociopolitical forces shaped the newsrooms of the 20th century.

A BRIEF HISTORY OF WOMEN IN THE NEWSROOM

Previous studies have discussed the experiences of women journalists when they entered newsrooms in the early 20th century, after the passage of the 19th amendment that allowed women to vote. These pioneers performed well in men-dominated newsrooms, yet they faced barriers arising from the rigid gender-stereotypical roles assigned to men and women during that era. In order to succeed, women journalists working in the period between the 1920s and 1940s adopted qualities usually ascribed to men, such as toughness and not showing emotion (Lumsden, 1995). They tried to navigate the line between traditional notions of femininity and the toughness expected of a reporter. As Lumsden (1995) found in her analysis of the lives of women reporters of this era, they labored hard to hide their anger at the instances of sex discrimination at work, continuously tried to prove their excellence, and consciously avoided challenging gender stereotypes lest they lose their tenuous position at their workplace. On one hand, the women faced pay discrimination and exclusion from professional events such as the White House Correspondents' Association Dinner, but on the other, they used their presence in the newsroom to lobby for more coverage of issues that affected women's and children's lives (Lumsden, 1995). In order to succeed in their chosen profession, women of this era favored individualism. They shunned feminist values and avoided forging communities with other women.

At the end of World War II, when the men returned home from the war, American society was overtaken by a new wave of conservatism. Postwar messages of women's empowerment coexisted with messages that the rightful place of women was in the home. The effects of this conservatism were felt within newsrooms, which had hired women staffers to fill the positions left empty by men correspondents who had been drafted for the war. According to the 1960 U.S. Census, 37% of reporters and editors working in newsrooms during this time were women. However, as Bradley (2005) argues, these numbers did not reflect the reality of women's position in the newsroom. They were assigned smaller roles and were more likely to be asked to cover stories in women's weekly magazines and women's sections of the newspaper than general news assignments. Newsrooms were mostly run by men editors who were hesitant to hire women for more prestigious general reporting assignments. Women in broadcast news seldom saw or heard their voices on air, and women's salaries remained far below those of men journalists. Overall, the condition of women journalists was similar to that of women in the newsroom at the beginning of the 19th century. African Americans in the newsroom fared even worse. Despite the Kerner Commission report of 1968, which had blamed the country's race-related riots on the media's stereotyping coverage of Blacks, African Americans made up only 2.6% of the staff in the newsroom in 1960 (Bradley, 2005).

In the 1970s, the equal rights legislation derived from the civil rights movements, and the attention garnered by the second wave of the women's rights movement, marked a change in the attitudes and bargaining powers of women who worked as reporters, editors, and photographers in newsrooms around the country. They began to organize and fight back against the men-dominated culture that prevented them from achieving professional success. Women journalists became activists, and they worked to diversify the news agenda to include stories on social problems, feminism, and human interest, in addition to stories about politics, scandal, and the government, which was the norm (Mills, 1997). Senior women journalists agitated for equal pay and were willing to file lawsuits to this end. This period was marked by changes in the news agenda: Black women began to be featured in mainstream women's magazines, women were hired as anchors on news programs, and feminist issues such as abortion received in-depth coverage in the news.

HOW GENDER SHAPES NEWSROOM EXPERIENCES

The opportunities that the women journalists talked about in this chapter received were shaped by prevalent ideas about gender and social roles. Some of these women described how gender considerations had shaped their relationships with their editors, colleagues, and sources and influenced the issues they wrote about. Existing research on gender in journalism has documented that men and women journalists tend to differ in terms of their newsroom experiences and how they cover the news. Women journalists tend to cite more women in their stories than men (Weaver & Wilhoit, 1996). Women journalists also tend to use a greater variety of sources, use fewer stereotypes in their content, emphasize personalization, and frame stories more positively than do men reporters (Correa & Harp, 2011; Rodgers & Thorson, 2003). Women editors are less likely to differentiate between men and women journalists when assigning stories, while men editors have a preference for negative stories (Craft & Wanta, 2004). However, other studies have found that men and women behave in similar ways as journalists (Hanitzsch & Hanusch, 2012) or that external factors such as sociocultural values, the size of the media organization, and the type of ownership affect the gendered patterns in news coverage.

Two models of socialization—the gender model and the job model—have been used to explain these gender-based differences in the newsroom (Rodgers & Thorson, 2003). The gender model posits that women and men socialize differently in professional spaces because they share different values and priorities.

Given the traditional social roles of caregiver and nurturer that women occupy in society, they are associated with traits such as empathy and warmth. Men, on the other hand, are traditionally associated with leadership roles and are perceived as naturally tough and assertive (Huddy & Terkildsen, 1993). These gendered perceptions affect men and women's professional lives. Women in the workplace are perceived as prioritizing interdependence, sharing, and nurturing behavior, while men are perceived as valuing independence and assertive behavior. Women also tend to place more value on cooperation and democratic structures at their workplaces than men. In addition, women and men differ in linguistic styles. While women tend to use indirect language and ask questions that invite elaboration and foster cooperation, men tend to be more direct in their language and use directives that could indicate impatience (Mulac et al., 2001). Applied to journalism, the gender model of socialization predicts that as a result of these gender-based differences, women and men will have different approaches to sourcing and framing news stories, and this will result in a difference in the content of news coverage. The gender model as a whole indicates that men and women differ in their level of commitment to work: Due to the differences in their socialization process, women prioritize their families over work, while men value commitment to work.

In contrast, the job model predicts that regardless of one's socialization, men and women will behave similarly if their experiences in the workplace are similar. Thus, workplaces that prioritize a masculine culture, such as networking on weekends or at the end of the workday, or forming informal communication channels that exclude women, tend to create lower levels of attitudinal commitment among women (Dodd-McCue & Wright, 1996). When applied to journalism, the job model predicts that gender differences in values and working styles are mediated by organizational factors such as ownership, size of the newsroom, audience demographics, and composition of the newsroom. In men-dominated newsrooms, women are expected to exhibit masculine behaviors in order to be accepted or promoted, but when the number of women or minorities in the newsroom goes up, expectations change. However, studies on the impact of women and minorities in the newsroom have found that the masculine culture of the newsroom is well-entrenched and difficult to change (Nishikawa et al., 2009).

In the sections below, I apply the gender and job theories of socialization to the oral histories of women journalists to determine the extent to which gender shaped their experiences in the newsroom.

Introduction to Journalism

Almost all journalists in this dataset described working in an overwhelmingly masculine culture. Their initial years were filled with struggles where they worked long hours for low or no pay, and worked hard to establish their journalistic credentials so they would be taken seriously by the men editors. Sportswriter Mary Garber started out as a society editor, covering dances and social events. She got a foothold in the sports section only as a result of World War II, which emptied the newsrooms of the men who were drafted into the war. She described this period as a time of "no discrimination" (C-SPAN, 1990), because women were doing everything at the newspaper. She acknowledged that during the course of her career she faced prejudices from people around her, and these had hurt her confidence. Yet she held herself partially responsible for the hostility she faced from colleagues. She explained her men colleagues' behavior thus:

> The problem was that neither of us knew quite how to accept the other. All of us had grown up in a male–female segregated society and all of a sudden, this woman comes into a previously male-dominated area and the men just didn't know what to do. I think I could have helped the situation a whole lot if I had been friendlier and spoken to them and told them who I was. (Browning, 2022a)

Though photojournalist Diana Walker started out in the 1970s—several decades after Garber—she faced a similar situation. As a freelance photographer for a political magazine in Washington, her job was poorly paid, but it gave her press credentials to shoot on Capitol Hill and the White House, and she used this opportunity to photograph events and build her portfolio, which eventually won her a contract at *Time* magazine.

Betsy Wade, who became the first woman copy editor at the *New York Times*, was among the top 10 women in her class of 1960 at Columbia, but she was rejected when she first applied to the *Times*. Her introduction to the newsroom was hostile. She described working in a filthy newsroom filled with scattered cigarette ends and spittoons, and men colleagues who used unprofessional language. In addition to the open hostility, Wade realized that there were double standards with regard to pay. Women journalists were barred from holding editor positions in the newsroom and were hired under the title of researcher. And though they did a lot of the work that was typically done by editors, they remained confined to the title and low pay of researchers.

Dorothy Gilliam's initiation into journalism was somewhat different from her white peers. Having grown up as a Black woman in a working-class family, she was unaccustomed to seeing Black people working as doctors or lawyers or occupying positions of power. But journalism made her feel powerful, and she received a lot of affirmation on seeing her name in print. Gilliam started out working as a secretary at a Black women's magazine, but when she tried to leverage this experience to get a reporting position at mainstream newspapers, she was rejected. So she decided to enroll at Columbia University to get the credentials she needed to be accepted in a mainstream newsroom. Her cohort was representative of real-world newsrooms of the times—it was white, male, and upper class. Gilliam described her experience in journalism school as "traumatic" and recalled trying to be equal to her classmates, who had a wide-ranging knowledge of culture and society, and to excel in her work. The sense that she did not fit in followed her from journalism school and stayed with her throughout her career as a journalist.

These accounts of women who entered journalism decades apart are uncannily similar and reflect how organizational structures affect whether one can enter the profession and be successful. Institutions with masculine structures create implicit signals about who is credible and acceptable as a journalist. These institutions rely on knowledge derived from socially constructed categories of gender to act as gatekeepers of the profession. Women who enter such environments are socialized from the very beginning to adopt the masculine culture or risk being left behind.

Navigating the Masculine Culture of the Newsroom

Traditional newsrooms were structured to promote the "man-as-norm and woman-as-interloper structure" (Ross, 2001, p. 535). Such environments encouraged conformity with the masculine norm and questioned behaviors that fell outside the strictly defined boundaries. Ross (2001) explains that women employ a number of strategies to navigate a gendered workplace. These include

> *incorporation* (one of the boys), which requires women to take on so-called masculine styles, values and reporting behaviours such as "objectivity";

feminist, in which journalists make a conscious decision to provide an alter-native voice, for example, writing on health in order to expose child abuse and rape; and *retreat*, where women choose to work as freelancers rather than con-tinue to fight battles in the workplace. (p. 535)

The oral histories of these six women journalists contained several descrip-tions of each of these types of behaviors. Interestingly, these behaviors varied depending on the era and the nature of the media organization. Women who worked in the early decades of the 20th century were more likely to adopt mas-culine norms unquestioningly and act as "one of the boys" in order to fit in. But women who worked in larger and urban newsrooms in the mid and latter de-cades of the century were more likely to exhibit feminist behaviors, or a mix of incorporation and feminist attitudes. Women who wanted to have a family life and children were most likely to exhibit retreat behaviors, as were senior jour-nalists who had spent their careers protesting benevolent sexism and outright hostility from colleagues but seen only incremental change.

In the interviews analyzed in this chapter, the women journalists mentioned using a variety of tactics to navigate hostility arising from gender differences. Some tried not to make too many waves; instead, they tried their best to get along with colleagues. Others refused outright to acknowledge the hostile work environment. Some women preferred using humor, or not reacting to perceived slights, while others tried doing their best work and working harder than anyone else. Some women also fought the system by building allies among men and per-sisting despite all odds. These tactics differed depending on the newsroom envi-ronment. For example, Mary Garber, who was the only woman in her newsroom, advised women to avoid looking for discrimination in the workplace. She said that women were inevitably going to run into discriminatory behavior, but they should try to roll with the punches and use their sense of humor to work around such situations. Similarly, Dorothy Gilliam, who was among the only women of color in the newsroom, did not share her traumas of reporting while Black with other people in the newsroom. Instead, she maintained a calm outwardly appear-ance even though she felt a lot of turmoil inside. Betsy Wade, as the first woman copy editor in the newsroom, dressed conservatively to avoid attracting atten-tion to herself. In all these instances, the women realized that as a result of being outnumbered, their voices were unlikely to be heard, pointing yet again to orga-nizational structures that affected their professional identities.

Many women interviewed for the project described facing discrimination when they decided to start a family and being forced to choose between their career and their family life. Most women in newsrooms in the 1940s through the early 1960s did not have children, and the early women reporters examined in this study, such as Ruth Cowan Nash and Mary Garber, decided not to marry or have children. As Nash mentioned, she "was very anxious to be a success in the writing business . . . and in those days the AP didn't want a married woman." Similarly, Betsy Wade recalled being fired from her job when she got married and had a child. Dorothy Gilliam, who wanted to work part-time while managing her children at home, was forced to quit her job when her editor complained that her situation was being perceived as unfair by the men journalists. After a hiatus of about seven years, she was hired back by the *Washington Post* as an editor in the style section, but this was possible only because of the Kerner Commission Report of 1968, which had prompted newspapers to hire more Black staff.

In the absence of a unified support structure that could support and advocate for them, some women created informal structures within and outside the newsroom to counter the masculine culture of the workplace. Women journalists rallied around other women and looked out for one another. Eileen Shanahan mentioned the existence of an informal "pinch list," an informal list of the names of men who were known for harassing women reporters. Shanahan said that this information circulated informally among women who covered Congress so they would know which men should never be interviewed alone, and would be prepared to tackle them.

Though the increasing number of women in the newsroom was beneficial to women journalists, some perceived a downside to this. As Mary Garber said, the position of young women sports writers is far more difficult today than in her days because people have come to realize that women sportswriters are here to stay. As the only woman in the newsroom, she found that people accommodated themselves to her presence, and she tried her best to fit in with them, but the presence of more women was perceived as a threat to the men-oriented newsroom culture.

Reflecting on her experiences as a woman in the newsroom, Garber said that one of the problems women face in modern newsrooms is the lack of acceptance from men sportswriters. When a school prohibits women journalists from entering the locker room, men dismiss it as the woman's fault, instead of treating it as a problem for journalists as a whole. Commenting on the situation, she said:

Journalist Dorothy Gilliam. (Courtesy of C-SPAN.)

I can't understand why the men don't realize this and why they aren't as willing to fight for our rights as they are for their own rights, but that isn't the way it works and they don't seem to realize that if I lose my rights, then they are going to lose theirs too. (Browning, 2022b)

The journalists who adopted activist roles toward the end of their careers were more likely to retreat from mainstream journalism and try to influence change from outside the institution. Dorothy Gilliam recalled that in the late 1970s, she observed an attitudinal change at the *Washington Post*, particularly a decline in support for civil rights, given the rise of the women's movement. Realizing that she no longer found fulfillment working at the newspaper, where she felt sidelined, she sought her calling elsewhere. She began teaching journalism, served on the boards of journalism education institutions, and wrote a book about media diversity—all efforts designed to improve the profession she had loved.

How Gender Shapes Reporting Assignments and Newsroom Interactions

Gender roles affect women journalists' interactions with their men editors, colleagues, and sources. Beasley and Gibbons (2003) found that men editors often perpetuated discrimination against women journalists but also that while this was often the case, there were some men editors who stood up for women staffers. Mary Garber spoke positively about her editors' contributions toward her career.

Journalist Eileen Shanahan. (Courtesy of C-SPAN.)

She recalled that in 1946, when she was denied entry into the press box because of her gender, her editor wrote to the athletic directors of Duke, Wake Forest, University of North Carolina, and North Carolina State University, saying that if they turned her away, they were turning away a member of the *Winston-Salem Journal-Sentinel* staff and not an individual. Garber recalled that this letter helped her gain acceptance at college sporting events.

Eileen Shanahan, who worked in the newsroom in the 1960s and 1970s, also found allies in some of her male colleagues. She recounted that when a male secretary of the U.S. Treasury had waved her away when she tried to ask a question at a press conference, a male colleague of hers had stepped in and asked that he respond to her question. And though she said she did not cover economics differently from a male reporter, she recounted an incident where she had lobbied to change the manner in which women were presented in unemployment statistics. While the category of "head of the household" included married men, it did not mention working women who supported their families. Shanahan brought this issue to the attention of the Bureau of Labor Statistics and lobbied successfully with other women to have it changed.

The journalists in this sample described a range of direct and indirect impacts of gender on their profession in terms of the content they produced and the assignments they received. Mary Garber mentioned that she was so grateful to her editor for facing negative comments, and taking a risk by having a woman on the staff as a sportswriter, that she developed a reputation for always saying good things about people and never being too critical.

Others, such as Betsy Wade, were slow to be promoted, despite being stellar workers. Their career trajectories were slowed down by men editors who doubted their journalistic skills, despite evidence to the contrary. Wade was paid below the prevailing scale at the time; however, due to the lack of precedent in the newsroom, and lack of data on women's employment, she was unable to advocate for herself. Having done a lot of difficult, sensitive work on the foreign copy desk where she edited stories on the Vietnam War, and handled high profile obituaries, she had made a reputation for herself as a hardworking, reliable, impartial editor. Yet no one considered her for the assistant editor position when it became available. When she expressed her interest in the position, the senior editor asked her if she was willing to give up her weekends for the job. Wade said she realized that the masculine culture of the newsroom did not leave room for family life, and the only way up the ladder was through working the late shift. However, she found another barrier in her way when the city editor declined to give her the late shift. He was unwilling to trust her because of a previous negative experience he had with a woman colleague. He also considered Wade unfit for the position as it involved exercising news judgment and deciding on the layout of stories—skills he felt women journalists lacked. She found few allies in the masculine culture of the newsroom, and for 20 years she was the only woman covering economic issues at the paper.

Photojournalist Diana Walker and reporter Ruth Cowan Nash described adapting so-called stereotypical feminine qualities to their advantage. Walker developed a specialty in being unobtrusive and taking "behind the scenes" photos, which were valued for their candid nature and authenticity. Referring to herself as "a stealth weapon," she said she perfected the art of blending into the background and never intruding upon her subjects. Nash, who covered World War II from the battlefield, said that though she would be present in the room while soldiers discussed their strategy, she made it a point to never intrude, because she didn't see much of a woman's angle in these stories. Since she was assigned to cover war stories from a woman's angle, she stuck to covering stories about nurses, hospitals, food, and civilian issues.

Gender also affected the women journalists' relationship with their sources. Mary Garber described being treated as a novelty as she was often the only woman sportswriter at a game. Since she was not allowed to enter the men players' dressing rooms, she had to make advance arrangements to speak to players and rely on coaches to hold their postgame conferences outside the dressing room. Garber recounted several instances of benevolent sexism in her interactions with sources. For example, she was once asked to sew a basketball player's ripped pants. On another occasion, a player sought her advice for asking a girl out on a date, and yet another sought encouragement from her when he was drafted to go to Vietnam.

As a Black woman, Dorothy Gilliam described being treated differently by Black sources. Some of the politicians she covered during her early days as a reporter expected her to give them special treatment, which made her uncomfortable as a journalist. She also described being assigned specifically to cover poverty and welfare stories. Though she enjoyed doing these stories, she was conscious that her career might be stifled if she was pigeonholed. Later in her career at the *Washington Post*, when she was hired to edit the style section, she focused on using that section to portray Black culture in a coherent manner.

CONCLUSION

The C-SPAN Video Library offers a great source of primary research material to answer questions about the evolution of journalism over time from women's perspectives. This study used an oral history approach to examine how gender affected the professional identities of women. Though the sample analyzed in this study offered rich details, it suffered from a lack of diversity. Only one Black woman's interview was available. The inclusion of interviews with more women of color will help answer additional questions about the intersectional nature of women journalists' experiences in the newsroom.

The findings in this essay show that the job model of socialization has a huge impact on shaping women journalists' identities and careers. These women's lived experiences in the newsroom affected the type of stories they produced. The masculine culture in which they were socialized left little room for questioning the norms, but despite that, these women succeeded in diversifying the news agenda, incorporating marginalized voices, and promoting issues that were traditionally not considered newsworthy. In doing this, these women were instrumental in changing the norms of journalism. Their perceptions of gender roles and the strategies they used to counter gender discrimination were influenced to a great extent by the prevailing sociopolitical forces, which acted as a powerful tool to cause significant shifts in the masculine newsroom culture.

REFERENCES

Armstrong, C. L., & McAdams, M. J. (2009). Blogs of information: How gender cues and individual motivations influence perceptions of credibility. *Journal of Computer-Mediated Communication, 14*(3), 435–456. https://doi.org/10.1111/j.1083-6101.2009 .01448.x

Barnes, L. (2016). An inexplicable gap: Journalism and gender in New Zealand. *Journalism, 18*(6), 736–753. https://doi.org/10.1177/1464884915620231

Beasley, M. H., & Gibbons, S. J. (2003). *Taking their place: A documentary history of women and journalism* (2nd ed.). Strata.

Bradley, P. (2005). *Women and the press: The struggle for equality.* Northwestern University Press.

Brann, M., & Himes, K. (2010). Perceived credibility of male versus female television newscasters. *Communication Research Reports, 27*(3), 243–252. https://doi.org/10 .1080/08824091003737869

Broussard, J. C. (2003). *Giving a voice to the voiceless: Four pioneering Black women journalists.* Routledge.

Browning, R. X. [RXB]. (2022a, March 14). *Clip of* Oral Histories: Mary Garber, Part 2 (July 3, 2011 [November 4, 1990]); *Garber on rights* [C-SPAN user video clip]. https://www.c-span.org/video/?c5005895/garber-rightsnewly%20second%20clip

Browning, R. X. [RXB]. (2022b, March 15). *Clip of* Oral Histories: Mary Garber, Part 1 (June 26, 2011 [November 4, 1990]); *Garber on locker room* [C-SPAN user video clip]. https://www.c-span.org/video/?c5005986/garber-locker-room

The Byline Blog. (2012). *The byline survey report, 2012: Who narrates the world?* https:// theopedproject.wordpress.com/2012/05/28/the-byline-survey-2011/

Correa, T., & Harp, D. (2011). Women matter in newsrooms: How power and critical mass relate to the coverage of the HPV vaccine. *Journalism & Mass Communication Quarterly, 88*, 301–319. https://doi.org/10.1177/107769901108800205

Craft, S., & Wanta, W. (2004). Women in the newsroom: Influences of female editors and reporters on the news agenda. *Journalism and Mass Communication Quarterly, 81*(1), 124–138. https://doi.org/10.1177/107769900408100109

C-SPAN (Producer). (1990, November 4). *Oral histories: Mary Garber, Part 2* [Video]. https://www.c-span.org/video/?299875-2/mary-garber-oral-history-interview -part-2

Dodd-McCue, D., & Wright, G. B. (1996). Men, women, and attitudinal commitment: The effects of workplace experiences and socialization. *Human Relations, 49*(8), 1065–1091. https://doi.org/10.1177/001872679604900803

Edy, C. (2019). Trust but verify: Myths and misinformation in the history of women war correspondents. *American Journalism, 36*(2), 242–251. https://doi.org/10.1080/08821127.2019.1602420

Engstrom, E., & Ferri, A. J. (1998). From barriers to challenges: Career perceptions of women TV news anchors. *Journalism & Mass Communication Quarterly, 75,* 789–802. https://doi.org/10.1177/107769909807500412

Everbach, T. (2006). The culture of a women-led newspaper: An ethnographic study of the *Sarasota Herald-Tribune. Journalism & Mass Communication Quarterly, 83*(3), 477–493. https://doi.org/10.1177/107769900608300301

Freedman, E., & Fico, F. (2005). Male and female sources in newspaper coverage of male and female candidates in open races for governor in 2002. *Mass Communication and Society, 8*(3), 257–272. https://doi.org/10.1207/s15327825mcs0803_5

Fuchs, P. B. (2003). Women in journalism oral history collection of the Washington Press Club Foundation. *Journalism History, 28*(4), 191–196, https://doi.org/10.1080/00947679.2003.12062612

Hanitzsch, T., & Hanusch, F. (2012). Does gender determine journalists' professional views? A reassessment based on cross-national evidence. *European Journal of Communication, 27*(3), 257–277. https://doi.org/10.1177/0267323112454804

Harp, D. (2007). *Desperately seeking women readers: US newspapers and the construction of a female readership.* Lexington Books.

Huddy, L., & Terkildsen, N. (1993). The consequences of gender stereotypes for women candidates at different levels and types of office. *Political Research Quarterly, 46*(3), 503–525. https://doi.org/10.1177/106591299304600304

Iiris, R., & Sinikka, T. (2018). Journalism and gender. Toward a multidimensional approach. *Nordicom Review, 39*(1), 67–79. https://doi.org/10.2478/nor-2018-0002.

Jenkins, J., Volz, Y., Finneman, T., Park, Y. J., & Sorbelli, K. (2018). Reconstructing collective professional identity: A case study of a women's journalist association in the post–second-wave feminist movement in the United States. *Media, Culture & Society, 40*(4), 600–616. https://doi.org/10.1177/0163443717724604

John, A. V. (2003). "Behind the locked door": Evelyn Sharp, suffragette and rebel journalist. *Women's History Review, 12*(1), 5–13. https://doi.org/10.1080/09612020300200344

Lumsden, L. (1995). "You're a tough guy, Mary—and a first-rate newspaperman": Gender and women journalists in the 1920s and 1930s. *Journalism & Mass Communication Quarterly, 72*(4), 913–921. https://doi.org/10.1177/107769909507200414

Meeks, L. (2013). He wrote, she wrote: Journalist gender, political office, and campaign news. *Journalism & Mass Communication Quarterly, 90*(1), 58–74. https://doi.org/10.1177/1077699012468695

Mills, K. (1997). What difference do women journalists make? In Norris, P. (Ed.) *Women, media, and politics* (pp. 41–56). Oxford University Press.

Mulac, A., Bradac, J. J., & Gibbons, P. (2001). Empirical support for the gender-as-culture hypothesis: An intercultural analysis of male/female language differences. *Human Communication Research, 27*(1), 121–152. https://doi.org/10.1111/j.1468-2958.2001.tb00778.x

Nicholson, J. O., Creedon, P. J., Lloyd, W. S., & Johnson, P. J. (Eds.). (2009). *The edge of change: Women in the twenty-first-century press.* University of Illinois Press.

Nishikawa, K. A., Towner, T. L., Clawson, R. A., & Waltenburg, E. N. (2009). Interviewing the interviewers: Journalistic norms and racial diversity in the newsroom. *The Howard Journal of Communications, 20*(3), 242–259. https://doi.org/10.1080/10646170903070175

Rodgers, S., & Thorson, E. (2003). A socialization perspective on male and female reporting. *Journal of Communication, 53*(4), 658–675. https://doi.org/10.1111/j.1460-2466.2003.tb02916.x

Ross, K. (2001). Women at work: Journalism as en-gendered practice. *Journalism Studies, 2*(4), 531–544. https://doi.org/10.1080/14616700120086404

Ruoho, I., & Torkkola, S. (2018). Journalism and gender: Toward a multidimensional approach. *Nordicom Review, 39*(1), 67–79. https://doi.org/10.2478/nor-2018-0002

Weaver, D. H., & Wilhoit, G. C. (1996). *The American journalist in the 1990s: U.S. news people at the end of an era.* Erlbaum.

Yow, V. (2015). *Recording oral history: A guide for the humanities and social sciences* (3rd ed.). Rowman & Littlefield.

9

MORAL SENTIMENTS OF U.S. CONGRESS'S FARM BILL DEBATES, 2012–2021

Jacob A. Miller-Klugesherz

INTRODUCTION

Farmers were in desperate need of help. Prices for goods plummeted, so farmers began plowing more ground to try to make up for lost income. Droughts came and remained. Wind swept plowed soil high into the sky and made little else visible but a bowl of dust. Then the Great Depression hit, and the U.S. federal government realized it could no longer idly stand by. The government scrambled to pass the Agricultural Adjustment Act of 1933, or as we know it today, the first ever Farm Bill (Farm Policy Facts, 2022).

Today, the Farm Bill is a marquee legislative responsibility of the agriculture committees of Congress. The Farm Bill is a comprehensive, omnibus package of agriculture, conservation, rural development, research, and food assistance. The Farm Bill is renewed about every five years, so it provides reliable opportunities for legislators to "comprehensively and periodically address agricultural and food issues" (Johnson & Monke, 2017, p. 2). There were 12 titles in the most recent, 2017–2018, Farm Bill: commodity programs, conservation, trade, nutrition programs, credit, rural development, research and related matters, forestry, energy, horticulture, crop insurance, and miscellaneous (Agriculture Improvement Act, 2018). Farm Bill debates occurred this year, in 2022, and the bill is expected to pass in September 2023.

The process by which provisions make it into Farm Bill markup and final legislation is decidedly moral. At its simplest, morality refers to what societies sanction as right or wrong. They are prevailing standards of behavior that allow people to live collectively. Specific group morals can form at any level, be it organizations, communities, or in this case, Congress's agriculture committees (Ahmed, 2021, p. 1). Moral choices have historically impacted *global* agri-food systems. Post–World War II competitive surplus commodity dumping established the "global food regime" (Friedmann, 1993). Most underdeveloped countries became dependent on exporting specialized crops and importing commodities. The regime promoted the spread of the "green revolution," typified by enhanced genetic varieties, industrial technologies, and chemical applications. Future agri-food decisions are largely confined to this globally dominant, moral framework. Given the Farm Bill's global scope, impact, and role as a precedent-setter for agriculture, it is crucial to better understand the morality latent in visceral agriculture committee debates.

Sociological theories of moral sentiments for institutions and organizations have long existed (e.g., Haveman & Rao, 1997; Wallwork, 1985). However, moral foundations theory (MFT) was initiated by social psychologists as a pluralist approach to understanding how moral foundations within political contexts evolve and persist within and across cultures over time. MFT posits that individuals have an initial "first draft" morality (Graham et al., 2012, p. 7) that is then edited by culture (p. 38–39) and finally institutionalized (p. 15). Haidt and Joseph (2004) compare each moral foundation to the five taste receptors; every person has all five, but the combination and degree of response differs for each person. The five widely accepted foundations and their (lowercase here) opposites are Care/harm, Fairness/cheating, Loyalty/betrayal, Authority/subversion, and Sanctity/degradation (Liberty/oppression is not yet widely accepted). Conservatives and liberals rely on different sets of moral foundations, with the former tending toward group-oriented morals and the latter toward individualities (Haidt & Graham, 2009). Several studies using multiple methods have found that liberals consistently showed greater endorsement and use of the Care/harm and Fairness/reciprocity foundations compared to the other three foundations, whereas conservatives endorsed and used the five foundations more equally (K. Johnson & Goldwasser, 2018; Roy & Goldwasser, 2021; Silver & Silver, 2017).

Moral sentiment scholars believe that our emotions and desires are crucial to morality's makeup, or that emotions are the primary source of moral knowledge (Kauppinen, 2018). A common method researchers use to identify a text's implicit morality is to analyze sentiments within it. MFT becomes *accessed* via sentiment analysis. Sentiment analysis has been used extensively in political and social media arenas for topic-specific issues. However, it has not been used to understand sentiment toward farms and farming generally. This study's core contribution is the examination of the relationship between legislators' latent, moral sentiments, their partisanship, and the legislation that directs the future of agriculture. Therefore, I ask:

RQ: What has been the U.S. Congress's moral sentiment toward American farms and farmers?

Answering this question is imperative given that Congress's emotive, moral disposition toward farms and farmers shapes the policy that constrains and enables farmers to put into practice the principles necessary to help alleviate the multiple, cascading ecological crises of our time (Burns, 2020), crises unimaginable to the 1933 Farm Bill framers. To answer the research question, I offer a literature review, methodology, results, and discussion.

LITERATURE REVIEW

Industrial agriculture has been the hegemonic moral, especially since President Nixon's USDA secretary, Earl Butz, and his 1970s dictum to farmers: "Get big or get out" (Philpott, 2008). The 1980s farm crisis was the result of the totalizing, moral sentiment for neoliberal, economic authority and its consequences for agricultural policy. The USDA's hegemony spread throughout the U.S. relatively unopposed but ran into movements of counter-hegemony. For instance, Wendell Berry (1977) lambasted the conventional agriculture's ideology, blaming it for the erosion of soil and culture. Jackson (1980) articulated the problems *of* agriculture and called for a perennial system. Counter-hegemonic moral frameworks paved the way for organic, sustainable, regenerative, and other "good food movements" (Preston, 2017). To expand on what is meant by morals, sentiments, and hegemony and their intertwinement in agriculture, this review covers (1) the sociology of politics and emotion and (2) the sentiment within moral foundations.

Sociology of Politics and Emotion

Democracy, as a sociological concept, "refers to a method for governing a collectivity" (Weinstein, 1996, p. 35). It is a method of "self-rule." Democratic groups establish their moral foundations and act for themselves in ways that reify—and (un)consciously spread—those foundations. MFT's psychosocial causal order suggests that individuals display openness, flexibility, and individual rights. These morals then scale and aggregate into an emergent, self-organizing, and democratic social systems. MFT's pluralistic approach supports multiple theories of democracy (Cunningham, 2002). They begin at different starting points but arrive at a similar conclusion: the collective's self-rule inevitably faces infinite complexity and messiness.

A psychosocial causal reordering helps us better understand how morals determine individual behavior from the top down. It is the preferred ordering since society's moral frameworks have the greatest influence over what individual farmers can and cannot do. Two examples illustrate this point. First, Bessire (2021, pp. 42–44) explains that "insurance farming" occurs when farmers are constrained to growing commodity crops, usually corn and soybeans, because those crops are covered by insurance. In contrast, alternative, perennial, and/or cover crop blends are rarely covered by insurance; thus, one barrier preventing large-scale transformation is guaranteed money for certain crops and not others (Carolan, 2005; Gosnell et al., 2019). As a second example, farmers in groundwater-depleting areas are put on a "production treadmill"—whereby farmers continue to pump depleting groundwater and install irrigation equipment—because the government pays them to do so (Sanderson et al., 2020; Sanderson & Hughes, 2019). These examples highlight that top-down policies can contradict or interfere with farmers' individual capacities.

Moral frameworks that have been bureaucratized and institutionalized (e.g., industrial agriculture) have power over individual farmer's moral determinations. Antonio Gramsci's theory of cultural hegemony is relevant here. Cultural hegemony holds that the ruling class injects the citizenry with its values, beliefs, attitudes, and ideology. U.S. hegemony not only affects its citizenry but other countries on the periphery of the Global North (Sebastian, 2021, pp. 9–10). Although federal politicians are *our* public servants, C. Wright Mills (2000) would remind us that politicians are among the "power elite." Lobbyists, backroom conversations, and revolving doors ensure that the elite write policy. Gilens and Page (2014, p. 564) found that "economic elites and organized groups representing business interests have substantial independent impacts on U.S. government policy, while average citizens and mass-based interest groups have little or no independent influence." The economic-political special interest block injects the citizenry with its ideologies filtered through media coverage, political rhetoric, and oligarchic mechanisms. The Farm Bureau is a louder voice than the Farmers Union due to the former's history of hiring and sponsoring the elite of industrial agriculture, the hegemon.

There is nothing rational about the hegemony of moral frameworks. Gramsci's writings focus on the affective dimensions of revolutionary aspirations (Adamson, 2014). Gramsci's *Prison Notebook* emphasizes the importance of discourse analysis to understand the emotions driving the oligarchical elite's hegemonic coercion to contest with a counterattack that maintains, in this case, the Care-laden morality of a democratic food system of, by, and for the people. As for sociology, although its foundations were primarily concerned with rationality (Weber, 1978), they left a trail of breadcrumbs on the role of emotion in social formation and influence. Later scholars collected these breadcrumbs and made "the sociology of emotion" subfield. It enjoys a lineage dating back to the 1970s (Shilling, 2014; Shott, 1979). Differentiation in emotions that allows for the emergence of meaning is socially constructed, and a cultural vocabulary around those sentiments forms (Gordon, 1992, p. 563). I briefly nod to this subfield for the primary purpose of highlighting that, contrary to most of sociology and especially its origins, the study of emotions is useful—if not crucial—to understanding how the U.S. Congress's sentiments toward farming result in policy that shapes the future of domestic and global agriculture.

Sentiment Within Moral Foundations

The theory of moral sentiments was first articulated in detail by Adam Smith (Cockfield et al., 2007). Smith (2005) detailed the impact of passions on economic activity (Barbalet, 2013). The sociology of morality built from this tradition to explain how individual valences of right and wrong structure society (Firey, 1945; Haveman & Rao, 1997; Hitlin & Vaisey, 2013; Kertzer et al., 2014). Because sociologists are more interested in how people pursue actions in the long run than at one moment in time, I am more interested in the development of morally institutional arrangements than in abstract scenarios (e.g., the classic train track scenario). Admittedly, this interest does make sociologists wade into "thick conceptions of morality" (Hitlin & Vaisey, 2013, p. 55).

A prominent, "thick" conception of morality is moral foundations theory. When MFT was proposed, it spread in popularity because its foundations held up *across cultures* and could be *quantitatively* assessed (Haidt, 2013; Haidt & Joseph, 2004). In the years since, MFT has been clarified, contested (Curry, 2019), and extended. For example, Landmann and Hess (2017) tested MFT with emotions and concluded that there are emotion-specific foundations (Care/harm) and emotion-unspecific foundations (Fairness, Authority and Loyalty). Studies within the MFT vein remain political in nature and emotional in context. Brady et al. (2017) found that the presence of moral-emotional language in political messages substantially increases their diffusion within (and less so between) ideological group boundaries. Authority has been found to be the prominent foundation for a vast majority of British parliamentarians' moral tweets when discussing the Brexit withdrawal agreement (van Vliet, 2021, p. 11). Alizadeh et al. (2019) found MFT's embeddedness in partisan Twitter users and extend the theory to political extremist groups. Kertzer et al. (2014) examined how the individualized morals of Care and Fairness especially shape foreign policy attitudes. For instance, university extension agencies and internationally focused programs (e.g., Kansas State University's International Grains Program) spread their morals through their industrialized and concentrated approach to agriculture. Given that Care has been found to be more used by liberals (Haidt & Graham, 2009), I posit the following:

H1a: Democratic sentiment will be the strongest within the Care foundation when discussing issues of agriculture.

Moreover, given Republicans' deference to the authoritative powers that run industrial agriculture (e.g., Farm Bureau, Bayer-Monsanto, Cargill), I predict the following:

H1b: Republican sentiment will be the strongest within the Authority foundation when discussing issues of agriculture.

Sentiment Analysis

Whether morality is dormant in all human expression or whether there is such a thing as amorality are topics for later discussion. However, it is difficult to contest that latent morals are communicated through emotive and visceral expressions, or sentiments. Gordon (1992, p. 566) defines sentiments as "socially constructed patterns of sensations, expressive gestures, and cultural meanings organized around a relationship to a social object, usually another person." In this case, congressional colleagues. Access to moral foundations is obtained by a variety of methods, chief among them sentiment analysis (SA).

SA is a machine-learning, textual analysis technique whereby embryonic expressions, emotions, and sentiments are extracted from text. According to Medhat et al., (2014, p. 1093), SA is the "computational study of people's opinions, attitudes and emotions toward an entity." Mäntylä et al. (2018) reviewed the evolution of SA: It began in studies on public opinion near the beginning of 20th century and in the text subjectivity analysis performed by the computational linguistics community in 1990s. A quantitative method, SA is used in several different fields: consumer research (Aaker et al., 2008; Büschken & Allenby, 2016), political science (Kertzer et al., 2014), media studies, disaster relief management (Beigi et al., 2016), finance (D'Andrea et al., 2015), linguistics (Taboada, 2016), and sociology (Haveman & Rao, 1997), especially social network analysis (Chakraborty et al., 2018; Mukkamala et al., 2014). SA has become an especially popular method given its compatibility with big data. Opinion mining of political rhetoric on Twitter has boomed in popularity in the past decade (Alsaeedi & Zubair, 2019), with scholars even assessing the real-time Twitter sentiment toward the candidates in the 2012 U.S. presidential election (Wang et al., 2012). Twitter has likely become more popular since contemporary political speeches use simpler language and express more sentiments than they previously did (Kansas State University, 2020). Given this finding, and the increasingly divisive, crude, and jarring political climate of the last decade, with the topic of agriculture as no exception (for instance, Congress's proposed "meatless Mondays" became a topic of fierce debate), I offer the following:

H2:   Moral sentiment toward farms and farming has increased since 2012.

That SA is commonly used to understand political expressions should come as no surprise. Political responses primarily express deeply held, primal, and often fear- or hope-based beliefs. Hearit and Buzzanell (2018, p. 57) used SA to analyze Chairman Greenspan's talk about uncertainties in the future. Using a dataset of 161,000 tweets authored by U.S. politicians, Roy and Goldwasser (2021) analyzed the politicians' sentiments toward the hot topics of gun control and immigration while utilizing MFT. They found a strong correlation between moral foundation usage and politicians' nuanced stances on a topic, and notable differences in moral foundation usage by different political parties toward the issues.

Frimer et al. (2015) conducted a textual analysis of all 124 million words spoken in the House of Representatives between 1996 and 2014 and found that declining levels of prosocial language strongly predicted public disapproval of Congress six months later. Frimer et al.'s (2015, p. 6591) finding that "prosocial language has an independent, direct effect on social approval" established the link between social response and congressional sentiment. Takikawa and Sakamoto's (2020) "moral-emotional foundations of political discourse" compared sentiments in floor debates and speeches between the U.S. and Japan since most SA has been done in the U.S. context. Their multilevel modeling findings lead them to conclude that the moral-emotional framework cannot be easily explained away by ideology alone. Finally, Jones's (2021) SA on factory farming found that corporations and nongovernmental organizations treat factory farming positively, whereas governmental bodies show nearly neutral scores. Given the past ferocity of Farm Bill debates as well as the overall negative and polarized nature of Congress, I predict the following:

H3:   Congress's negative moral sentiment toward farms and farming has linearly increased since 2012.

To test these hypotheses, I offer the following methodological approach.

METHODOLOGY

Dataset and Procedure

I employed textual analyses using video clips from the C-SPAN Video Library to assemble my sample. The search timeframe was from April 1, 1971, to April 30, 2021, but video clip dates only ranged from 2012 to 2021. I searched using the keywords "farm" and "farming" under "Clips" in the C-SPAN Video Library. I limited the series to the U.S. House and Senate, yielding 278 clips. Fifty-five videos were excluded from the initial 278—1 video was unavailable for download, 8 were on irrelevant topics, another 8 were simple roll call votes, and 38 were duplicates. Their exclusion left a remaining total of $N = 223$ videos for analysis, 132 for the House and 89 for the Senate. Video clips are valuable because they retain the passion, emotion, and energy of the argument. They are also a valuable pedagogical tool.

TABLE 9.1 *Number of Videos and Runtimes by Year*

Year	Number of videos	% of total videos	Total runtime	% of total time
2012	20	8.97	141 minutes, 39 seconds	5.74
2013	65	29.15	605 minutes, 54 seconds	24.56
2014	20	8.97	305 minutes, 57 seconds	12.40
2015	7	3.14	22 minutes, 20 seconds	0.91
2016	3	1.35	21 minutes, 55 seconds	0.89
2017	5	2.24	49 minutes, 57 seconds	2.03
2018	74	33.18	1,053 minutes, 43 seconds	42.72
2019	12	5.38	118 minutes, 58 seconds	4.82
2020	14	6.28	65 minutes, 29 seconds	2.65
2021*	3	1.35	80 minutes, 41 seconds	3.27
Total	223	*100*	*41 hours, 6 minutes, 33 seconds*	*100*

*Through July.

The average video length was 10 minutes and 34 seconds, with the shortest running just 6 seconds and the longest running 8 hours and 31 minutes. Overall, there were 41 hours, 6 minutes, and 33 seconds of total runtime (Table 9.1), 8,482 unique words, and 307,256 total words (excluding numbers but not fragments). "Year" refers not to the date clipped but date created. The years 2012, 2013, 2017, and 2018 have, by far, the most videos and runtime. This makes sense because Congress passed Farm Bills in 2014 and 2018 and most of the videos in those years consisted of Farm Bill debate, statements, and appeals. Transcripts were uploaded into Atlas.ti v.9 (2021), a leading qualitative analysis software.

Analysis

Two primary modes of textual analysis were utilized: (1) textual sentiment analysis and (2) text search by coding for emergent issues.

(1) Textual sentiment analysis

SA measures the "polarity" and "tonality" of texts by identifying the expressions people use to discuss other people, things, or events (Haselmayer & Jenny,

2017, p. 2625). The scientific method of quantitative content analysis is a systematic and reproducible way to understand the latent meaning of texts. It allows for the "separation of the researcher from the text," even though neither the "conceptualization of the content" nor interpretation of results is free from researcher subjectivity (Hearit & Buzzanell, 2018, pp. 51–52; Krippendorf, 2012). The core assumption of textual, discursive, and sentiment analyses is that researchers treat "text as data" (Grimmer & Stewart, 2013, p. 2). The era of big data enables researchers to amass a sample (r) far more representative of the population (P) than smaller, more localized datasets (Mukkamala et al., 2014). However, automated methods of analyzing big data are no substitute for careful thought, close reading, and context-specific validation. There are several limitations to the a priori assumption of text as data, chief among them that the text is reduced to a "bag of words" and detached from its sentence–paragraph contexts and temporal ordering (Mukkamala et al., 2014, p. 6). These limitations and others will be extrapolated in the discussion section of this essay. Despite these qualifications, SA is one of the best textual methods for uncovering moral foundations.

VALANCED SENTIMENT ANALYSIS

I performed a valanced SA to uncover Congress's tonality related to farming and farmers over time using Atlas.ti's SA feature (Kalpokas & Radivojevic, 2021). Valanced SA simply categorizes the expressed sentiment (positive, negative, or neutral) of a particular paragraph or sentence. Instead of analyzing the sentiment per word—as Jones (2021) does—I analyzed by sentence. Sentence-level analysis has been found to be more "distinguished and coherent" than sampling at the word level (Büschken & Allenby, 2016, p. 1). Although word-level analysis is used for the next SA technique, sentence-level was chosen for valanced SA. This is because data were clumped into long paragraphs and sentiments range widely within. The word-level SA was not used because it is too fine-grained and reductionistic (Thelwall et al., 2010). Atlas.ti's natural language processing engine, AtlasspaCy, generates the outputs by frequency, meaning each video is assigned a certain number of positive, neutral, or negative sentiments. I then divided each by the total sum and multiplied by 100 to calculate the rate.

EXTENDED MORAL FOUNDATIONS DICTIONARY

Researchers have assessed the impact positive and negative sentiments have on behaviors. However, Villarroel Ordenes et al. (2017, p. 6) argued that these simple, valanced words "mask the effects of further language granularities," such as the strength or conviction with which consumers express their sentiment (Thelwall et al., 2010). Positive and negative removes what the emotion is used for and instead takes a macro approach at identifying the overall tone of a particular person or political party. A valanced approach alone is not sufficient to effectively uncover moral sentiments. Therefore, I utilize Hopp et al.'s (2021) extended Moral Foundations Dictionary (eMFD), developed as a new dictionary built from annotations of moral content by a large, diverse crowd (p. 244).[1] Hopp et al. (2021, p. 235) explain that their crowd-sourced eMFD is a useful tool that can identify and relay the large-scale judgments of moral sentiments in a text and that eMFD overcomes the limitations of previous dictionary attempts. Hopp et al.'s dictionary is available as an open source .csv file.[2] The dictionary contains a composite score ranging from −1 (most negative) to +1 (most positive), denoting the average sentiment score of "the annotations . . . in a foundation-specific fashion" (Hopp et al., 2021, p. 238).

Grimmer and Stewart (2013) warned that for dictionary methods to work well, the scores attached to words must closely align with how the words are used in a particular context. The eMFT dictionary is a context-*independent* dictionary but is still valid for three reasons. First, Hopp et al. (2021, p. 238) used the Valence Aware Dictionary for Sentiment Reasoning (VADER) package to extract words deemed moral by virtue or vice (i.e., positive or negative), and words that could not be assigned either were dropped. Second, Hopp et al. (p. 242) sourced news articles from outlets ranging the partisan spectrum, so the extracted words did not skew toward one party. Finally, Jones (2021, p. 5) too used VADER as his core sentiment identifier for topics related to factory farming. For these reasons the eMFT dictionary is valid for this study's context.

The final step was to create document groups based on political party and year. There were total unique words for Democrats ($N = 6{,}493$), Republicans ($N = 6{,}273$), and bipartisans ($N = 8{,}433$), including repeat words. The words were then matched with eMFD, which excluded those words, fragments, and numerical values included in the text but *not* in the eMFD. The remaining word totals are as follows: Democrats ($N = 2{,}192$), Republicans ($N = 2{,}150$), and bipartisans ($N = 2{,}576$). Moral foundations probability and sentiment scores were multiplied by their frequency count to factor frequency into the weight of the scores, then aggregated by their mean score. I chose not to calculate "nonmoral"/"amoral" percentages or scores because I maintain the ontological position that amorality cannot exist.

(2) Text search by coding for emergent issues

Qualitative tools are simply that—tools. Because my methodological approach has followed the lead of the foremost qualitative and coding research (Davidson, 2009; Merrigan & Hutson, 2008), I also follow its caution: tools are no substitute for close analysis of the text. Therefore, manual coding was performed to (1) clean up textual errors, (2) identify one or two core issues per clip (depending on the length and range of core topics) and the periphery codes of "anti-Democrat" and "anti-Republican," and (3) ascertain exemplary quotations in their own context.

FINDINGS

Valanced Sentiment Analysis

Positive, negative, and neutral sentiments from 2012–2021 varied little between Democrats, Republicans, and bipartisans. Democrats showed the most negative sentiment (48.13%). Republicans were the most positive (35.75%) and the most neutral (20.82%). For Congress as a whole, over time valanced sentiment largely remained consistent (see Figure 9.1). Over time, linear trend lines for neutral ($R2 = -0.059$) and negative ($R2 = -0.056$) sentiments slightly decreased, but slightly increased for positive sentiments ($R2 = 0.001$) (see Figure 9.2).

Independent sample t-tests were performed to see if there were statistically significant differences in valanced sentiment rates between all those belonging to a specific political party and all others *not* in that party (see Table 9.2). There were statistically significant differences in negative sentiment among Democrats ($M_{diff} = 3.75$) and Republicans ($M_{diff} = -4.68$), and neutral sentiment among Democrats ($M_{diff} = -2.15$). In other words, Democrats were, on average, 3.75% more negative than non-Democrats, Republicans were 4.68% less negative than non-Republicans, and Democrats were 2.15% less neutral than non-Democrats.

Extended Moral Foundations Dictionary Sentiment Analysis

Figure 9.3 displays the evolution of Congress's moral sentiment over time. All moral sentiments except Loyalty increased over time: Care ($R2 = 0.003$), Fairness ($R2 = 0.02$), Loyalty ($R2 = -0.022$), Authority ($R2 = 0.013$), and Sanctity ($R2 = 0.057$). The 2016 spike was an outlier, since that year saw only three clips

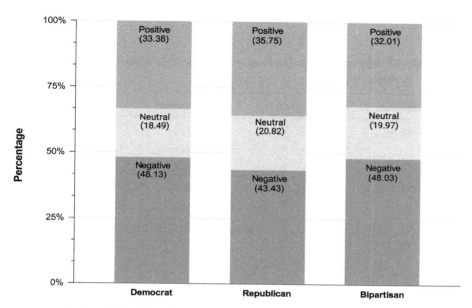

FIGURE 9.1 Valanced rates of U.S. congressional party sentiment toward farming, 2012–2021.

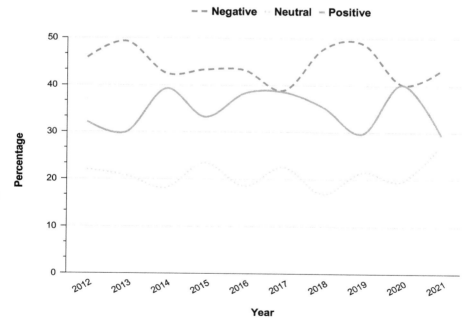

FIGURE 9.2 Valanced rates of U.S. congressional party sentiment toward farming over time.

TABLE 9.2 *Independent Sample t-Tests (equal variances assumed) for Valanced Sentiment Rates by Political Party*

Sentiment rate (%)	Party	Mean difference[1]	Standard error difference
Negative	D	3.75*	1.81
	R	−4.68*	1.88
	B	1.68†	3.17
Neutral	D	−2.15*	1.08
	R	2.13†	1.13
	B	0.59†	1.90
Positive	D	−1.60†	1.70
	R	2.56†	1.77
	B	−2.27†	2.95

[1]Mean difference subtracts the nonparty from party. In other words, a *positive* mean value indicates that Democratic (D), Republican (R), and bipartisan (B) legislators express *higher* rates than non-Democrats, non-Republicans, and non-bipartisan members, respectively. Thus, a *negative* mean value indicates members of the political parties express *lower* rates than members not of those parties.

*$p < .05$.

†Not significant.

comprising a mere 0.89% of total runtime. Care and Sanctity remained negative over time, indicating the prevalence of their opposites: harm and degradation. eMFD also includes a vector scale that captures the probabilities that words belong to a given moral foundation, reflected in Figure 9.4. Care and Fairness had the greatest probability, and Sanctity the lowest.

Figures 9.5 and 9.6 highlight the eMFD *probabilities* and word *sentiment* scores by partisanship, respectively. Words used by Democrats are more likely to fall within the Care and Fairness foundations than words used by Republicans or those in bipartisan clips. Harm and degradation are the sentiments most used by Democrats compared to the other two groups, whereas Fairness, Loyalty, and Authority are most used by Republicans, comparatively.

Text Search for Emergent Issues

Minnesota, Texas, and California were the three states mentioned or represented the most in the text, and Idaho, Utah, and Wyoming the three least (see Figure 9.7). This makes sense given that the congressional leadership during this decade

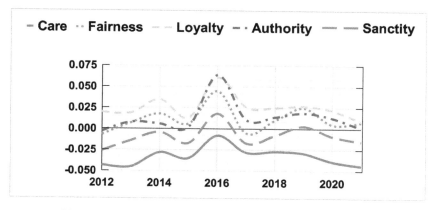

FIGURE 9.3 Congress's moral sentiment from 2012 to 2021 (aggregated, mean values).

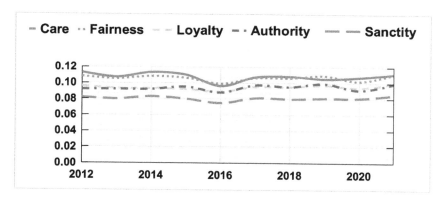

FIGURE 9.4 Vector scale of the probability that the words fall within the moral foundation (aggregated, mean values).

are largely from Minnesota, Texas, and California and because the states ranked fifth, third, and first, respectively, for the largest agricultural industries (Gallagher, 2021).

Manual coding identified that passing the Farm Bill was the most common ($N = 72$), followed by farm subsidies ($N = 46$) and amending the Farm Bill ($N = 46$) (see Figure 9.8). Sen. Dick Durbin (D-IL) captured the overall sentiment Democrats had toward farm subsidies and insurance for large farms:

 Anytime you put the two words "Federal Insurance" in the same sentence, I advise my colleagues step back and ask some questions. (C-SPAN User-Created Clip, 2014)

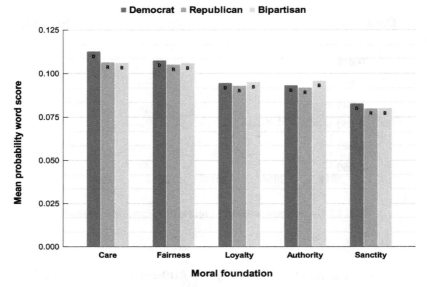

FIGURE 9.5 *Probability* that words fall within MFD foundation, sorted by party (mean values).

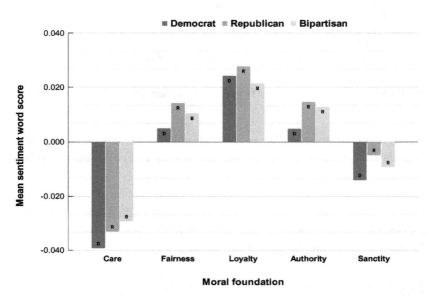

FIGURE 9.6 eMFD foundation *sentiment* word scores by party (aggregated, mean values).

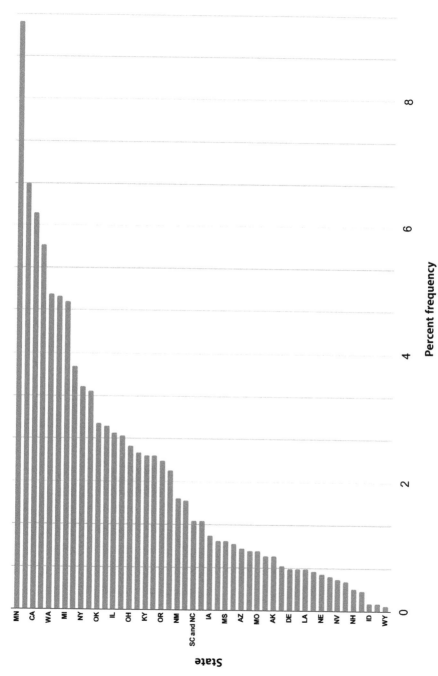

FIGURE 9.7 Frequency of states represented.

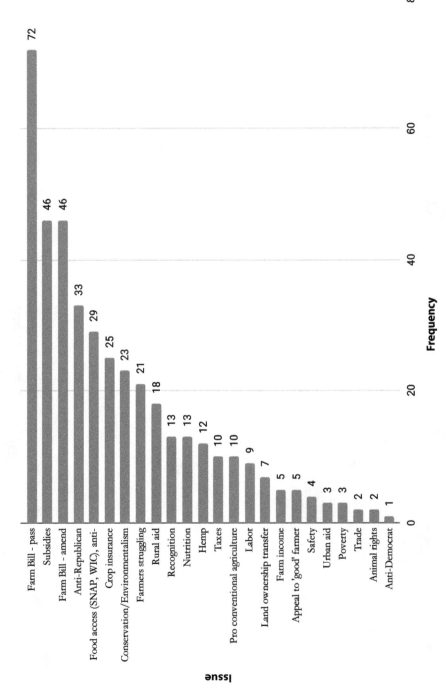

FIGURE 9.8 Frequency of core issues (themes). *Note:* "Anti-Republican" and "anti-Democrat" were not considered core issues but rather directly expressed, anti-party sentiments peripheral to the core issues. All exhaustive instances of anti-party sentiment were recorded.

Anti-Republican sentiment ($N = 33$) was much more frequent than anti-Democratic sentiment ($N = 1$). The frequency of anti-Republican sentiment was often the result of emotional arguments countering the Republicans' hesitancy—and sometimes vitriol—toward increasing allocations for food access and welfare programs ($N = 29$). Republicans generally thought that welfare programs would lead to more welfare abusers. For instance, Rep. Joni Ernst (R-IA) said (see Figure 9.8):

 I'm reminded of the 28-year-old, lobster-eating, Cadillac Escalade–driving surfer from San Diego, California, who had not worked in over a year and was receiving food stamps. He was unabashedly abusing the system and taking benefits away from those that need those benefits the most. . . . We should not allow this type of behavior to continue. (C-SPAN User-Created Clip, 2018b)

Sen. Jim Inhofe (R-OK) was blunter:

 I encourage my colleagues to vote for this amendment and turn the Farm Bill into a Farm Bill instead of a charity bill. (C-SPAN User-Created Clip, 2013a)

Rep. Jackie Speier's (D-CA) pointed out Republicans' hypocrisy (see Figure 9.9):

 My Republican colleagues have a point. It's terrible that some people take advantage of free food and drink to continue their slothful lifestyles. I agree, this conduct must stop. Of course, members of Congress can attend lunches and receptions with free food and drink every single day, and sleep on the taxpayer's dime in their offices. (C-SPAN User-Created Clip, 2018a)

Sen. Debbie Stabenow (D-MI), ranking member of the Senate Agriculture Committee, displayed on many an occasion anti-Republican sentiment. For instance, she said:

 The same Republicans who refuse to fix the sequester refuse to work with us to get the economy moving. . . . Again, they're trying to take temporary food assistance away from the children and their families who are out of work. (C-SPAN User-Created Clip, 2013b)

FIGURE 9.9 Rep. Jackie Speier challenges Republicans on food access. (Courtesy of C-SPAN.)

DISCUSSION

We can now answer our research question(s): *What has been the U.S. Congress's moral sentiment toward American farms and farmers?* Overall, moral sentiment has increased over the past decade. Democrats displayed greater harm and degradation sentiment scores, whereas Republicans had greater Authority, Loyalty, and Sanctity scores. For hypotheses 1a and 2, we can reject the null and accept the alternative, whereas for 1b and 3 we fail to reject the null (see Table 9.3).

These findings contribute to research on moral sentiment of agriculture policy discourse. They show that moral sentimentalism has increased over time

TABLE 9.3 *Results of Hypotheses*

H0	Hypothesis	Result
1a	Democratic sentiment will be strongest within the Care foundation when discussing issues of agriculture	Reject null, accept alternative
1b	Republican sentiment will be the strongest within the Authority foundation when discussing issues of agriculture	Fail to reject null
2	Moral sentiment toward farms and farming has increased since 2012	Reject null, accept alternative
3	Congress's negative moral sentiment toward farms and farming has linearly increased since 2012	Fail to reject null

for all foundations *except* for Loyalty, even though Republicans' Loyalty sentiment score was the strongest. Republicans expressed greater sentiment scores for Authority and Loyalty, confirming previous findings (Graham et al., 2012). Once again, it is confirmed that Republicans will remain loyal. The question becomes, *to whom* are they loyal? Who comprises the in-group? The list is long, yet primary suspects include party leadership, previous rationales for Farm Bill titles, or dominant agricultural organizations. Regardless, these fall within the hegemonic, industrial agriculture model. Even most of the conservation titles are not accepted by the counter-hegemonic agricultural movement (such as regenerative agriculture). Higher Authority sentiment scores signify that they view this hegemonic way of farming as powerfully purposeful, legitimate, and right. A certain circular logic begets inertia—it is right now because it was right before. This was most clear in the debates about adding additional dollars to the nutrition programs. Republicans thought it too expensive and more than what was necessary, even though that which was "necessary" was determined by previous Farm Bills.

All parties expressed degradation, though Democrats more so than Republicans. They considered the agricultural system, as represented by the Farm Bill, to be less pure or holy than did Republicans. This logic extends from Republicans' higher Authority scores, suggesting that Democrats believe that greater degradation is occurring in the hegemonic agriculture systems. Democrats more readily assume the counter-hegemonic stance that industrial agriculture does more harm than good (critiques *of*), whereas Republicans appeal to industrial agriculture's inertia, espousing its strengths and how to improve its weaknesses (critiques *within*).

Democrats' Care/harm sentiment scores confirm previous findings of their reliance on Care foundations. It suggests that Democrats rely on the language of (in)justice and fairness even when discussing the Farm Bill. Moreover, Democrats were more negative than Republicans and less neutral than non-Democrats. They viewed the agriculture issues as least fair. These findings indicate that Democrats focused on the harm done to small farms, food stamp recipients, or the environment. Moral foundations quantify the emotionally charged nature of Democratic discourse, and in so doing help confirm Republican perception of Democrats as overconcerned with political correctness, injustices, and solving social maladies.

Considering congressional sentiment as a whole, a few longitudinal trends stand out. First, in the 2012 Farm Bill discussions, Congress's sentiment toward Fairness and Authority promoted their opposites, cheating and subversion. This indicates greater overall skepticism of hegemonic agriculture, as it was being presented in Farm Bill debates, compared to recent years. Second, if the oscillation pattern holds true for the future, then we will continue to see the peak of moral sentiments every five years leading up to the Farm Bill debates. This observation is intuitive yet beckons us to recognize an important point: the Farm Bill is more emotionally charged and sentiment-laden than other agriculture bills. Is this the case for other omnibus bills? Do they follow the same trend? I hypothesize yes, but that is a future study. Future studies could also explore crowdsourced, moral foundations of policy alternatives to the 5-year Farm Bill, such as the 50-year Farm Bill (Miller, 2020). This is necessary to make future, counter-hegemonic potentialities less abstract and, perhaps someday, able to be realized.

We are likely to see the increased use of machine learning (ML) techniques to predict future moral sentiments among political discourse (Liu et al., 2018; Rudkowsky et al., 2017). This could be done with issues related to agriculture so that organizations, institutions, and individuals wishing to reform some part of the agriculture system could have some advantage in preparing their messaging. However, there are some ML considerations that need to be addressed. Moral foundations expressed in greater frequency or severity (emphasis) today constrain or enable those expressed at future dates. Liken it to a choose-your-own-moral-sentiment adventure, whereupon the read pages influence the next but cannot be unread. The paradox is that analyzing the constriction of future options based on past actions requires present constriction, nominalization, and parsimony—that is, greater reductionism over time. However, it is impossible to reduce every unit of analysis (word, sentence, or paragraph) of every title in the bill down to moral sentiments. Moreover, a word dictionary is not a senator (a crowdsource of $N = 1$). Studies pursuing predictive ML models on moral foundations in political discourse must not lose sight of theory in the excitement of using innovative research tools.

In terms of a practical, political implication, one must first establish whether increased moral sentimentalism in Congress is acceptable or a problem worthy of social correction. If one deems it a problem worthy of correction, then there are steps citizens can take in their own advocacy (e.g., phone calls, emails, town halls) to reduce or retool their moral appeals. For instance, our study found that, unsurprisingly, Democrats heavily defer to the Care foundation. This unbalance causes a rift between them and Republicans, who are more balanced across all moral foundations (Haidt & Graham, 2009). Democrats wishing to increase the impact of their advocacy messaging to Republican legislators might consider reducing their reliance on Care. Similarly, Republicans wishing to effectively persuade Democrats may consider using fewer appeals to Loyalty and Authority. Before implementing these practical messaging techniques, one must ask: Does it make sense to adapt one's moral foundations to the other party in hopes of persuading them? Moreover, adaptation to achieve persuasion assumes that if one party adapted enough of its moral sentiments to fit the other side, then there exists the possibility of bipartisanship or reaching across the aisle, which has become rarer, even nonexistent. Perhaps moral foundations are merely descriptive of the polarization issues embedded in our politics, and perhaps not as likely to be acted upon for persuasive corrections. But when has "perhaps" ever stopped a dedicated advocate?

There are two final points of discussion concerning the MFT framework of moral formation. First, critics of MFT argue that morality forms based on *cooperation*, not contrast (Curry, 2019; Curry et al., 2019). For instance, Curry et al. (2019) found that their Morality-as-Cooperation Questionnaire (MAC-Q), containing seven moral factors, did better at comprehensively assessing moral foundations compared to MFT. Future studies could compare the e-MFT (established in 2021) to the MAC-Q and other moral dictionaries. Second, MFT and other areas studying morals should continue wrestling with central questions of framing morality. Can truly amoral contexts exist, especially in Congress? Can amorality begin as a first draft in a person's mind and remain amoral when culturally edited as the person engages in relational and social experiences? How does amorality scale, especially in an increasingly partisan and emotive political milieu?

LIMITATIONS

While any qualified scholar could identify several limitations, I focus on three.

First, words included in the texts but not in the eMFD were excluded from analysis. Hopp et al. (2021) made eMFD available for scholars to apply to various contexts. However, more methodological discussion is needed as to whether previously understudied topics, such as Farm Bill discourse, should require their own validated dictionary or whether context-independence is acceptable so long as authors justify the dictionary's fit to their research content and context.

Second, the sample clips may not be representative of the population of congressional sentiment toward farming due to the potential selection bias of those clipping the videos. People clip videos that catch their attention. Clipped videos likely display more expressive moral flareups than the average congressional segment and thus could include more outliers and extreme sentiments than are typical. The findings might show an effect that may not exist in the population. Therefore, this study is most likely to commit a false positive (Type 1 error).

Third, the moral valence of vice–virtue, positive–negative is imperfect because it removes the context in which the meaning gives rise (Grimmer & Stewart, 2013). Therefore, these findings are constrained to general moral sentiments of parties within the congressional chamber. The findings *should not be applied* to the congresspersons themselves. The detached boundary of the discourse about the foundations therefore limits the study to which moral arguments were used, but not which types of virtues were favored by each side.

Taking these limitations seriously should not be reason for dismissal of this essay's findings and significance.

CONCLUSION

This essay has examined the moral sentiment among and between U.S. Senate and House members, Republicans, Democrats, and bipartisan moments. It did so by utilizing content and textual sentiment analyses of 223 C-SPAN video clips (approximately 41 hours) related to farms and farming. This essay's main contribution is that it uses the eMFT to analyze changes in sentiment over time in a previously unstudied context of attitudes expressed in Farm Bill discourse toward farmers and farming in general. It contains relevant implications for sociologists, political scientists, communication studies scholars and rhetoricians, and scholars of other disciplines studying morals, sentiments, cultural hegemony, political attitudes, and textual/discourse analysis. Its findings may be useful for those who work in areas of political rhetoric/communication or political advocacy, or for workers in congressional offices. Farmers, and those in agricultural sectors, need government assistance as much now (or more) than they did in 1933. *Why?*, *How much?*, *When?*, and *For whom?* are the real questions, forever contingent on latent, moral sentiments espoused through fiery debate.

ACKNOWLEDGMENTS

I would like to thank C-SPAN for the grant that enabled me to pursue this research and its presentation. Much thanks to colleague Abigail Weiser for her help with downloading and categorizing C-SPAN videos and for her input on the initial stages of the project. Finally, this study was supported in part by National Science Foundation grant #1828571 and its involved members.

NOTES

1. The authors' procedure of building a sentiment dictionary included five steps: (1) sampling sentences from the domain of interest; (2) crowdcoding the sentiment strength of sentences; (3) estimating a sentence tonality score; (4) estimating a word tonality score; and (5) discriminating between important and unimportant words.

2. See https://github.com/medianeuroscience/emfd/blob/master/dictionaries/emfd _amp.csv.

REFERENCES

Aaker, J., Drolet, A., & Griffin, D. (2008). Recalling mixed emotions. *Journal of Consumer Research*, 35(2), 268–278. https://doi.org/10.1086/588570

Adamson, W. L. (2014). *Hegemony and revolution: Antonio Gramsci's political and cultural theory*. Echo Point Books & Media.

Agriculture Improvement Act of 2018, H.R.2, U.S. House of Representatives, 115th, P.L. 115-334 (2018). https://www.congress.gov/bill/115th-congress/house-bill/2

Ahmed, A. (2021, February 23). *Ethics, morals, principles, values, virtues, and beliefs. What is the difference?* Values Institute. https://values.institute/ethics-morals-principles -values-virtues-and-beliefs-what-is-the-difference/

Alizadeh, M., Weber, I., Cioffi-Revilla, C., Fortunato, S., & Macy, M. (2019). Psychology and morality of political extremists: Evidence from Twitter language analysis of alt-right and Antifa. *EPJ Data Science*, 8(1), 17. https://doi.org/10.1140/epjds/s13688 -019-0193-9

Alsaeedi, A., & Zubair, M. (2019). A study on sentiment analysis techniques of Twitter data. *International Journal of Advanced Computer Science and Applications*, 10(2), 361–374. https://doi.org/10.14569/IJACSA.2019.0100248

ATLAS.ti. (2021). Sentiment analysis. In *ATLAS.Ti 9 user manual*. https://doc.atlasti. com/ManualMac.v9/SearchAndCode/SearchAndCodeSentimentAnalysis.html

Barbalet, J. (2013). Adam Smith: Theorie der ethischen Gefühle. In K. Senge & R. Schützeichel, (Eds.), *Hauptwerke der Emotionssoziologie* (pp. 333–339). Springer VS. https://doi.org/10.1007/978-3-531-93439-6_46

Beigi, G., Hu, X., Maciejewski, R., & Liu, H. (2016). An overview of sentiment analysis in social media and its applications in disaster relief. In W. Pedrycz & S.-M. Chen (Eds.), *Sentiment analysis and ontology engineering: An environment of computa-*

tional intelligence (pp. 313–340). Springer International Publishing. https://doi.org
/10.1007/978-3-319-30319-2_13

Berry, W. (1977). *The unsettling of America: Culture and agriculture* (1st ed.). Sierra
Club Books.

Bessire, L. (2021). *Running out: In Search of water on the high plains*. Princeton University Press.

Brady, W. J., Wills, J. A., Jost, J. T., Tucker, J. A., & Bavel, J. J. V. (2017). Emotion shapes
the diffusion of moralized content in social networks. *Proceedings of the National
Academy of Sciences, 114*(28), 7313–7318. https://doi.org/10.1073/pnas.1618923114

Burns, E. A. (2020). Thinking sociologically about regenerative agriculture. *New Zealand Sociology, 35*(2), 189–213.

Büschken, J., & Allenby, G. M. (2016). Sentence-based text analysis for customer reviews. *Marketing Science, 35*(6), 953–975. https://doi.org/10.1287/mksc.2016.0993

Carolan, M. S. (2005). Barriers to the adoption of sustainable agriculture on rented
land: An examination of contesting social fields. *Rural Sociology, 70*(3), 387–413.
https://doi.org/10.1526/0036011054831233

Chakraborty, K., Bhattacharyya, S., Bag, R., & Hassanien, A. A. (2018). Sentiment
analysis on a set of movie reviews using deep learning techniques. In N. Dey, S.
Borah, R. Babo, & A. S. Ashour (Eds.), *Social network analytics: Computational
research methods and techniques* (pp. 127–147). Academic Press.

Cockfield, G., Firth, A., & Laurent, J. (2007). *New perspectives on Adam Smith's* The
Theory of Moral Sentiments. Edward Elgar Publishing.

C-SPAN User-Created Clip. (2013a, May 22). *Clip of* Senate Session (May 22, 2013); *User
clip: Sen. Inhofe—SNAP program—Farm Bill* [C-SPAN user video clip]. https://
www.c-span.org/video/?c4452740/user-clip-sen-inhofe-snap-program-farm-bill

C-SPAN User-Created Clip. (2013b, September 18). *Clip of* Senate Session (September 18,
2013); *User Clip: Sen. Stabenow addresses Farm Bill issues* [C-SPAN user video clip].
https://www.c-span.org/video/?c4465233/user-clip-sen-stabenow-addresses-farm
-bill-issues

C-SPAN User-Created Clip. (2014, February 4). *Clip of* Senate Session, Part 1 (February
4, 2014); *User clip: Sen. Durbin highlights the Farm Bills* [C-SPAN user video clip].
https://www.c-span.org/video/?c4483391/user-clip-sen-durbin-highlights-farm-bill

C-SPAN User-Created Clip. (2018a, May 17). *Clip of* Morning Hour (May 17, 2018); *User
Clip: Jackie Spear challenges the proposed Farm Bill and members of Congress on the
House floor* [C-SPAN user video clip]. https://www.c-span.org/video/?c4729988/user
-clip-jackie-spear-challenges-proposed-farm-bill-members-congress-house-floor

C-SPAN User-Created Clip. (2018b, June 28). *Clip of* Senate Session (June 28, 2018); *User* clip: Sen. *Joni Ernst Farm Bill work requirements* [C-SPAN user video clip]. https://www.c-span.org/video/?c4738049/user-clip-sen-joni-ernst-farm-bill-work-requirements

Cunningham, F. (2002). *Theories of democracy: A critical introduction*. Routledge. http://untag-smd.ac.id/files/Perpustakaan_Digital_1/DEMOCRACY%20Theories%20of%20Democracy~%20A%20Critical%20Introduction%20-%20Routledge.pdf

Curry, O. S. (2019, March 26). *What's wrong with moral foundations theory, and how to get moral psychology right*. Behavioral Scientist. https://behavioralscientist.org/whats-wrong-with-moral-foundations-theory-and-how-to-get-moral-psychology-right/

Curry, O. S., Jones Chesters, M., & Van Lissa, C. J. (2019). Mapping morality with a compass: Testing the theory of "morality-as-cooperation" with a new questionnaire. *Journal of Research in Personality*, *78*, 106–124. https://doi.org/10.1016/j.jrp.2018.10.008

D'Andrea, A., Ferri, F., Grifoni, P., & Guzzo, T. (2015). Approaches, tools and applications for sentiment analysis implementation. *International Journal of Computer Applications*, *125*(3), 26–33. https://doi.org/10.5120/ijca2015905866

Davidson, C. (2009). Transcription: Imperatives for qualitative research. *International Journal of Qualitative Methods*, *8*(2), 35–52. https://doi.org/10.1177/160940690900800206

Farm Policy Facts. (2022). *Farm Bill: A short history and summary*. https://www.farmpolicyfacts.org/farm-policy-history/

Firey, W. (1945). Sentiment and symbolism as ecological variables. *American Sociological Review*, *10*(2), 140–148. https://doi.org/10.2307/2085629

Friedmann, H. (1993). The political economy of food: A global crisis. *New Left Review*, *1*(197), 19. https://newleftreview.org/issues/i197/articles/harriet-friedmann-the-political-economy-of-food-a-global-crisis

Frimer, J. A., Aquino, K., Gebauer, J. E., Zhu, L., & Oakes, H. (2015). A decline in prosocial language helps explain public disapproval of the US Congress. *Proceedings of the National Academy of Sciences of the United States of America*, *112*(21), 6591–6594. https://doi.org/10.1073/pnas.1500355112

Gallagher, K. (2021, April 3). *States with the biggest agriculture industry*. Stacker. https://stacker.com/stories/3183/states-biggest-agriculture-industry

Gilens, M., & Page, B. I. (2014). Testing theories of American politics: Elites, interest groups, and average citizens. *Perspectives on Politics*, *12*(3), 564–581. https://doi.org/10.1017/S1537592714001595

Gordon, S. L. (1992). The sociology of sentiments and emotion. In M. Rosenberg & R. H. Turner (Eds.), *Social psychology: Sociological perspectives* (1st ed., pp. 562–592). Routledge. https://doi.org/10.4324/9781315129723-18

Gosnell, H., Gill, N., & Voyer, M. (2019). Transformational adaptation on the farm: Processes of change and persistence in transitions to "climate-smart" regenerative agriculture. *Global Environmental Change, 59*, 101965. https://doi.org/10.1016/j.glo envcha.2019.101965

Graham, J., Haidt, J., Koleva, S., Motyl, M., Iyer, R., Wojcik, S. P., & Ditto, P. H. (2012). Moral foundations theory: The pragmatic validity of moral pluralism. *Advances in Experimental Social Psychology, 47*, 55–130. https://doi.org/10.1016/B978-0-12 -407236-7.00002-4

Grimmer, J., & Stewart, B. M. (2013). Text as data: The promise and pitfalls of automatic content analysis methods for political texts. *Political Analysis, 21*(3), 267–297. https://doi.org/10.1093/pan/mps028

Haidt, J. (2013). *The righteous mind: Why good people are divided by science and religion*. Penguin Random House.

Haidt, J., & Graham, J. (2009). Planet of the Durkheimians, Where community, authority, and sacredness are foundations of morality. In J. T. Jost, A. C. Kay, & H. Thorisdottir (Eds.), *Social and psychological bases of ideology and system justification* (pp. 371–401). Oxford University Press.

Haidt, J., & Joseph, C. (2004). Intuitive ethics: How innately prepared intuitions generate culturally variable virtues. *Daedalus, 133*, 55–56. https://doi.org/10.1162/00115 26042365555

Haselmayer, M., & Jenny, M. (2017). Sentiment analysis of political communication: Combining a dictionary approach with crowdcoding. *Quality & Quantity, 51*(6), 2623–2646. https://doi.org/10.1007/s11135-016-0412-4

Haveman, H. A., & Rao, H. (1997). Structuring a theory of moral sentiments: Institutional and organizational coevolution in the early thrift industry. *American Journal of Sociology, 102*(6), 1606–1651. https://doi.org/10.1086/231128

Hearit, L. B., & Buzzanell, P. M. (2018). Communication as an economic tool: Chairman Greenspan's talk about uncertainties in future U.S. conditions. In R. X. Browning (Ed.), *The year in C-SPAN archives research: Volume 4* (pp. 45–84). Purdue University Press. https://docs.lib.purdue.edu/ccse/vol4/iss1/1

Hitlin, S., & Vaisey, S. (2013). The new sociology of morality. *Annual Review of Sociology, 39*(1), 51–68. https://doi.org/10.1146/annurev-soc-071312-145628

Hopp, F. R., Fisher, J. T., Cornell, D., Huskey, R., & Weber, R. (2021). The extended Moral Foundations Dictionary (eMFD): Development and applications of a crowd-sourced approach to extracting moral intuitions from text. *Behavior Research Methods, 53*(1), 232–246. https://doi.org/10.3758/s13428-020-01433-0

Jackson, W. (1980). *New roots for agriculture*. University of Nebraska Press.

Jibben, B. (2020, September 3). *USDA says farm income is increasing, gov. payments are a record*. AgWeb. https://www.agweb.com/news/policy/usda-says-farm-income -increasing-gov-payments-are-record

Johnson, K., & Goldwasser, D. (2018). Classification of moral foundations in microb-log political discourse. In *Proceedings of the 56th Annual Meeting of the Association for Computational Linguistics (Volume 1: Long papers)* (pp. 720–730). Association for Computational Linguistics. https://doi.org/10.18653/v1/P18-1067

Johnson, R., & Monke, J. (2017). *What is the farm bill?* (No. RS22131; p. 16). Congressional Research Service.

Jones, C. (2021). Problems and solutions in factory farming: The role of institutions, capital, and rhetoric. *Inquiries Journal, 13*(1), 1–9. http://www.inquiriesjournal.com /articles/1856/problems-and-solutions-in-factory-farming-the-role-of-institutions -capital-and-rhetoric

Kalpokas, N., & Radivojevic, I. (2021, March 9). *Sentiment analysis in ATLAS.ti cloud*. ATLAS.ti. https://atlasti.com/2021/03/09/35383/

Kansas State University. (2020, August 18). *Computer analysis shows that political speeches now use simpler language, express more sentiments*. News and Communications Services. https://www.k-state.edu/media/newsreleases/2020-08/political -speech-analysis81820.html

Kauppinen, A. (2018). Moral sentimentalism. In E. N. Zalta (Ed.), *Stanford encyclopedia of philosophy* (Winter 2018). Metaphysics Research Lab, Stanford University. https://plato.stanford.edu/archives/win2018/entries/moral-sentimentalism/

Kertzer, J. D., Powers, K. E., Rathbun, B. C., & Iyer, R. (2014). Moral support: How moral values shape foreign policy attitudes. *The Journal of Politics, 76*(3), 825–840. https://doi.org/10.1017/S0022381614000073

Krippendorf, K. (2012). *Content analysis: An introduction to its methodology* (3rd ed.). Sage.

Landmann, H., & Hess, U. (2017). Testing moral foundation theory. Are specific emotions elicited by specific moral transgressions? *Journal of Moral Education, 47*(1), 34–47. https://doi.org/10.1080/03057240.2017.1350569

Liu, L., Zhang, D., & Song, W. (2018). Modeling sentiment association in discourse for humor recognition. In *Proceedings of the 56th Annual Meeting of the Association for Computational Linguistics (Volume 2: Short papers)* (pp. 586–591). Association for Computational Linguistics. https://doi.org/10.18653/v1/P18-2093

Mäntylä, M. V., Graziotin, D., & Kuutila, M. (2018). The evolution of sentiment analysis—A review of research topics, venues, and top cited papers. *Computer Science Review, 27*, 16–32. https://doi.org/10.1016/j.cosrev.2017.10.002

Medhat, W., Hassan, A., & Korashy, H. (2014). Sentiment analysis algorithms and applications: A survey. *Ain Shams Engineering Journal, 5*(4), 1093–1113. https://doi.org/10.1016/j.asej.2014.04.011

Merrigan, G., & Hutson, C. L. (2008). Content analysis. In *Communication Research Methods* (2nd ed., pp. 147–162). Oxford University Press.

Miller, J. A. (2020). Examining the narrative persuasiveness of the 50-year Farm Bill. *Northwest Journal of Communication, 41*(1), 97–129.

Mills, C. W. (2000). *The power elite* (New ed.). Oxford University Press.

Mukkamala, R. R., Hussain, A., & Vatrapu, R. (2014). Fuzzy-set based sentiment analysis of big social data. In *2014 IEEE 18th International Enterprise Distributed Object Computing Conference* (pp. 71–80). IEEE. https://doi.org/10.1109/EDOC.2014.19

Philpott, T. (2008, February 8). *A reflection on the lasting legacy of 1970s USDA Secretary Earl Butz.* Grist. https://grist.org/article/the-butz-stops-here/

Preston, B. (2017). *The new farm: Our ten years on the front lines of the good food revolution.* Abrams Press.

Roy, S., & Goldwasser, D. (2021). Analysis of nuanced stances and sentiment towards entities of US politicians through the lens of moral foundation theory. In *Proceedings of the Ninth International Workshop on Natural Language Processing for Social Media* (pp. 1–13). https://doi.org/10.18653/v1/2021.socialnlp-1.1

Rudkowsky, E., Haselmayer, M., Wastian, M., Jenny, M., Emrich, S., & Sedlmair, M. (2017, May 25–29). *Supervised sentiment analysis of parliamentary speeches and news reports* [Paper presentation]. 67th Annual Conference of the International Communication Association (ICA), Panel on "Automatic Sentiment Analysis," 15. https://www.vis.uni-stuttgart.de/documentcenter/staff/sedlmaml/papers/rudkowsy2017sentiment.pdf

Sanderson, M. R., Griggs, B. W., & Miller, J. A. (2020, November 9). *Farmers are depleting the Ogallala Aquifer because the government pays them to do it.* The Conversation. http://theconversation.com/farmers-are-depleting-the-ogallala-aquifer-because-the-government-pays-them-to-do-it-145501

Sanderson, M. R., & Hughes, V. (2019). Race to the bottom (of the well): Groundwater in an agricultural production treadmill. *Social Problems, 66*(3), 392–410. https://doi.org/10.1093/socpro/spy011

Sebastian, T. (2021). *Everyday food pratices: Commercialisation and consumption in the periphery of the global north.* Lexington Books.

Shilling, C. (2014). The two traditions in the sociology of emotions. *The Sociological Review, 50*(S2), 10–32. https://doi.org/10.1111/j.1467-954X.2002.tb03589.x

Shott, S. (1979). Emotion and social life: A symbolic interactionist analysis. *American Journal of Sociology, 84*(6), 1317–1334. https://doi.org/10.1086/226936

Silver, J. R., & Silver, E. (2017). Why are conservatives more punitive than liberals? A moral foundations approach. *Law and Human Behavior, 41*(3), 258–272. https://doi .org/10.1037/lhb0000232

Smith, A. (2005). *The theory of moral sentiments* [1759] (6th ed. [1790]). MetaLibri.

Taboada, M. (2016). Sentiment analysis: An overview from linguistics. *Annual Review of Linguistics, 2*(1), 325–347. https://doi.org/10.1146/annurev-linguistics-011415-040518

Takikawa, H., & Sakamoto, T. (2020). The moral–emotional foundations of political discourse: A comparative analysis of the speech records of the U.S. and the Japanese legislatures. *Quality & Quantity, 54*(2), 547–566. https://doi.org/10.1007/s11135 -019-00912-7

Thelwall, M., Buckley, K., Paltoglou, G., Cai, D., & Kappas, A. (2010). Sentiment strength detection in short informal text. *Journal of the American Society for Information Science and Technology, 61*(12), 2544–2558. https://doi.org/10.1002/asi.21416

van Vliet, L. (2021). Moral expressions in 280 characters or less: An analysis of politician tweets following the 2016 Brexit referendum vote. *Frontiers in Big Data, 4,* 699653. https://doi.org/10.3389/fdata.2021.699653

Villarroel Ordenes, F., Ludwig, S., de Ruyter, K., Grewal, D., & Wetzels, M. (2017). Unveiling what is written in the stars: Analyzing explicit, implicit, and discourse patterns of sentiment in social media. *Journal of Consumer Research, 43*(6), 875–894. https://doi.org/10.1093/jcr/ucw070

Wallwork, E. (1985). Sentiment and structure: A Durkheimian critique of Kohlberg's moral theory. *Journal of Moral Education, 14*(2), 87–101. https://doi.org/10.1080 /0305724850140202

Wang, H., Can, D., Kazemzadeh, A., Bar, F., & Narayanan, S. (2012). A system for real-time Twitter sentiment analysis of 2012 U.S. presidential election cycle. In *Proceedings of the ACL 2012 System Demonstrations* (pp. 115–120). https://aclanthology .org/P12-3020

Weber, M. (1978). *Economy and society* [1922] (G. Roth & C. Wittich, Eds.). University of California Press.

Weinstein, J. (1996). The place of democracy in applied sociology. *Journal of Applied Sociology, 13*(1), 31–55.

10

DETECTING NONVERBAL AGGRESSION IN PRESIDENTIAL DEBATE

A Demonstration and Rationale for a CCSE Data Co-op

Erik P. Bucy, Dhavan V. Shah, Zhongkai Sun, William A. Sethares,
Porismita Borah, Sang Jung Kim, and Zening Duan

Until recently, presidential debates were high stakes but somewhat staid affairs where candidates exchanged views and engaged in rhetorical give and take involving acclaims, some attacks on the opponent, and defenses (Benoit, 2016). Rather than plot how to best assail and dominate the opponent, debate strategy focused on playing up a candidate's favorable qualities and issues—and guarding against gaffes, misdelivered lines, or verbal blunders (Schroeder, 2008). In this "polite era" of politics, moments and displays of overt aggression were rare and typically involved quippy one-liners or sharply focused zingers that were fleeting in delivery (Seiter & Weger, 2020). During the 2000 presidential debates, for example, Vice President Al Gore was widely criticized for leaving his podium to step into the personal space of George W. Bush in an attempt to rattle the Texas governor. Bush shrugged off Gore's space violation with a nonchalant look and continued without any sign of discomfort. The moment, which backfired on Gore, was seen as an ineffectual but aggressive attempt to intimidate the less experienced Bush.

Fast-forward to 2016, when the arrival of Donald Trump as the Republican presidential nominee saw a dramatic shift in the tenor and conduct of candidate behavior (Bucy et al., 2020; Oliver & Rahn, 2016). As documented in a detailed nonverbal comparison of the 2012 and 2016 presidential debates, Trump's nonverbal communication style was consistent in its anger, defiance, and aggression—and at a level of expressive intensity that outpaced not only Hillary Clinton in their 2016 debate encounters but also Mitt Romney and Barack Obama in the first presidential debate of 2012 (Bucy et al., 2020; Shah et al., 2016). In the second, town hall–style debate of 2016, Trump further unnerved his opponent by repeatedly violating her personal space and looming behind her during many of her speaking segments (Bucy & Gong, 2018). Trump was even more aggressive in the 2020 debates against Joe Biden; indeed, the first debate was so antagonistic, interruption-filled, and hostile in tone that the *New York Times* characterized the 90-minute encounter as a political "dumpster fire" (Poniewozik, 2020).

Despite verbal answers that were frequently superficial or factually incorrect, Trump's nonverbal expressiveness was an important factor in his ability to bond supporters to his cause and hold media attention throughout his election and presidency (Bucy et al., 2020; Hall et al., 2016). This quality of embodiment is of growing interest politically as populist candidates who are more physically expressive grow in popularity globally. Indeed, over the past decade, research in nonverbal communication and biobehavioral responses has made significant strides in refining our understanding of the ways in which embodied political performance draws attention, evokes emotion, rallies support, and leads to electoral success (Bucy, 2022). Detailed coding of candidate behavior and rhetoric has been linked with social media commentary during debates, showing the verbal, tonal, and nonverbal dimensions of candidate communication that shape viewer response (Bucy et al., 2020; Shah et al., 2016). Using time-series analysis that syncs the action on the main screen of television with the flow of social media response on the "second screen," this emerging literature finds that tonal (e.g., voice tone and interruptions) and nonverbal (e.g., facial expressions and physical gestures) indicators of political performance are more consequential in predicting the volume and valence of Twitter response than verbal indicators of rhetorical functions at different time lags.

At the same time, computational analyses of political performance, including large-scale computer vision and machine learning studies of political imagery and voice tone (e.g., candidate behavior and legislator movement within representative chambers), are uncovering patterns of expression and response that are not readily apparent in everyday observations (see Dietrich et al., 2019; Joo et al., 2019; Kang et al., 2020). Although computational work on political behavior and image analysis generally requires much larger data samples than studies based on human coding, so far there has been very little research examining longitudinal trends in political communication and behavior that leverages both a larger sample size and an analysis that compares across time periods. The demonstration project described here addresses this technical limitation by applying machine learning techniques based on human coding to the first general election debate of every U.S. presidential election since the Ford–Carter encounters of 1976. We do so as a proof of concept toward the development of a data archive that would spur further research integrating political science and communication science with computer vision and multimodal classification in computational social science.

In computer science, it is common practice to provide data sets and computer code that are detailed enough for results to be duplicated, verified, and extended. Bringing such an open science approach to social and political research, we propose a plan for sharing our findings and raw data—derived from an analysis of presidential debate video from the C-SPAN Video Library—with the wider research community in the form of a CCSE (Center for C-SPAN Scholarship & Engagement) Data Co-op (Bucy & Shah, 2021) to enable more rigorous empirical examinations of televised political events and interdisciplinary engagement with computational approaches to political video analysis.

The formation of such a data co-op would, to our knowledge, be a first-of-its-kind resource specifically dedicated to the analysis of political video. (For discussions of data co-ops in the social sciences, see King & Persily, 2020; Levi & Rajala, 2020.) While other digital archives of political materials exist at universities (e.g., the Julian P. Kanter Political Commercial Archive at the University of Oklahoma) and through museums of broadcasting (e.g., the Museum of the Moving Image in New York), they have not yet taken the next step of serving as a site for the research community to work collaboratively to tackle problems at the intersection of multiple fields that utilize data science and social science knowledge and techniques.

LITERATURE REVIEW

In the following sections, we briefly review the open science approach to research, then summarize our hand coding of televised candidate behavior in presidential debates over time. Following this discussion, we describe how our manual annotations of candidate behavior can be used to train a machine classifier, which from a sample of behavioral indicators learns to detect candidate facial displays and gestures across entire debates, enabling efficient assessment of candidate behavior over time. The diagnostic utility of this approach to debate analysis is demonstrated with a presentation of results from a computational model of aggressive and affiliative candidate behaviors from 1976 to 2020, showing a high level of accuracy in classifying affiliative behaviors prior to 2016 and aggressive behaviors in 2016 and 2020. The different layers of data constituting the CCSE Data Co-op are then diagrammed and described, with concluding comments focused on the benefits of the open science approach to empirical research enabled by the creation of this data co-op.

OPEN SCIENCE

Questions concerning the replicability of results in experimental psychology have led in recent years to what some have characterized as a "replication crisis" (Shrout & Rodgers, 2018) or "credibility revolution" (Vazire, 2018) that ultimately spread across the social sciences, spurring a wider movement toward open science as a means for advancing rigorous inquiry. Open science approaches to quantitative research can be summarized as practices focusing on open data, open study materials, open code repositories, and preregistration of study plans and study designs.

In this context, open science refers to easily accessible data sets, study stimuli, questionnaires and scales, coding and measurement instruments, and other research resources that would allow another research team to replicate the same study and analysis to confirm and verify results. Preregistration and publication of study protocols refers to the filing of a predetermined study design and analysis plan that, if closely followed, leaves little to no room for ad hoc statistical modeling, data removal, unplanned data exploration, or other ways of "p hacking"—looking for tests that yield significant differences rather than sticking with predetermined tests that are theoretically derived. Open science procedures "are thought of as a means to improve the credibility of research—for example, through increasing reproducibility (i.e., ensuring that a reanalysis of the same data results in the same conclusions) and/or replicability (i.e., ensuring that an empirical replication of a study leads to the same conclusions)" (Engzell & Rohrer, 2021, p. 297).

Open science also refers to other practices and goals aimed at enhancing inclusivity, including open access to published journal articles free of pay walls and accessible educational resources, particularly in less affluent regions and institutions. A recent Open Scholarship initiative within the International Communication Association, one of the leading professional associations in media and communication studies, formulated a statement emphasizing the orientation of open science toward

> advancing scholarship through transparency, wide-ranging collaboration, and a focus on the creation of public goods. It is about sharing knowledge about our research process, being up front about research ideas, transparent and thoughtful about analyzing our materials, and ensuring that, when possible, data and instruments are available for future scholars to learn from and to challenge. (de Vreese, 2021)

The benefits of a more accessible, transparent approach to research extend beyond research credibility and inclusivity to enhanced efficiency, an expanded analytical scope, and the ability to conduct cumulative rather than piecemeal research. In addition, refinement of techniques and discovery of new findings are accelerated and amplified when researchers from divergent backgrounds work together in common cause from a resourced starting point. As observed by Engzell and Rohrer, "Sharing of data and other materials reduces duplicate work and increases the yield from a given dataset, enables pooling of evidence, imposes greater self-scrutiny, and allows others to adapt and build on existing efforts" (2021, p. 299). The advantages are especially salient for early career and under-resourced researchers.

Problems such as failure to replicate (Open Science Collaboration, 2015) encouraged the discussion about open science in the social sciences around 2012 (Markowitz et al., 2021). Similar problems and conversations took place in communication research (Lewis, 2020). Indeed, a range of scholars now advocate for open science in the field of communication (Bowman & Spence, 2020; Dienlin et al., 2021; Lewis, 2020; McEwan, et al., 2018). Despite many advantages of open science, it is not a common practice in communication research (Markowitz et al., 2021). Examining research from 26 journals between 2010 and 2020, Markowitz and colleagues (2021) concluded that only 5.1% of published papers used open science practices. At the same time, data co-ops have been forming around a growing number of fields, particularly in computational areas (Ligett & Nissim, 2020). These trends demonstrate the scarcity of open science approaches in media and communication and the opportunity to offer new resources for interdisciplinary research and engagement.

TELEVISED CANDIDATE BEHAVIOR, 1976–2020

With these principles in mind, we set out to create a longitudinal data set of visual, verbal, and tonal coding of candidate behavior encompassing the entire era of televised presidential debates, excepting the 1960 debates. We intentionally left out the 1960 Kennedy–Nixon debates because there was a 16-year break between these first televised candidate encounters and the next set of debates, in 1976, between Gerald Ford and Jimmy Carter. Given our interest in trends, it is also notable that 1976 was the first year that presidential debates were broadcast in color, leading us to focus on 1976 to 2020.

The behaviors coded for this project began with a detailed analysis of the first 2016 presidential debate between Donald Trump and Hillary Clinton (Bucy et al., 2020). That analysis focused on the transgressive performative style that Trump brought to the debate stage—namely, his violation of normative boundaries, particularly those related to protocol and politeness, and open displays of frustration and anger. Together, the variables analyzed in this work indexed the visual (nonverbal) and tonal markers of outrage that give political populism its distinctive flair. Behavioral indicators, tonal maneuvers, and hostile verbal strategies such as put-downs, were grouped together into three major dimensions identified in analysis of populist communications—simplification, emotionalization, and negativity (see Engesser et al., 2017). For the longitudinal analysis here, we focus on emotionalization and negativity to develop indices of nonverbal and tonal aggression over time.

As we noted in our earlier study of the 2016 debates, emotionalization should be evident in the anger that populists direct toward adversaries (e.g., elites and outsiders), embodied by facial displays of anger/threat and defiance gestures that evoke an antagonistic relationship between the candidate, opponent, or implied nemeses. Emotionalization might also be indicated by a negative or excited tone of voice, interruptions signaling impatience with formality and decorum, and inappropriate put-downs, side comments, and nonverbal behavior that are essentially norm-violating and incompatible with the rhetorical context of formal debate.

In addition to voice tone, negativity may be visible in antagonistic expressions and defiant gestures that communicate zeal for political battle. Verbally, negativity is also manifested in angry language that paints adversaries and opponents in hostile, resentful terms and (in the context of populism) blames elites for the current state of society as bleak and broken. Outrage may also be stoked by ad hominem attacks against the opponent, which perform the service of reducing the prestige of one's rival while increasing the likelihood of supporters' engagement, which is similar to the rallying effect that negative displays have in bonding followers to leaders (see Sullivan, 1996; Valentino et al., 2011).

For our longitudinal analysis, we coded for 14 different candidate behaviors across a dozen first debates from 1976 to 2020, including nonverbal behaviors (angry/threatening facial expressions, defiance gestures, shows of nonverbal disagreement, inappropriate displays, opponent wave-offs), tonal gambits (angry/threatening voice tone, interruptions of various kinds), and verbal assaults (opponent put-downs or character attacks). To track positive interactions, we also coded for happiness/reassurance displays, affinity gestures, and communal behaviors. (For detailed definitions of all these variables, see Bucy et al., 2020; Bucy & Gong, 2016; Shah et al., 2016.)

For our manual coding we randomly selected a 20% sample of each first debate for each election year ($N = 12$ debates, with two candidates per debate coded separately, excluding 1992, which featured three candidates), amounting to roughly 3.5 hours of debate content total. Similar to our prior studies, all candidate behaviors were coded at 10-second segments, where behaviors were coded nominally for presence or absence (not duration). Figure 10.1 illustrates the cumulative trends in candidate behavior over time, focusing on nonverbal and verbal + tonal aggression by year, along with the affiliative behaviors we tracked. Trends show relative stability in aggressive behaviors from 1976 to 2012 and then an enormous upward spike in 2016 and 2020, particularly in forms of nonverbal aggression. Affiliative behaviors are more subject to shifts over time, including dips in 1980 (Carter vs. Reagan), 1992 (Bush vs. Clinton vs. Perot), 2004 (G. W. Bush vs. Gore), and 2020 (Biden vs. Trump).

As the graphs in Figure 10.1 show, our manual coding reveals a sudden shift in aggressive tone and behavior by candidates in presidential debates in the two most recent election cycles. The increase in incivility was not gradual, as would be suggested by a consistent, rising pattern. Rather, the transformation to an "impolite" era of politics occurred abruptly with the ascension of Donald Trump. As outlined above, this hand-coded content also served a second purpose, with the random sample of 10-second segments covering 20% of each first presidential debate from 1976 to 2020 used to train a machine classifier to perform a granular examination of the visual, tonal, and verbal content of each debate subjected to analysis. The ability to pair social scientists interested in biobehavioral approaches to politics and communication with computer scientists interested in

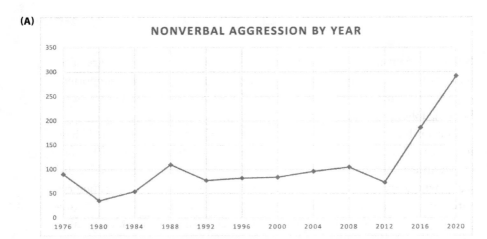

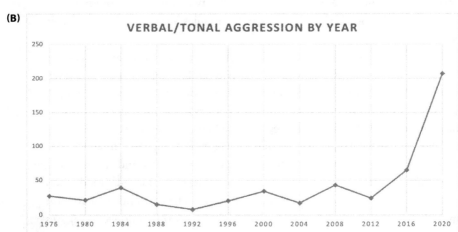

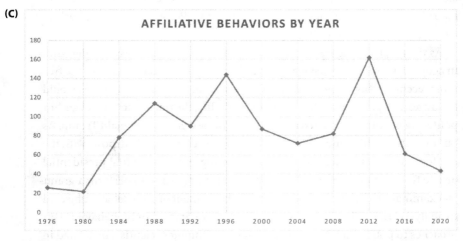

FIGURE 10.1 Nonverbal aggression by year (a); verbal/tonal aggression by year (b); and affiliative behaviors by year (c).

developing computer vision and multimodal classification techniques is high-lighted by the possibilities of our two-step approach, which employs coding of C-SPAN video as training data.

TRAINING A COMPUTER VISION CLASSIFIER

Using our 20% manual coding sample to train a classifier (see Sun et al., 2019), we were able to generate a promising set of findings following a machine learn-ing approach adapted from Sun and colleagues (2019). A notable result of this effort to generate a multimodal classifier from our manual coding of candidate behavior is the demarcation of the debates into two distinct eras. Table 10.1 shows that the detection model performs at 84% accuracy prior to 2016 for nonaggres-sive behaviors (i.e., happy/reassuring facial expressions and voice tone), but for aggressive behaviors (i.e., angry/threatening facial expressions and voice tone, plus verbal put-downs and additional measures of vocal performance) the per-formance for 2016 and 2020 improves to 92% classification accuracy. The low ac-curacy scores for aggressive behaviors prior to 2016 are likely due to the fact that they appeared very infrequently.

Thus, there appear to be two phases of politics indicated by our initial analy-sis, one (prior to 2016) polite and characterized by more affiliative behaviors and the other (during the Trump era) impolite and characterized by more candidate aggression. We are confident that the visual, verbal, and tonal behaviors charac-terizing each era are meaningfully detected by our approach—and that a larger

TABLE 10.1 *Detection Model Performance*

	F1 — before (aggressive)	F1 — after (aggressive)	F1 — before (nonaggressive)	F1 — after (nonaggressive)	Overall F1 — before	Overall F1 — after
Prior to 2016	0.66	0.59	0.81	0.84	0.75	0.76
2016 and 2020	0.90	0.92	0.60	0.64	0.85	0.87
All data	0.85	0.86	0.76	0.80	0.83	0.84

Note: Columns with a "before" notation indicate results based on a 10% manual coding sample, whereas columns with an "after" notation indicate results based on a 20% coding sample. This stemmed from an iterative approach in determining how much content to code from each debate. F1, a statistical measure used to rate performance, is defined as the harmonic mean between precision and recall. The higher the F1 coefficient, the more accurate the detection model performance.

sample of human coding would improve overall model performance even further. Performance could also be improved by further benchmarking efforts by computer scientists working to develop computer vision and multimodal classifiers.

PRESIDENTIAL DEBATE DATA CO-OP

As this brief demonstration suggests, longitudinal coding of nonverbal candidate behavior in presidential debates not only reveals shifting patterns of debate performance in recent elections but also how these same data can be used in computational social science applications. Given this potential, and confirmatory results of related computational studies of political behavior (see Dietrich et al., 2019; Joo et al., 2019; Kang et al., 2020), we advance the formation of a data co-op, housed by the Center for C-SPAN Scholarship & Engagement (CCSE) at Purdue University (Bucy & Shah, 2021).

Funding from a CCSE small grant has already facilitated manual coding of 20% of the first presidential debates from 1976 to 2020. With the formation of the data co-op, we will make our coded data available as training sets for computational researchers to explore further refinements of our detection techniques with the goal of enhancing detection accuracy and precision. The impact of such publicly available data, both the political video and training set data, may extend well beyond the political analysis of debates. For example, researchers in multimodal sentiment or vocal analysis may find this a unique resource. Coding of other aspects of visual politics beyond presidential debates using the C-SPAN Video Library would give the data co-op breadth and allow researchers from various disciplines to explore the potential of computer vision analysis.

As envisioned, the CCSE Data Co-op will consist of multiple layers of raw data, including images from the presidential debate videos, audio recordings and audio processing files, debate transcripts, and linguistic processing data. The CCSE Data Co-op would serve as a repository for C-SPAN videos and the corresponding image, audio, and text layers, along with manual coding of these data for the purposes of building training models (see Figure 10.2). Such models might include the development of computer vision classifiers based on the image layer or verbal aggression based on a combination of the audio and text layers. Our manual coding of candidate nonverbal behaviors and tonal features would serve as the initial training set data, which could be used in computational analyses of multimodal classification.

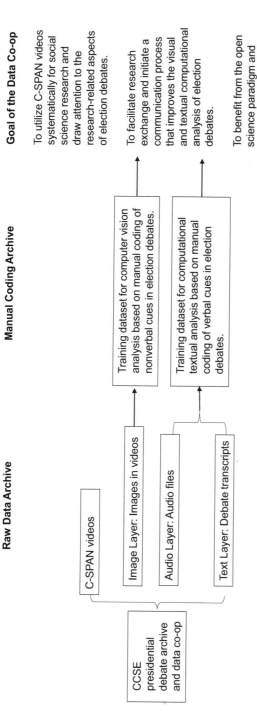

FIGURE 10.2 Visualization of the CCSE Data Co-op.

On the data co-op site, links will also be provided to open source tools used for analysis of facial displays, audio processing, and text analysis such as Torchaudio for acoustic features and OpenFace for facial action features. The goal of this one-stop shop approach is to facilitate greater cooperation between researchers performing manual coding on the social scientific side and those on the computational side working in data science. Ultimately, the CCSE Data Co-op would facilitate research related to election debates, strengthen both visual and textual analyses of these high-stakes moments of political deliberation and confrontation, and help broaden the appeal and accessibility of both computational research and behavioral analysis of politics. Once established, the data co-op could also easily be expanded beyond debates. New research teams could form around thematic research streams, such as the rise of political aggression, gender dynamics in politics, or the evolution of leadership styles.

DISCUSSION

Although our primary intent with this project is to improve the efficiency and accuracy of computer vision detection and multimodal classification systems to eventually enable rapid and near real-time analysis of political events by providing a one-stop shop for researchers interested in presidential debates, there are many other benefits to forming a data co-op related to the open science framework. As summarized by Engzell and Rohrer (2021), these include harnessing tacit knowledge that exists within the research community by enabling many minds to engage with similar questions at low cost, improving problematic research practices that lead to difficulties with replication and confirmation of previous results, enabling research areas to grow faster and more efficiently by reducing the amount of duplicate work and wasted efforts at reinventing the wheel, and fostering a more inclusive and democratic research environment by expanding access to information and lowering barriers to entry.

Over time, the development of the CCSE Data Co-op could just be the beginning of a much broader collaborative research effort. As of this writing, the C-SPAN Video Library contains over 277,000 hours of political video, including coverage of U.S. presidential campaigns, elections, and administrations but also extensive video records of all three branches of American government, special hearings and investigations, impeachments, foreign leader addresses to Congress, prime ministers' questions from the U.K., historical documentaries, panels and discussions, specials on First Ladies, African American history, student leaders, the Civil War, and other specials covering the gamut of political content and culture. Over time, the CCSE Data Co-op idea could extend to these and other areas of American political life and bring the open science framework to the analysis of video from a variety of different perspectives and approaches at scale.

ACKNOWLEDGMENT

We wish to thank Duncan Prettyman for his assistance with manual coding of the debates.

REFERENCES

Benoit, W. L. (2016). Political election debates. In G. Mazzoleni (Ed.), *The international encyclopedia of political communication*. John Wiley & Sons. https://doi.org/10.1002/9781118541555.wbiepc127

Bowman, N. D., & Spence, P. R. (2020). Challenges and best practices associated with sharing research materials and research data for communication scholars. *Communication Studies, 71*, 708–716. https://doi.org/10.1080/10510974.2020.1799488

Bucy, E. P. (2022). Embodied politics and emotional expression in the populist era: Research advances amid a disruptive decade. In K. Döveling & E. Konijn (Eds.), *Routledge international handbook of emotions and media* (2nd ed.; pp. 247–266). Routledge.

Bucy, E. P., Foley, J. M., Lukito, J., Doroshenko, L., Shah, D. V., Pevehouse, J. C. W., & Wells, C. (2020). Performing populism: Trump's transgressive debate style and the dynamics of Twitter response. *New Media & Society, 22*(4), 634–658. https://doi.org/10.1177/1461444819893984

Bucy, E. P., & Gong, Z. H. (2016). Image bite analysis of presidential debates. In R. X. Browning (Ed.), *Exploring the C-SPAN Archives: Advancing the research agenda* (pp. 45–75). Purdue University Press.

Bucy, E. P., & Shah, D. V. (2021, September 27). *Creating a C-SPAN presidential debate co-op: A new open-science resource for political scholarship* [Paper presentation]. Center for C-SPAN Scholarship & Engagement Workshop. Purdue University, West Lafayette, IN. https://www.purdue.edu/amap/events/2021-Fall-CSPAN-workshop-flyer.pdf

De Vreese, C. (2021). *Open scholarship: Report of the ICA Open Access and Open Scholarship Task Force*. International Communication Association. https://www.icahdq .org/general/custom.asp?page=OpenScholarship

Dienlin, T., Johannes, N., Bowman, N. D., Masur, P. K., Engesser, S., Kumpel, A. S., . . . de Vreese, C. (2021). An agenda for open science in communication. *Journal of Communication, 71*(1), 1–26. https://doi.org/10.1093/joc/jqz052

Dietrich, B. J., Hayes, M., & O'Brien, D. Z. (2019). Pitch perfect: Vocal pitch and the emotional intensity of congressional speech. *American Political Science Review, 113*(4), 941–962. https://doi.org/10.1017/S0003055419000467

Engesser, S., Fawzi, N., & Larsson. A. O. (2017). Populist online communication: Introduction to the special issue. *Information, Communication & Society, 20*(9), 1279–1292. https://doi.org/10.1080/1369118X.2017.1328525

Engzell, P., & Rohrer, J. (2021). Improving social science: Lessons from the open science movement. *PS: Political Science & Politics, 54*(2), 297–300. https://doi.org/10 .1017/S1049096520000967

Hall, K., Goldstein, D. M., & Ingram, M. B. (2016). The hands of Donald Trump: Entertainment, gesture, spectacle. *HAU: Journal of Ethnographic Theory, 6*(2), 71–100. https://doi.org/10.14318/hau6.2.009

Joo, J., Bucy, E. P., & Seidel, C. (2019). Automated coding of televised leader displays: Detecting nonverbal political behavior with computer vision. *International Journal of Communication, 13*, 4044–4066. https://ijoc.org/index.php/ijoc/article/view/10725

Kang, Z., Indudhara, C., Mahorker, K., Bucy, E. P., & Joo, J. (2020). Understanding political communication styles in televised debates via body movements. In A. Bartoli & A. Fusiello (Eds.), Computer vision: ECCV 2020 workshops, *Lecture Notes in Computer Science, Vol. 12535* (pp. 788–793). Springer, Cham. https://doi.org/10 .1007/978-3-030-66415-2_55

King, G., & Persily, N. (2020). A new model for industry-academic partnerships. *PS: Political Science & Politics, 53*(4), 703–709. https://doi.org/10.1017/S1049096519001021

Levi, M., & Rajala, B. (2020). Alternatives to Social Science One. *PS: Political Science & Politics, 53*(4), 710–711. https://doi.org/10.1017/S1049096520000438

Lewis, N. A. (2020). Open communication science: A primer on why and some recommendations for how. *Communication Methods and Measures, 14*(2), 71–82. https:// doi.org/10.1080/19312458.2019.1685660

Ligett, K., & Nissim, K. (2020, November 24). *Data co-ops: Challenges and how to get there* [Video]. YouTube. https://www.youtube.com/watch?v=ZZugFpAOA64

Markowitz, D. M., Song, H., & Taylor, S. H. (2021). Tracing the adoption and effects of open science in communication research. *Journal of Communication, 71*(5), 739–763. https://doi.org/10.1093/joc/jqab030

McEwan, B., Carpenter, C. J., & Westerman, D. (2018). On replication in communication science. *Communication Studies, 69*(3), 235–241. https://doi.org/10.1080/10510974.2018.1464938

Oliver, J. E., & Rahn, W. M. (2016). Rise of the *Trumpenvolk*: Populism in the 2016 election. *The Annals, 667*(1), 189–206. https://doi.org/10.1177/0002716216662639

Open Science Collaboration. (2015). Estimating the reproducibility of psychological science. *Science, 349*(6251). https://doi.org/10.1126/science.aac4716

Poniewozik, J. (2020, September 30). Donald Trump burns the first debate down. *New York Times*. https://www.nytimes.com/2020/09/30/arts/television/donald-trump-debate.html

Schroeder, A. (2008). *Presidential debates: Fifty years of high-risk TV* (2nd ed.). Columbia University Press.

Seiter, J. S., & Weger, H. Jr. (2020). *Nonverbal communication in political debates*. Lexington Books.

Shah, D. V., Hanna, A., Bucy, E. P., Lassen, D. S., Van Thomme, J., Bialik, K., Yang, J. H., & Pevehouse, J. (2016). Dual screening during presidential debates: Political nonverbals and the volume and valence of online expression. *American Behavioral Scientist, 60*(14), 1816–1843. https://doi.org/10.1177/0002764216676245

Shrout, P. E., & Rodgers, J. L. (2018). Psychology, science, and knowledge construction: Broadening perspectives from the replication crisis. *Annual Review of Psychology, 69*, 487–510. https://doi.org/10.1146/annurev-psych-122216-011845

Sullivan, D. G. (1996). Emotional responses to the nonverbal behavior of French and American political leaders. *Political Behavior, 18*(3), 311–325. https://doi.org/10.1007/BF01498604

Sun, Z., Sarma, P., Sethares, W., & Bucy, E. P. (2019, September). *Multimodal sentiment analysis using deep canonical correlation analysis* [Paper presentation]. International Speech Communication Association, INTERSPEECH 2019. Graz, Austria.

Valentino, N. A., Brader, T., Groenendyk, E. W., Gregorowicz, K., & Hutchings, V. L. (2011). Election night's alright for fighting: The role of emotions in political participation. *Journal of Politics, 73*(1), 156–170. https://doi.org/10.1017/S0022381610000939

Vazire, S. (2018). Implications of the credibility revolution for productivity, creativity, and progress. *Perspectives on Psychological Science, 13*(4), 411–417. https://doi.org/10.1177/1745691617751884

CONCLUSION

Through the 10 essays in this volume, we have seen scholars advance our understanding of politics, communication, and history by using the C-SPAN Video Library. Each has used a slightly different approach to address a different question. What unifies these essays is the use of the records originally created by C-SPAN to document the public affairs events of our day. Some have recounted history. Others examined gender in campaigns and in the newsroom. We have learned about agriculture policy and the spectacle of congressional hearings. Finally, we saw a proposal for a new data co-op to advance the study of elections through a repository of video coding and results.

Where do we go from here? With each volume—this is the eighth—we see scholars approaching new topics with new techniques. The Center for C-SPAN Scholarship & Engagement (CCSE), which sponsors the research conference where these essays are first presented, also holds a series of workshops through the academic year. These workshops are designed to introduce faculty and students to software and techniques that can be used to analyze the videos and text from the C-SPAN Video Library. Video recordings of these workshops are available at the CCSE website at Purdue University. In the past year, we held workshops on video and audio processing as tools become more readily available to analyze the video directly.

This year we saw three historians use the collection to analyze conventions, campaigns, and the history of cable news coverage. Additionally, another scholar analyzed the evolution of Senator Kennedy's views on health care. Each year, there is more history being archived and the collection reaches further back in time, making it more valuable as a look at our history.

Impeachments, wars, Supreme Court justice nominations, political campaigns, congressional debates, hearings, presidential addresses to the nation, and speeches by Supreme Court justices all are recorded, indexed, and made available for research. We invite you to think of the questions that these videos can answer, the techniques used to tease out those answers, and the possibility of participating in future conferences and volumes. The C-SPAN Video Library is there for your access and research.

CONTRIBUTORS

Sheri Bleam earned an MA in rhetoric at Central Michigan University and a PhD in communication and rhetorical processes at Wayne State University after completing a BA in communication arts at Wright State University. She then served in the Adrian College professoriate for four decades, during which time she developed and implemented a communication arts program. Bleam concentrated her professional efforts in several areas, including the establishment and growth of a faculty for her new department, a continued broadening of departmental and interdepartmental offerings in communication arts, and an ongoing, reflective program of research regarding growth and change in higher education. She also consulted for over a decade with the NCA Institute for Faculty Development. Recently, Bleam was honored to collaborate with her home institution's team of architects and IT personnel as they prepared for a new academic building on the Adrian College campus—the Center for Communication Arts.

Porismita Borah is an associate professor at the Edward R. Murrow College of Communication and a graduate faculty member in the Prevention Science program at Washington State University. Her research focuses on digital media effects in the context of both politics and health. Borah's recent work focuses on problematic information, including mis/disinformation, hate speech, and incivility. Her work has been published in top journals such as the *Journal of Communication, Political Communication, Journal of Computer-Mediated Communication*, and *New Media and Society*. Borah has received funding from multiple sources, including the National Institutes of Health and the National Science Foundation, for her research. Borah is currently editor-in-chief of the *International Journal of Public Opinion Research*.

Kathryn Cramer Brownell is an associate professor of history at Purdue University and an editor at *Made By History* at *The Washington Post*. Her research and teaching focus on the intersections between media, politics, and popular culture, with a particular emphasis on the American presidency. Her first book, *Showbiz Politics: Hollywood in American Political Life* (University of North Carolina Press, 2014), examines the institutionalization of entertainment styles and structures in American politics and the rise of the celebrity presidency. She is now completing a new book project on the political history of cable television.

Erik P. Bucy is the Marshall and Sharleen Formby Regents Professor of Strategic Communication in the College of Media and Communication at Texas Tech University. He teaches and conducts research on disinformation, visual communication, political nonverbal behavior, and public opinion about the press. Bucy is the author of *Image Bite Politics: News and the Visual Framing of Elections* (with Maria Grabe, 2009) and editor of the *Sourcebook for Political Communication Research* (with R. Lance Holbert, 2013). Bucy is the past editor of the Cambridge-published journal *Politics and the Life Sciences* and recently guest-edited a special issue of the *International Journal of Press/Politics* on visual politics. He is currently producing a series of news literacy videos in conjunction with KTTZ-TV in Lubbock, Texas, to combat misinformation and enhance public understanding of journalism. Bucy has held fellowships at the London School of Economics and University of Oxford and was recently named an honorary fellow of the Mass Communication Research Center at the University of Wisconsin–Madison.

Zening Duan is a doctoral student in mass communication at the University of Wisconsin–Madison, School of Journalism and Mass Communication. Duan's research interest is twofold: Under the first research line, he examines the position and impact of emerging media technologies (e.g., bots and recommendation systems) in the hybrid and high-choice media ecology. Under the second research line, he explores how Americans express and act on controversial politics and politicized public health issues, including election debates, protests, and the COVID-19 pandemic. Duan has been trained in both quantitative and computational social science methods. Some of his ongoing works attempt to explain the macro/micro factors of public opinion dynamics and (mis)information diffusion.

Matthew George is a senior communication studies and Spanish double major at Young Harris College, in Young Harris, Georgia. He is a tutor for communication studies, Spanish, and writing and also works as a policy analyst for the Council of State Governments. With many aspirations, George intends to graduate in December 2022 and is currently exploring future options. He has earned the Georgia Youth Leadership award for demonstrating exemplary leadership excellence and has earned dean's and president's list designations four consecutive semesters. George is a rising scholar in communication studies and looks forward to new and upcoming research within the field.

Joshua Guitar earned his MA and PhD in communication from Wayne State University after completing a BA in communication at Adrian College. He currently serves as an assistant professor of communication at Kean University in Union, New Jersey, where he teaches courses in rhetoric, critical media studies, and political communication. Guitar employs both classical and critical methods of rhetorical inquiry to examine mediated political discourse, oftentimes to interrogate the rhetorical manifestations of ideology that inhibit democratic discourse, civil liberties, and political equity. His research has been featured in communication journals such as *Critical Studies in Media Communication, First Amendment Studies*, and *Western Journal of Communication*. His most recent work is *Dissent, Discourse, and Democracy: Whistleblowers as Sites of Political Contestation*, published by Lexington Books in 2021.

Heather Hendershot is a professor of film and media at Massachusetts Institute of Technology. She is a former editor of *Cinema Journal*, the official publication of the Society for Cinema and Media Studies, and she has held fellowships at NYU, Princeton, Stanford, and Harvard; Hendershot has also been a Guggenheim fellow. Her two most recent books are *Open to Debate: How William F. Buckley Put Liberal America on the Firing Line* (HarperCollins, 2016) and *When the News Broke: Chicago 1968 and the Polarizing of America* (University of Chicago, 2022).

Jennifer Hopper is an associate professor of political science at Southern Connecticut State University, where she regularly teaches courses in American government, the U.S. presidency, Congress and the legislative process, and media and politics. She is the author of *Presidential Framing in the 21st Century News Media: The Politics of the Affordable Care Act* (Routledge, 2017). Her scholarship has also appeared in *White House Studies*, *Social Science History*, and the *International Journal of Communication*. Her research interests focus on political communication, the presidency, and the U.S. news media, particularly as they relate to health care politics and policy.

Sang Jung Kim is a PhD candidate at the University of Wisconsin–Madison, School of Journalism and Mass Communication. Kim studies the interaction between technology, politics, and social identity. She explores the identities of message creators and message receivers on social media platforms—including racial identity, gender identity, and political identity—and utilizes both experimental methods and computational approaches to understand how consumers and creators of such content introduce and are impacted by biases. Her works have been published in *Information, Communication & Society*, *International Journal of Press/Politics*, *Journal of Communication*, and *Journal of Computer Mediated Communication*.

Jared McDonald is an assistant professor of political science and international affairs at the University of Mary Washington. His research examines how American voters evaluate politicians and hold them accountable in an environment increasingly characterized by high levels of polarization and strong partisan identities. His work has been published in the *Journal of Politics*, *Public Administration Review*, and *Political Behavior*, among others.

Jacob A. Miller-Klugesherz is a PhD student at Kansas State University on an NSF-sponsored NRT-R3 research traineeship. He researches the barriers to regenerative agriculture adoption, community, and personal well-being, absentee ownership's effects on conservation, and the moral foundations of the policy-making process related to agriculture and climate change. Visit his personal website at https://jam199540.wixsite.com/personalsite. Miller-Klugesherz is a sixth-generation Kansan. His nonacademic interests include cooking and all things basketball.

Newly Paul is an assistant professor of journalism in the Mayborn School of Journalism at the University of North Texas. She teaches various levels of undergraduate classes, such as introduction to media writing, copyediting, principles of news, and minorities in media. She graduated with a PhD in media and public affairs from the Manship School of Mass Communication at Louisiana State University. Her research interests lie in the areas of political communication and media coverage of minorities. Broadly, she examines questions such as *How do minority women running for political office represent themselves to voters? How does newsroom diversity affect news coverage? How do the media cover minority groups?* and *What are the implications of media coverage on readers?* Her research has won grants and awards and has been published in journals such as *Political Research Quarterly, Journalism and Mass Communication Quarterly, Journal of Computer Mediated Communication,* and *Atlantic Journal of Communication.* Before joining academia, Paul was a journalist and worked in newsrooms in New Delhi and Los Angeles, where she covered a number of beats, including city government, crime, education, and politics

Allison Perlman is an associate professor of history and film and media studies at the University of California, Irvine. She is the author of *Public Interests: Media Advocacy and Struggles over US Television* (Rutgers UP, 2016). She is currently working on two projects related to the history of U.S. public media.

Zachary Scott is a postdoctoral fellow in the College of the Environment and Life Sciences at the University of Rhode Island. He received his PhD in government and politics from the University of Maryland in 2020. His research interests include political communication, mass media, presidential primary campaigns, political elite rhetoric, and political parties. His research has been published in *American Politics Research,* the *Journal of Elections, Parties, and Public Opinion, Journalism & Mass Communication Quarterly,* and *Electoral Studies.*

William A. Sethares received his PhD in electrical engineering from Cornell University. He has worked at the Raytheon Company designing image processing systems and is currently a professor in the Department of Electrical and Computer Engineering at the University of Wisconsin–Madison. Sethares has held visiting positions at the Australian National University in Canberra, the Technical Institute in Gdansk Poland, New York University in Abu Dhabi, the Institute for Applied Mathematics in Ankara Turkey, and the NASA Ames Research Center in Mountain View, California. He is currently a scientific researcher at the Rijksmuseum in Amsterdam and is an Honorary International Chair Professor at the National Taipei University of Technology in Taiwan. His research interests include adaptation and learning in speech and signal processing, decision and estimation in imaging and audio systems, and text and language processing for social media. Sethares is the author of four books holds six patents.

Dhavan V. Shah is Maier-Bascom Professor at the University of Wisconsin–Madison, where he is the director of the Mass Communication Research Center (MCRC), research director of the Center for Communication and Civic Renewal (CCCR), and scientific director in the Center for Health Enhancement System Studies (CHESS). An abiding interest in the intersecting power of framing and social capital has shaped his research in three areas: the influence of message construction and processing, the communication dynamics shaping civic participation, and the effects of computer-mediated interactions on chronic disease management. This work has generated grants totaling nearly $50 million from private foundations and federal governments. He often applies computational approaches to social science questions, using digital trace data, natural language processing, network mapping, and predictive analytics to study politics and health. Shah is appointed in the School of Journalism and Mass Communication, with affiliations in Industrial and Systems Engineering, Marketing, and Political Science.

Madeline Studebaker earned her BA in communication with a concentration in media studies from Young Harris College in Young Harris, Georgia, in May 2022. As an undergraduate research assistant in the Communication Studies Department, Studebaker enjoyed being involved in projects employing feminist and rhetorical approaches, for which she was named a Distinguished Undergraduate Research Scholar. She coauthored and presented "Abstracting AOC: Reifying the Reactionary Rhetoric of Patriarchal Ideology" at the Southern States Communication Association in 2022. Studebaker plans to pursue the critical rhetoric of neocolonialism, one of her primary academic interests, at the graduate level.

Zhongkai Sun is an applied computational scientist at Amazon Alexa AI. Sun received his PhD in electrical and computer engineering from the University of Wisconsin–Madison. At Madison, he worked as a research assistant on interdisciplinary teams in computer science and journalism/mass communication. His research interests include multimodal information (visual, audio, text)–based analysis involving the detection of sentiment, word meaning shift, and video style. His research also encompasses the classification and sentiment analysis of tweets. Sun's academic studies have performed multimodal language and sentiment analysis using deep canonical correlation, a data analysis technique that projects two modalities into a space in which they are maximally correlated. Among other journals, his work has been published in the *Journal of Computer-Mediated Communication*, *International Journal of Communication*, and *Journal of Quantitative Description*.

Jenna Thomas recently graduated with a BA in communication studies from Young Harris College located in Young Harris, Georgia. She primarily researches political ideologies and mediated campaigns through critical and rhetorical methods. As a communication scholar exemplar, Thomas thoroughly enjoyed her role as a research assistant within the Department of Communication Studies. Because of this opportunity, she has found a passion for research and wants to continue looking at media through critical and rhetorical methods she learned under her mentor and Dr. Joshua Guitar. Thomas currently lives in McLean, Virginia, where she works as an event coordinator and remains open to future academic research opportunities.

Whitney Tipton holds a PhD in communication and information studies with an emphasis in organizational communication, and a master's degree in strategic communication and leadership. Since moving to Indiana, Tipton has been involved with voter registration and engagement efforts through UIndy Votes!, where she helps students design engaging voter registration drive materials, conducts research about voter attitudes, and works with community organizations to help register more Hoosiers. Tipton is an assistant professor of communication at the University of Indianapolis, where she also advises the Public Relations Student Society of America.

Stephanie Wideman holds a PhD in communication studies with an emphasis in rhetoric from Wayne State University. She received her MA degree in political science with an emphasis in public administration and her BA in communication with an emphasis in public relations from the University of West Florida. She currently resides in Indianapolis and is an assistant professor and director of the Forensics Speech and Debate Team at the University of Indianapolis. Throughout her collegiate career, Wideman competed with and then coached several speech and debate teams. Her time engaging in this activity contributes to her research interests that lie at the nexus of argumentation studies, visual rhetoric, gender, and politics.

Laura Merrifield Wilson is an associate professor of political science at the University of Indianapolis, where she also serves as the pre-law advisor and codirector of the Gender Center. Her specializations include gender politics, campaigns and elections, and state government. In addition to these academic specialties, she has a passion for social justice issues, civic engagement, and service learning. Wilson earned her bachelor's in theatre (2008) and master's in political science (2010) from Ohio University and her master's in women's studies (2014), master's in public administration (2012), and PhD in American politics (2014) from the University of Alabama. Wilson is a regular panelist on CBS 4's/Fox 59's *IN Focus* on Sunday mornings and is the producer and host of WICR 88.7's *Positively Politics* on Saturdays at 11:30 a.m. She is the current president of the Indiana Political Science Association, where she has been on the executive board since 2015, and an active board member of the Indiana Social Science Association.

INDEX

CPSIA information can be obtained
at www.ICGtesting.com
Printed in the USA
LVHW020238151122
733111LV00003B/358